BEYOND
SURVIVAL

LABOR AND HUMAN RESOURCES SERIES

BEYOND SURVIVAL

Wage Labor in the Late Twentieth Century

CYRUS BINA
Harvard University

LAURIE CLEMENTS
University of Iowa

CHUCK DAVIS
University of Minnesota

editors

M.E. Sharpe
Armonk, New York
London, England

Library of Congress Cataloging-in-Publication Data

Beyond survival : wage labor in the late twentieth century /
Cyrus Bina, Laurie Clements, and Chuck Davis, editors.
p.   cm.
Includes bibliographical references and index.
ISBN 1-56324-515-9 (hardcover : alk. paper).
ISBN 1-56324-516-7 (pbk. : alk. paper)
1. Labor—Congresses.   2. Labor market—Congresses.   3. Industrial
relations—Congresses.   4. Trade-unions—Congresses.
5. Labor—United States—Congresses.   6. Labor market—United States—
Congresses.   7. Industrial relations—United States—Congresses.
8. Trade-unions—United States—Congresses.   I. Bina, Cyrus, 1946–   .
II. Clements, Laurie 1950–   .   III. Davis, Chuck, 1954–
HD4813.B49   1996
331—dc20   95-42401
CIP
Printed in the United States of America

The paper used in this publication meets the minimum requirements of
American National Standard for Information Sciences—
Permanence of Paper for Printed Library Materials,
ANSI Z 39.48-1984.

∞

MV (c)   10   9   8   7   6   5   4   3   2   1
MV (p)   10   9   8   7   6   5   4   3   2   1

"Five men," he said, "can produce bread for a thousand. One man can produce cotton cloth for two hundred and fifty people, woolens for three hundred, and boots and shoes for a thousand. One would conclude from this that under a capable management of society modern civilized man would be a great deal better off than the caveman. But is he?"

—Jack London, *The Iron Heel*
(Chicago: Lawrence Hill Books, n.d.;
originally published 1907), p. 56

Is a tractor bad? Is the power that turns the long furrows wrong? If this tractor were ours it would be good—not mine, but ours. If our tractor turned the long furrows of our land, it would be good. Not my land, but ours. We could love that tractor then as we have loved this land when it was ours. But this tractor does two things—it turns the land and turns us off the land. There is little difference between this tractor and a tank. The people are driven, intimidated, hurt by both. We must think about this.

—John Steinbeck, *The Grapes of Wrath*
(New York: Penguin Books, 1976;
originally published 1939), pp. 205–6

WILLY: Funny, y'know? After all the highways, and the trains, and the appointments, and the years, you end up worth more dead than alive.

—Arthur Miller, *Death of a Salesman,* Act Two
(New York: Penguin Books, 1976;
originally published 1949), p. 98

Contents

Acknowledgments

The book's development began in the fall of 1990 as a publicized "call for papers" in conjunction with a conference titled "Labor Confronts the 1990s." The conference was the Midwest–Southern Regional meeting of the University and College Labor Education Association (UCLEA) and was held at the University of Iowa, Iowa City. The objective was to bring together and establish dialogue between labor educators and political economists to develop a theoretically informed practice necessary for labor's revitalization. The conference format enabled participants and presenters to share ideas and experiences surrounding the dynamics of the U.S. labor movement's decline, and explore practical plans of action for labor's renewal. The efforts of Roberta Till-Retz, who coordinated the conference, Clara Oleson, and Steve Dohrmann contributed significantly to the success of that program.

In the period following the conference, additional authors were solicited to participate in this collective effort. All the book's chapters were prepared exclusively for this volume, and the editors would like to thank the contributors: David C. Ranney, Norman Eiger, Michele I. Naples, David Fairris, Victor G. Devinatz, Philip Garrahan, Paul Stewart, Vernon Mogensen, Elaine Bernard, and David Schultz for their diligence and unwavering support in the completion of this project. However, the editors are not responsible for the views expressed by the contributors.

The purpose and to some extent the contents of this volume have been influenced by the work of several contemporary scholars/activists. We would like to thank Ben Fine, Anwar Shaikh, Kim Moody, Willi Semmler, and John Weeks for their ideological, methodological, theoretical, and practical guidance to the subject matter. Their assistance has been invaluable. Additionally, insights provided by Berch Berberoglu, Howard Botwinick, James Cypher, Reza Fazeli, Susan Himmelweit, Stephen Marglin, Patrick Mason, Juliet Schor, Bryan Snyder, John Willoughby, and Behzad Yaghmaian have been much appreciated.

The editorial assistance from M.E. Sharpe, Inc., Publisher, has been both professional and extremely supportive, and we would like to offer a special thanks to Richard D. Bartel for believing in the book, and to Karen Byrnes,

Esther L. Clark, Christine Florie, and Stephen Dalphin for their perseverance in seeing the project completed.

We would also like to thank Dawn Addy, Bobby Bina, Penny Jo Hage, and Joyce Hegstrom for providing technical assistance.

Finally, a special thanks to our graduate students; and to all the workers who have attended classes, seminars, and conferences of the editors and taught them the real meaning of solidarity, struggle, and survival.

BEYOND SURVIVAL

Introduction—Beyond Survival: Toward the Revitalization of Labor

Understanding labor's past, present, and its future revitalization requires a critical analysis that has to do with the nature of wage labor vis-à-vis capital, along with the corresponding labor organizations around the globe. One such approach is provided by the social relations school, which looks upon capitalism in terms of a historically defined mode of accumulation based on wage labor, rather than a natural or randomly given system of direct and transparent relations. Capitalism is a global social relation based on the antagonism between capital and labor, which is contingent on the subsumption and subordination of the latter by the former. The control and domination of labor by capital is the inner developmental force of capital as an inescapable social form.[1] This is accomplished through material production and its accompanied ideological reinforcement that puts the world of *technological change* at the center of socioeconomic life, rendering the use of education and skills accumulated by workers redundant and reducing the value of labor power—the socially necessary labor time (per unit of output)—on an ever increasing universal scale. Trade unions emerged as a challenge to capital as a social relation, and play a pivotal role in the struggle against the effects of subsumption and subordination of labor under capital.

Capitalism is restructuring on a global scale to increase production of relative surplus value and, consequently, profit. This is occurring through the construction of a new international division of labor: "the restructuring of productive capital internationally and nationally to increase profitability as an element of the *global whole*," supported by "the construction and consolidation of a new international role for financial capital."[2] The transnationalization of capital as a social relation has had a devastating effect on the value of labor power. The forces of capital accumulation and global competition are driving the majority of the

3

world's population into abject poverty. Global economic growth has fallen well below the levels of the 1950s and 1960s, "world per capita income fell in 1993 for the fourth straight year,"[3] and the world is now in the worst employment crisis since the Great Depression of the 1930s. Thirty percent of the global labor force is either unemployed or underemployed, and there is growing labor market inequality. "The gulf between the world's haves and have-nots is widening rather than narrowing."[4] The rate of capital accumulation and increased capitalist competition have exerted downward pressure on the value of labor power expressed in declining real incomes for workers worldwide as a result of the rise in the global reserve army of labor, and the intensification of the labor process. These trends are illustrative of the long-term systemic development of capital as a global social relation.[5]

The effects of capitalist restructuring are clearly evident in the United States. As of March 1995, four years after the last recession, the official unemployment rate was still above the prerecession low of 5 percent. The result is that since 1972, real average weekly earnings of nonsupervisory workers have declined by 20 percent. At present, nominal wages *and* benefits for the average worker have fallen for the first time since computation was being done in 1987, and after adjusting for inflation, represent a 3 percent decline in purchasing power.[6] The number of full-time workers earning below the poverty level has increased by 35 percent since 1972. The latest data from the U.S. Census Bureau show that 18 percent of all year-round workers over the age of sixteen earn incomes below the poverty line. Between 1979 and 1992, the ranks of these workers rose by 44 percent.[7] The number of workers without health insurance or pension coverage likewise has grown. Capitalist restructuring has led to layoffs and outsourcing of jobs, and the replacement of workers with part-time/temporary employees who earn significantly less than the former full-time employees. The number of contingent workers—workers who generally lack a permanent attachment to an employer and work on a temporary or contract basis—has increased by 33 percent. In 1993, contingent workers made up one-third of the workforce, up from a quarter in 1988.[8] Workers who have been forced to find new jobs because of restructuring have taken, on average, a 20 percent pay cut.[9]

To make up for a declining standard of living, workers are working longer hours. In September and October of 1994, the U.S. Bureau of Labor Statistics estimated factory workers put in an average of four hours and forty-two minutes of overtime a week, the most ever registered in the 38 years during which the agency has kept track. By May 1995, average hours worked by all full-time workers was forty-three hours and twenty-four minutes per week.[10] Additionally, since 1970 the rate of labor force participation has risen by 10 percent as workers attempt to alleviate declining real wages.[11]

Social capital's global strategy for reducing the value of labor power continually degraded the standard of living for workers and increased wealth and income inequality. In the United States, the assets of the wealthiest 1 percent of the population have grown as the population below the poverty line has swollen.[12] The portion of the increase in national income going to labor is the smallest of any expansion in the past twenty years. In the first quarter of 1995, corporate profits were up 14 percent over 1994. Worker productivity has reached a new, higher level. Yet the improvement in productivity has not been passed on to workers—"The owners of capital are registering huge gains while ordinary working Americans are seeing their incomes fall."[13] In October of 1994, U.S. Labor Secretary Robert Reich commented on this development in the United States:

> We have the most unequal distribution of income of any industrial nation in the world. . . . Unless we turn this situation around we're going to have a two-tiered society; we can't be a prosperous or stable society with a huge gap between the very rich and everyone else. . . . As the economy grows, people who work the machines and clean the offices and provide the basic goods and services are supposed to share in the gains, but that hasn't been happening.[14]

Since the late 1970s the connection between increases in labor productivity and the return going to labor has been cut in the United States. Increases in real wages are normally limited by improvements in labor productivity and, there-fore, remain within the bounds of capitalist profitability. However, productivity increases are transformed into wage increases only when workers have the power to establish this linkage.[15] Labor productivity has outstripped real com-pensation since the late 1970s, and at an accelerating rate after 1987. Between March of 1994 and March of 1995, average real wages and salaries fell 2 percent while labor productivity rose by 2 percent. For two decades, declining unit labor costs have increased the profitability of capital in the United States.[16]

Struggles of labor organizations by their very nature embrace a fundamental class dynamic that is absolutely critical to the improvement in the general wage level. Union density declined from a high of 34 percent of the total workforce in 1956, to 15.5 percent in 1995. This has significantly eroded labor's bargaining power. Capitalist competition, labor-saving technical change, and the downward pressure of the reserve army of the unemployed have forced down real wages as labor productivity has grown.[17]

The Role of the State

State policies are integrally related to the global restructuring of capital, the devaluation of labor power, and the growth in inequality of income and wealth. These policies can be understood in the relation of the state to the trans-nationalization of capital.[18] The character of state intervention has shifted in line with the changing balance of class forces. Power has moved decisively toward global capital.[19] State intervention on behalf of global capital undermines the power of workers and their organizations. Trade liberalization policies, for example, increasingly promote a global low-wage and expendable laborforce. The redefinition of subsistence and, therefore, value of labor power is, in part, a product of public policy. "It is this combined impact of government-empowered employers and government-disempowered employees that has created, maintained, and now expands the world of marginal incomes and high unemployment."[20]

In the United States, the state has intervened in such a way as to encourage and facilitate class polarization and growth of the low-wage workforce. The orchestration of unemployment through monetary policy, tax reform benefiting the wealthy, cuts in social spending, deregulation, privatization, attacks on trade unions, and hemispheric and global trade liberalization represent a consolidation of state intervention to benefit global capital and weaken organized labor. They represent new forms of intervention, not the state's withdrawal from economic activity.[21]

Government support of these policies has been framed in terms of the need to effectively compete in the world economy. Competitiveness is defined from capital's perspective to sustain long-term profitability. Competition is the coercive force of global capital and the accumulation process. This is masked by defining competition in nationalistic terms, where nation-states are characterized as competing with each other, and the nation's relative competitiveness is derived from increasing profitability. In reality, however, as Paul Burkett has astutely observed:

> the whole ideology of competitiveness serves to divide and rule workers, both domestically and internationally. Its real purpose is to facilitate acquiescence to the redistribution of income from wages to profits and to an economy which is increasingly incapable of producing positions of material comfort (not to speak of human fulfillment) for all but a shrinking minority. When taken to its logical conclusion the competitiveness strategy leads to a reduction of workers' living standards to the lowest common denominator internationally.[22]

"New" Industrial Relations

In the United States, one way the state has endorsed capital's low-wage strategy of competition is by supporting and proposing initiatives to promote labor-management cooperation and productivity. The proposition is if U.S. industry is to reach relative competitiveness on a world scale, it must achieve more effective labor relations. Effective labor relations are defined primarily as improvements in labor productivity and labor control. Increasing labor productivity—both in terms of quantity of output and quality of performance—emphasizes cooperation between labor and capital. The path to global competitiveness, according to the state, requires a new era of nonadversarial labor relations based on "teamwork and mutual respect," where a workplace is envisioned "in which happy workers and fair-minded managers labor together harmoniously to increase corporate productivity and competitiveness."[23] A more cooperative industrial relations system that encourages and increases worker participation is projected as a way to improve labor productivity, profitability, and capital's global competitiveness. Labor organizations are viewed positively as long as they are seen as facilitating such goals. Increased productivity is based on worker involvement in workplace decision making; and, according to this perspective, unions provide the best structure or vehicle for genuine employee involvement. As former U.S. labor secretary Ray Marshall recommends, "high-performance organizations require much greater worker involvement, which, in turn, is the most effective if workers have an independent source of power to represent their interests."[24] Little if any notice, however, is given to the basic reason for the existence of unions: protecting and representing the needs of their membership in a conflictual environment.[25]

History has shown that when organized labor succeeds, it is not through cooperating with management to make the employer more competitive. Rather, its power has been derived from the acceptance of the adversarial nature of its relation with capital, and from its reliance on independent labor organization based on labor's distinct and incompatible interests with management. U.S. labor history, past and present, has been marked by hostility and conflict between labor and capital, with a fundamental contempt expressèd for labor unions, in conjunction with a general unwillingness to accept and respect their existence. Yet the state feels compelled to convince labor that what is good for capital is good for wage labor. It is more than coincidental that this approach to industrial relations has arisen in an unprecedented period of global economic integration, restructuring, and competition. The fundamental underlying reason labor-management cooperation, increased productivity, and global competition are articulated together at the same time is that they are all part of the same vision—the drive to achieve unfettered freedom for social capital to exploit labor everywhere and to accumulate wealth, beyond the boundaries of nation-states, throughout the world.[26]

The attempt has been to create a caricature of labor unions as integral to and necessary for social capital's effective economic performance while, in actuality, it amounts to an ample opportunity to undermine the integrity and power of workers. Unfortunately, part of the labor movement supports this effort, and views labor's long-term survival, and the solution to the nation's economic problems of poverty, inequality, and low-wage economic development, to be dependent, in part, on a move toward a more nonadversarial approach to unionism that allows for more management "flexibility," "labor-management partnerships," and the "high-performance workplace." The tragic irony is that while recognizing that capital attempts, either with state assistance or acquiescence, to bludgeon labor organizations to death, capitalist ideology of cooperation and competitiveness continues to be accepted as a matter of faith.

Bound by the tradition of business unionism—unwillingness to accept the relationship between capital and labor as fundamentally antagonistic—certain elements within the labor movement continue to extend their hand of cooperation to capital, and to work with business and government as partners in order to succeed in a world of capitalist competition. Business unionists fail to see the self-defeating and contradictory nature of partnership with capital when the maximization of profits and minimization of costs through labor productivity are all at the expense of workers. Working together for goals of increased productivity and quality are emphasized, while simultaneously, decline in unit labor costs, and competition among workers compel the unions to become subordinated to capitalist objectives. By requiring workers to compete with each other under a regime of labor-management participation, the collective power of unions is undermined. Traditional collective bargaining, on the other hand, attempts to take labor out of capitalist competition by establishing standards and, hence, minimizing competition among workers in the labor market. The policies according to "new" industrial relations have the opposite effect. They require workers to adopt capitalist norms of competition that put workers at each others' throats. The "new American workplace" "has actually drawn a blueprint for the fragmentation of labor organization and the dispersal of its real power."[27]

The "new" regime of industrial relations is characterized by an alleged fundamental reconciliation of interests between capital and labor—where mutual interests are emphasized, and the existing fundamental, irreconcilable antagonism between labor and capital is ignored.[28] The reality has shown otherwise. Capital as a social relation remains committed to expanding the production of surplus value through deepening the real subsumption and subordination of labor under capital—cheapening the value of labor power. The "new" approach to industrial relations is not so new after all. To be more competitive and more effective, workers have always been asked to participate in their own further subjugation under capital; to cooperate fully in the further exploitation of themselves by increasing the production of relative surplus value.

Strategies for Renewal

The chapters in this book offer a fresh and innovative approach to the dynamics of labor's decline and proposals for policy initiatives necessary for labor's revitalization. Emphasizing the conscious restructuring of capitalism on a global scale and its effect on class relations, the contributions challenge traditional economics and industrial relations' wisdom and develop alternative theoretical and practical plans of action for labor as we approach the twenty-first century. Addressing general as well as specific issues of concern for labor in a variety of contexts, the book provides the basis for theoretically informed practice. A common thread that binds all of the selections is the recognition of the fundamental antagonism between capital and labor, and a commitment to independent, militant, adversarial unionism.

In the opening chapter, Cyrus Bina and Chuck Davis have gone beyond the internationalization of circuits of social capital, drawing on the transformation of world economy since the 1970s, proposing a unified conceptual framework compatible with it. They calibrate the global economy in terms of global competition and cheapening of labor power, and show how the transnationalization of the labor process is intimately related to the universalization of class struggle. The result, they argue, has also been the establishment of a newly formed global social relation with its own technological and institutional power structure, beyond the boundaries of nation-states. Globalization is a process that renders obsolete the international system centered around the building blocks of nation-state and national economy.

According to Bina and Davis, globalization in capitalism is a macro phenomenon that is universally contingent on the cheapening of labor power through ceaseless technological revolutions—hence the need for crises of restructuring in the face of symptoms such as the swollen ranks of the unemployed or the contingent armies of the working poor everywhere.

They further maintain that the post–World War II economy (and polity) known as *Pax Americana,* while facilitating the spread of globalization, has ultimately led to its own demise in terms of loss of hegemony and global relevance. The postwar American labor aristocracy, they point out, has been dependent on the hegemony of Pax Americana. Hence Bina and Davis, within a unifying framework, attribute the fall of the U.S. labor aristocracy to the rise of the globalizaton process, and point to labor's revitalization through international labor solidarity.

In chapter 2, David Ranney combines the effects of globalization and the predicament of U.S. labor in the devalorization of capital. He defines devalorization as "the restructuring and/or destruction of firms, infrastructure, industrial capital, and driving down wages and living standards worldwide." Well informed of the instabilities that are embedded in the periodic crises of restructuring, Ranney provides a critique of the existing theories and policies, from "smokestack chasing" to "capacity building," profit squeeze, profit cycle, etc., before offering an alternative view, centered on the emergence of "supranational" corporations and the domestic "deindustrialization." Here deindustrialization is clearly the flip side of transnationalization. Consequently, the management decisions to close the domestic factories seem "reasonable" and, indeed, "fit in with a rational global strategy for capital as a collective entity." As for the labor agenda, he cautions about illusion of the generation of wealth according to just principles. As the size of the pie shrinks through devalorization, he warns, many workers—having no awareness about the limits of capitalism— may resort to all sorts of chauvinism in pursuit of their own "share." Hence, Ranney's singular emphasis is on the role of intellectuals and activists "to clarify the nature of the present situation."

In chapter 3, Laurie Clements points out that the shift to the right in the political arena has had a profound effect on the public sector. Over the past two decades, deregulation and privatization have become more pervasive elements that have affected government at all levels. The call from the Clinton administration to "reinvent government" is, he argues, an extension of the developments that occurred under the Reagan and Bush administrations. He suggests that this has led to a resurgence in political entrepreneurialism in which all parts of the public sector are being encouraged to structure their activities in line with private business practice.

Clements argues that this development has had an adverse impact on the public sector, which has become ever more squeezed of resources. Government is expected to do ever more with less. The faith in the market has become a national myopia, but he maintains that this has had the effect of changing and restructuring the role of government to more finely tune its policies to meet the needs of private capital. He remarks that under Reagan and Bush, the retreat from Keynesianism was more ideological than real, and contends that the demand to downsize government, deregulate, and privatize are part of a "grand illusion" that simply reducing government would enhance the economic well-being of the populace.

Clements concludes that while the problems of government administration are real, privatization and deregulation are quick-fix solutions to complex issues and are rooted in political opportunism. These solutions are based on an ideology of privilege that has already led to the greatest concentration of wealth in the twentieth century. This has been accompanied by social and urban devastation, and political alienation. Government must become proactive to solve the problems facing the nation. If government policies continue to be reconfigured to better serve the needs of the wealthy, the real losers are those most in need in our society.

In chapter 4, Norman Eiger provides a critique of developments that have occurred in Sweden over the past fifteen years. He argues that the Swedish model has gone through dramatic changes. He details the major policy initiatives developed by the Swedish trade union movement and the Social Democratic Party. The commitment to full employment was a cornerstone of the policy, and workplace programs were also designed to serve broader social ends. Active labor market policies facilitated the movement of workers by providing incentives to relocate, training, employment service support, and the use of the state as employer of last resort. Unions cooperated with wage restraint in inflationary periods. The labor movement, however, pushed for greater influence over investment policies of Swedish corporations, which culminated in the Meidner Plan in the late 1970s.

The plan was abandoned, as the free market ideology that affected many Western economies in the 1980s influenced Swedish economic policymakers. The use of rising unemployment to fight inflation quickly found its way into the Swedish model, leaving it unrecognizable to its earlier supporters. The Swedish adjustment has fallen into line with other Western economies—higher unemployment, protection of the currency in international markets, and the distribution of wealth toward the owners of capital. Sweden developed its own version of "Reaganomics." Eiger suggests this results from the global restructuring of capital as Sweden's own large corporations have come to increasingly dominate the economy, and following the lead of other multinational corporations, increasingly locate their investments abroad. These changes, as the author outlines, have had broad-based repercussions in the political and social welfare arenas.

Eiger concludes that a fundamental transition has occurred in the economic and labor market dimensions of the model. The attempt to move beyond reformism toward social ownership and democratic control of the economy was soundly defeated, leaving international capital interests to drive the economy. Similar profound changes have occurred in the political dimension of the model, although the institutional welfare state appears to have been the lasting legacy of Sweden's challenge to the hegemony of capital.

In chapter 5, Michele Naples deals with the labor relations in U.S. coal mining in terms of a paradigm known as the social structure of accumulation (SSA). From the framework of SSA, she introduces a set of ten generalizations that, in her view, would draw a parallel between the "institutionalization" of the SSA-type social relations, and ups and downs of labor in U.S. coal mining since World War II. Five periods are distinguished: (1) the period of contention before the dominance of postwar SSA; (2) the period of truce between coal operators and the union; (3) the unraveling of the truce; (4) the period of subsequent stalemate between coal operators and the union; and (5) the beginning of new experiments in labor relations by Pittston, giving a pivotal position to the Pittston strike of 1989. Naples also contrasts the SSA framework with other approaches to labor relations, including neoclassical theory, the institutionalist school, traditional Marxian theory, and the regulation school.

In chapter 6, David Fairris provides a historical perspective on the changing structure of workplace relations in the mass-production sector of the economy. He suggests that the active participation of rank-and-file workers in their unions gave way to a centralization of power within unions that emasculated their power on the shop floor. Unions became more bureaucratically centralized and labor relations more codified. Fairris refers to this development as "shop floor contractualism" in which conflict on the floor was increasingly managed. Collective bargaining, to use C. Wright Mills's phrase, became a drainage channel for discontent, in which the grievance procedure served to channel disputes into a more manageable form. A new "accord" was forged that had important long-term consequences for shop floor labor relations, particularly the erosion of rank-and-file power at the point of production, and the appropriation of working conditions by employers in the labor process. This resulted, in the 1960s, he argues, in an increase in the level of shop floor discontent manifest in strikes over working conditions, wildcat stoppages, and an increased tension between

rank-and-file workers and labor leadership. It also served to depreciate productivity and reduce profit rates.

Fairris suggests that these changes provided the undercurrent for management
programs promoting labor-management cooperation in the form of various quality programs in the 1970s and 1980s. This created a challenge to the contractualism of the 1950s and 1960s and resulted in significant concessions by unions as
competition, both domestic and international, intensified. But whereas these developments have restored the decentralized bargaining of earlier decades, they
more severely constrain independent worker activity.

Fairris concludes by projecting that the nature of the relationship between
capital and labor at the point of production needs further change. He explores
German and Japanese models of labor relations and concludes that the German
model, while not ideally transferable to an American context, offers a high
degree of plant-level organization that possesses significant power over determining shop floor outcomes. However, he is under no illusion that change can
only be achieved through concerted activity at the point of production, in the
broader community, and through the political process.

In chapter 7, Victor Devinatz points out important lessons to be learned from
the institutionalization of collective bargaining. He suggests that the roots of the
current crisis in the American labor movement can be traced back to the 1940s
and 1950s, when the collective bargaining agreement had to be regarded as the
"workplace rule of law." He offers a historical perspective by comparing the
experience of two Harvester plants organized by the UAW and the FE.

Devinatz suggests that the FE approach to bargaining was to reject the incorporation of unions into the economic status quo, a position, he suggests, more
readily accepted by the UAW. This led to the UAW becoming increasingly
bureaucratized as industrial conflict became ever more institutionalized. When
the FE refused to sign the anticommunist affidavit, the CIO gave the UAW permission to raid the FE locals. Devinatz contends that the position of the UAW was
consolidated in the industry but that power was increasingly removed from the
rank and file. This process was replicated in other sectors of the labor movement.
The erosion of shop floor power, however, became a major factor in reducing the
ability of unions to withstand the onslaught of concessions in the 1980s. His final
contention is that there is a need to rekindle the spirit of shop floor militancy that
has not been seen in the American trade union movement for decades.

In chapter 8, Philip Garrahan and Paul Stewart demonstrate that "employee autonomy, upskilling, and knowledge enhancement" are factors that
must be considered in a viable managerial strategy and its underlying manufacturing techniques. They argue that beneath the "flexible" and autonomous
facade of lean production methods (LPMs), led by Japanese car manufacturers, there is a sinister side that can be attributed to a new mode of subordination,
self-surveillance, work intensification, and the exclusion of independent unions.
The case in point is Nissan's giant production facility in Sunderland, United

Kingdom, where "the company ethos—the 'Nissan Way'—is foregrounded at an early stage in the recruitment and training of new employees." Yet Garrahan and Stewart report that the Nissan workers they interviewed "were anything but a happy family working as a team."

This case study also sheds light on the interface of two overlapping dynamics in the global labor process, namely the region-locale peculiarities and capital-labor specificity. As a result, LPMs in auto manufacturing are to be viewed as a worldwide management initiative—indeed, a unified global theme capable of emerging in many divergent local variations.

Vernon Mogensen argues that the new "information age" has blurred the distinction between the assembly line and the modern office of today, thus subjecting the white-collar workers to, more or less, the same problems that governed the lives of traditional industrial workers. This is the subject of chapter 9. Similarly, it has also created a two-tier pool of deskilled, degraded, stressful, and expendable workers hostage to constant monitoring. The advancement of technology here has not apparently been liberating at all. Instead, it has greatly improved on the Taylorism of the old days.

He details the introduction of the video display terminal (VDT) in the "office of the future" by demonstrating its manifold outcomes, such as lack of career advancement, "technostress," total submission to management, and abnormal miscarriages for U.S. office workers, some 80 percent of whom are women.

Mogensen maintains that the key to organizing U.S. office workers is a full-scale coordination and firm alliance with their foreign counterparts. "Without such effort," he points out, "domestic attempts are bound to fail since work can be readily exported." What are the major labor issues in this particular sector? He points to reproductive and ergonomic hazards of VDT-related work, comparable worth, parental leave, day-care provision, and national health care. Given that only 13.8 percent of the clerical workers in the United States are organized, the field is open, but the challenge for organized labor is how to articulate a unifying common ground that will be acceptable to all clerical workers and their industrial counterparts across the globe.

Offering a Canadian perspective on current challenges in the workplace, in chapter 10, Elaine Bernard provides a case study report of her research into management resistance to change. She argues and demonstrates that while much research focuses on worker resistance, much needs to be done to review managerial Luddism. Bernard argues that the driving force behind management resistance is the fact that work is being "re-Taylorized," with the new systems challenging the authority of middle management. The threat is manifest in the use of centralized databases that allow senior management greater control over both costs and personnel, including middle management. This, she suggests, is a conscious management choice for purposes of control, not an inherent characteristic of the control system itself in terms of improved productivity and efficiency.

At the same time, Bernard argues, workers are increasingly encroaching on management authority. Middle managers are often not informed of the implications of the changes that are being made, and frequently they do not have input into the design process of new work systems. She also found that while middle management complained that workers resisted change, this was not sustained by the research; even where jobs were at stake, workers were more positive toward technological innovation that would make their jobs easier or more interesting than were middle management. Her contention is that management resistance is rooted in the antidemocratic and authoritarian organizational structures of control that dominate workplaces. Computerization is welcomed by managers insofar as it enhances their control over workers and the production process. She concludes that new technology has become a "contested terrain" that workers seek to control work processes and management seeks to control workers.

Finally, in chapter 11, David Schultz shows an alternative avenue to support labor, capitalizing on the legal remedies against plant closing. Today, U.S. workers and their communities are bearing the brunt of the relocation of manufacturing plants. This has been continuously going on since the early 1970s. The social cost of unemployment has not only left a heavy burden on the shoulders of working people but also has created devastating effects on the lives of communities all over this nation. As Schultz observes, "the impacts of these closings are known to include such symptoms as chronic unemployment, reduced incomes, loss of savings and other property, and physical and mental health problems, [notably] alcoholism, physical abuse, divorce, and even suicide." All these make up the cost of globalization, a capitalist strategy that has set forth many new fault lines in our society.

This chapter provides two sets of remedies: the use of eminent domain, and the claim of infringement on community property rights. Schultz explains the legal cases that set forth the precedents for exercising the option of eminent domain, namely *Berman* v. *Parker,* a U.S. Supreme Court decision in 1954, expanded by *Poletown Neighborhood Council* v. *City of Detroit, City of Oakland* v. *Oakland Raiders,* and *Hawaii Housing Authority* v. *Midkiff.* Similarly, he introduces the reader to the realms of breach of contract, promissory estoppel, and the implied contract, through all of which the assertion of rights to the community property seems applicable. He cites *United Steel Workers of America* v. *U.S. Steel Corp.* not as a lost cause but as a full-length mirror reflecting the reactionary political atmosphere that, from time to time, runs the judicial system of this country. Yet Schultz appeals to "a conscious strategy of litigation to pursue test cases that would be most favorable to establishing property or contractual rights" for labor.

Conclusions

Beyond Survival: Strategy for Labor's Revitalization

The continued deterioration of working-class life under capitalism poses a serious challenge to organized labor. The failure of the labor movement to achieve its economic, political, and social goals has led to the following conclusion: no longer business as usual. As Howard Botwinick has succinctly stated, there is a

> [need] to develop viable strategies for militant, adversarial unionism in today's increasingly competitive environment. [A need to] provide coherent alternatives to corporate calls for wage concessions, team concepts, and other forms of nonadversarial labor relations that are now supposedly required to "beat the competition." ... the continued failure to develop viable labor strategies to effectively confront the forces of capitalist competition is proving to be devastating for the labor movement.[29]

Given the continued existence of conflict between labor and capital, the imperative to avoid company unions through independent labor organization is as strong as ever. Equally serious is the need for labor to organize on the same scale as capital. This is necessary to take wages and working conditions out of competition. Labor must organize globally to accomplish this task. Stewart Acuff describes the nature of increased militancy and wider worker organization needed for labor to achieve its goals:

> What is militancy? It is our refusal to play by their rules. It is our refusal to be bound by their constraints. It is our refusal to allow them to set the terms and conditions of our struggle. Militancy includes the collectivization of our individual anger. It includes the conscious disruption of business as usual. It includes the breaking of the civic order or civil peace. It is the mobilization of our members and other constituents in nonviolent direct action and struggle. Militancy is one of the most effective means we have for altering the distribution of wealth and building power for our institutions and people. It is our responsibility to mobilize our members to struggle collectively for their future.[30]

Defending and demanding a better standard of living and a better way of life for workers require organization inside and outside the workplace. Supportive labor law reform is not enough. Successful organization requires a new orientation for labor built on democratic participation; militant, tactical innovation; strong labor-community alliances/coalitions based on rank-and-file and grassroots involvement; independent political action founded on a labor-based political party; and, most importantly, international labor solidarity.

Positive developments are occurring within the house of labor. Many labor organizations have already adopted a more expanded perspective on organizing. More must follow. Finding the right combination of local, national, and international efforts to revitalize the labor movement will require a process of economic and political experimentation that may even include a tendency toward the transformation of capitalist social relations. Yet the end of capital as a social relation requires revolutionary change.

The very first step toward the revitalization of labor is the recognition of the historical fact that fundamentally there is no reconciliation between the interests of labor and those of capital, and that despite the sincere attempts of one side or the other in restraining itself from plunging into daily antagonisms that are brought to bear by the existing mode of accumulation, all the policies that are based on social harmony remain illusive, if not tantamount to outright lies. The reason is that the very existence of wage labor, a category *par excellence* in capitalism, embodies the seed of all antagonisms that would ramify the capitalist society. By recognizing this simple fact, workers and their organizations will be able to conduct themselves for better survival.

—The Editors
1995

Notes

1. Ben Fine, *Economic Theory and Ideology.* (London: Edward Arnold, 1980), ch. 1.

2. Ben Fine and Laurence Harris, "Ideology and Markets: Economic Theory and the 'New Right,' " in Ralph Miliband, Leo Panich, and John Saville, eds., *Socialist Register* (London: Merlin Press, 1987), 367, emphasis added.

3. Noam Chomsky, "Rollback IV," *Z Magazine* 8, no. 5 (May 1995): 18.

4. *ILO Washington Focus* (Winter 1995), 2.

5. Cyrus Bina, "On Sand Castles and Sand-Castle Conjectures: A Rejoinder," *Arab Studies Quarterly,* 17, nos. 1 & 2 (Winter, Spring 1995): 167–71.

6. *Minneapolis Star Tribune* (June 27, 1995) 1D, citing the U.S. Dept. of Labor.

7. Rick Mercier, "Welfare Reform," *Z Magazine* 7, no. 9 (September 1994): 26.

8. Holly Sklar, "Disposable Workers," *Z Magazine,* (January 1994): 37.

9. *Minneapolis Star Tribune* (June 27, 1995): 1D.

10. *LRA's Economic Notes* (May 1995).

11. John McDermott, "And the Poor Get Poorer," *The Nation* 259, no. 16 (November 14, 1994): 577.

12. *LRA's Economic Notes* (May 1995).

13. Quote from U.S. Labor Secretary Robert Reich in *Minneapolis Star Tribune* (June 27, 1995): 1D.

14. Quoted in "Income Distribution," *Too Much Newsletter* 1, no. 1 (Spring 1995): 2.

15. Rick Mercier, "Welfare Reform."

16. See Keith Bradsher, "Productivity Is All, But It Doesn't Pay Well," The *New York Times* (June 25, 1995) 4; and Howard Botwinick, *Persistent Inequalities: Wage Disparity Under Capitalist Competition*, Princeton, NJ: Princeton University Press, 1993, 9.

17. Botwinick, *Persistent Inequalities,* 260

18. John Holloway, "Global Capital and the Nation State," *Capital & Class,* 52 (Spring 1994): 23, 32.

19. Fine and Harris, "Ideology and Markets," 369, 367.

20. McDermott, "And the Poor Get Poorer," 580.

21. Fine and Harris, "Ideology and Markets," 368, 369.

22. Paul Burkett, "The Strange U.S. Economic Recovery and Clintonomics Historically Considered," *Capital & Class,* 52 (Spring 1994): 13.

23. Laura McClure, "Clinton Administration's Labor Policy: Cooperate!" *Z Magazine* (May 1994): 48.

24. Christopher Schenk, reviewing *Unions and Economic Competitiveness,* ed. Lawrence Mishel and Paula Voos (Armonk, NY: M.E. Sharpe, Inc., 1992) in *Capital & Class,* 53 (Summer 1994), 140–142.

25. Ibid.

26. Robert E. Wages, " 'Cooperationism' an Ideological Smokescreen," *OCAW Reporter* (May–June 1995): 4.

27. See Kim Moody, "New Unionism or No Unionism At All," *Labor Notes* (December 1988): 15; and "AFL-CIO Committee on the Evolution of Work, A Report," *The New American Workplace: A Labor Perspective* (February 1994).

28. See Tony Smith, "Flexible Production and the Capital/Wage Labour Relation in Manufacturing," *Capital & Class* 53 (Summer 1994): 39–63.

29. Botwinick, *Persistent Inequalities,* 7.

30. Stewart Acuff, "We're not going to play by their rules," *JwJ Newsletter, I'll Be There,* 7, no. 3 (July 1994).

1

Wage Labor and Global Capital: Global Competition and Universalization of the Labor Movement

Cyrus Bina and Chuck Davis

Introduction

Historically, the development of capitalism has provided the preconditions for the collective organization of workers, as the structures of labor organizations have by necessity evolved to meet the capitalist challenge. Thus the global evolution of the capital-labor relation has a profound influence on the nature of the class struggle. Capitalist competition has continuously pitted worker against worker, attempting to drive wages, conditions of work, and the quality of life to the lowest possible level—first locally, then regionally, nationally, and internationally. In combating the extraction of absolute and relative surplus value, workers have often conducted economic and, in many cases, political struggle to regulate and improve the terms and conditions under which they are obliged to dispose of their labor power. What is significant is that by transcending capitalist competition for labor power, the expression of trade union unity limits the ability of capital to minimize the value of labor power, which, in concrete and historical terms, counters capital's demand for increased control and domination of the labor process. This is particularly true in the present era. "Workers of the world, unite" ipso facto is becoming increasingly relevant and applicable as capital transcends the boundaries of nation-states. The transnationalization of capitalist relations—that is, the emergence of a *global* tendency to *real* subsumption of labor under capital (production of relative surplus value)—brings the common interests of workers in different countries into sharper focus. Workers are commonly affected by the global integration of labor processes; this elevates the

19

objective conditions for labor solidarity to an international level. On an international basis, workers are integrated into a new relationship. If workers can confront transnational capital with their own international organizations, they can begin to mitigate the deleterious effects of capital's worldwide mobility. At the stage of transnationalization (i.e., the global integration of social capital), labor organizations must play a central role to enhance the capacity of the working class worldwide in order to transform capitalist social relations.

However, the organizational capacity for the development of working-class consciousness at the national and global levels has yet to be realized. The discrepancy between the material foundation of the transnationalization of capitalist relations and the historical record of working-class nationalism in large part remains. It can be interpreted as an indicator of the contradictory balance of class forces, the backwardness of the labor movement itself, and the anachronistic worker and union appeal to nationalism. For labor organizations to succeed rudimentarily along economic and political lines, they must shed their historic roles as being largely *national* and *nationalistic* in structure and orientation.[1]

For capital, *sui generis*, to become a *de facto* global entity there has to be a global circuit in all its forms that would, in turn, unify the spheres of circulation and production: commodity capital, money capital, and productive capital. This has been historically accomplished through the internationalization of productive capital that fulfilled the completion of the globalization of capital in all its social forms.[2] This has resulted *inter alia* in colossal and integrated entities known as transnational corporations (TNCs), which operate throughout the world. To be sure, TNCs are cumulative effects of the transnationalization of capital in all its forms. Yet, while their emergence is contingent on the transnationalization of both commodity and money capitals, they would acquire a contemporary status via transnationalization of productive capital—including the globalization of technology. Having direct control over many different labor processes around the globe, transnational social capital (not to be confused with a single TNC) tends to exploit labor power worldwide. Tension between transnational capital and domestic capital, and the problematic role of the state in attempting to remedy this conflict, cannot be ignored. However, this issue exists at a more concrete level of inquiry, and therefore its analysis, being beyond the scope of this chapter, must come later. Here, contrary to the characterization offered by some writers, global capital is not an algebraic or a geometrical summation of the existing national capitals that are moving constantly across the globe from one country to another.[3] It is rather an organic supranational socioeconomic entity that intimately corresponds to the structure of global social relations. Thus we maintain that the most appropriate unit of analysis is none other than the globalized labor process. If capital is a global entity with its own global strategy, so there must be a corresponding global strategy for labor's revitalization.[4]

In what follows, in the first four sections we shall attempt to present a theoretical framework for the study of the labor process and competition in global capitalism. In the next three sections we shall focus on current problems, and the potential for revitalization of U.S. labor and the unity of labor in the context of the transnational economy. The last section carries our concluding remarks.

Competition, Globalization, and the Labor Process

Capitalist relations of production generate labor processes that are conducive to the development of capitalism beyond the boundaries of the nation-state. As a result, it is necessary to recognize the specific mechanisms through which the unfolding of the above process takes shape, and to investigate the consequences of this development for the world economy. Additionally, it is instructive to examine whether a greater integration of world capitalism will lead to further competition or monopoly.

For obvious reasons, the above issues have far-reaching implications for labor and its global strategies vis-à-vis capital. But strategies have to be set within a conceptual framework. The theoretical arguments of "monopoly capital," "dependency theory," or, for instance, the "theory of transnationalization of capital," provide different answers to the problems associated with working-class struggle.

We contend that, in appraising the role of competition in contemporary capitalism, radical economic theory is as confused as its counterpart in mainstream neoclassical economics. Radical theory, devoid of an independent conception of competition, relies on the textbook idealization of competition in terms of an axiomatically designated *spectrum* of competition-monopoly. *Competition* is defined as the absence of monopoly in a tautological manner, implying a division of capitalism into *laissez-faire* and *monopoly* stages, thus distinguishing its nineteenth-century and twentieth-century phases of development in an antithetical manner.[5] Yet radical theory accomplishes this in an ahistorical manner based on ideal types that are contrary to actual competition under capitalism. The idealization of competition thus parallels the idealization of its point of departure, monopoly.

For example, there are inconsistencies in characterizing national economies as monopolistic while considering the world economy as competitive, by simply relying on the number of firms (or production units) within each transnational industry. This makes a significant difference in explaining the origins and development of the transnational labor process. Correspondingly, this sort of analysis embodies its own strategic remedies for the revitalization of the labor movement.[6]

The seemingly appealing periodization of capitalism into the phases of *laissez-faire* and *monopoly* not only mischaracterizes capitalism but also reverses the order of its historical development. Anticipating this well over a century ago in *Grundrisse,* Marx pointedly explains:

> But free competition is the adequate form of the production process of capital. The further it is developed, the purer the forms in which its motion appear. . . .

As long as capital is weak, it still itself relies on the crutches of past modes of production, or of those which will pass with its rise. As soon as it feels strong, it throws away the crutches, and moves in accordance with its own laws.[7]

Marx also shows how this "adequate form of the production process of capital" develops from a single branch of a particular industry to become a worldwide phenomenon. The following passage illustrates his argument:

Within a single society ... the mode of production of capital develops in one branch of industry. ... Nevertheless, it is (1) its necessary tendency to conquer the mode of production in all respects, to bring them under the rule of capital. Within a given national society this already necessarily arises from the transformation ... of all labor into wage labor; (2) as to external markets, capital imposes this propagation of its mode of production through *international competition*. Competition is the mode generally in which capital secures the *victory of its mode of production* [emphasis added].[8]

According to Marx, competition is a *permanent* feature of the capitalist mode of production, regardless of the differences in cultural, legal, institutional, and historical characteristics that usually separate capitalist societies from one another. To secure its victory, fundamentally, *social capital* propagates its mode of production across the boundaries of nation-states through competition for labor power, the *sine qua non* of surplus value or lifeline of capitalism.

This is a very basic characteristic of capital as a social relation. Therefore, to uncover the origin of competition, as opposed to its manifested forms, "one has to start from the level of capital as a whole," that is, to start with competition of social capital for labor power.[9] This, of course, is intimately related to the crucial question of why the transnationalization process must be identified as a macro problem whose totality is not reducible to the summation of its constituent parts.[10] In other words, Marx's theory of competition has two levels: (1) the level of capital in general, which pertains to the most fundamental characteristic of this mode of production, that is, competition of social capital for labor power; and (2) the level of individual capital, which is the point of departure of capitalist production and thereby arises from the above level in terms of the coercive encounters of many capitals.[11]

The material basis for the transnationalized labor processes is historically contingent on the "victory" of the capitalist mode of production and the establishment of competition for labor power globally. Competition associated with capital in general, that is, the essential competition of capital for *labor power,* embodies the historical tendency of *cheapening* labor power, whereas competition for *cheap labor* (a prevailing issue in the development literature) is competition at the level of many capitals; it is competition among individual capitals for an entity that has *prior existence* by way of "primitive accumulation" or because of the circumstances that surround its low reproduction cost. What turns labor power into capital in a broad macroeconomic framework is not the interaction of individual capitals but rather the organic unity of social capital as a whole. Here, competition germane to this unity exists prior to the competition of constituent parts. Within the context of transnationalization and the current global crisis of accumulation, there have been profound attempts by capital to devalue labor power domestically and internationally in both the advanced and less developed capitalist countries.

Competition at the level of social capital originates from the production process, *differentia specifica,* founded on *wage labor* and, accordingly, *unfolds* within the realm of distribution (through exchange). As soon as the mode of production becomes secure, the study of global competition among many capitals can no longer be isolated from the analysis of competition associated with capital as a whole. This also applies to struggles in political and ideological arenas. Within a globalized labor process, wage labor simultaneously confronts capital in general and capital in its specific forms. Economic struggles soon embrace a political dimension. Here, the struggle between labor and capital reaches beyond the confines of the workplace.

There are two significant dimensions associated with such struggles: (1) the activities aimed at *individual capital* for the purpose of better economic and working conditions in a single workplace or industry, and (2) the activities aimed directly at *capital in general* for improvement in the working and living conditions of *workers in general.* The latter type of struggle coalesces the working class and provides the material basis of political struggles that transcend the traditional boundaries of the workplace. Economic struggles are transformed into political ones. Marx illustrates this development in a letter to Friedrich Bolte (November 23, 1871):

> [On the one hand,] every movement in which the working class as a class confronts the ruling classes and tries to constrain them by pressure from without is a political movement. For instance, the attempt by strikes, etc., in a particular factory or even in a particular trade to compel individual capitalists to reduce the working day, is a purely economic movement. On the other hand, the movement to force through an eight-hour, etc., *law* is a *political* movement. And in this way out of the separate economic movements of the workers there grows up everywhere a *political* movement, that is to say, a *class* movement [emphases in original].[12]

Because of transnationalization, the struggles against capital in general necessarily take on a worldwide political dimension. It provides the fundamental ingredients for working-class unity on a global scale. In today's objective conditions of global competition, such struggles can no longer remain within the narrow limits of nationalism or the selfish confines of economism, sexism, and racial prejudice. These struggles, therefore, must be able to turn the table of competition against *capital,* thus transforming its effects, from dividing into consolidating.

Cheapening of Labor Power and Spatial Mobility

To understand the transnational character of the labor process, one has to grasp (1) the transformation of *work* itself in the advanced capitalist countries (ACCs), and (2) the emerging global integration of capital, including the spread of capitalist social relations into the former colonies, semicolonies, and less developed countries (LDCs). Undue emphasis on the role of the advanced nations that mistakenly equates transnational social capital with transnational corporations provides an inadequate basis for the study of the transnationalization of labor process.[13] The need is to focus on the *relationship* and the organic connection between capitalism in the advanced capitalist countries and in the Third World, beyond the boundaries of the nation-states—that is, on the global conquest of the capitalist mode of production, not distinctions created by national boundaries or symptomatic distinctions that are often put forth in terms of regional trading blocs, or the center-periphery dichotomy. Such a conquest has always been made in uneven pace.

At the present stage of global capitalism, the centerpiece of global accumulation is the unifying control of the emerging transnational labor processes, and the growing domination of capital over labor internationally. This collectively represents the social character of global capital. The resultant transnational labor process is, *prima facie,* a point of departure of the transnationalization of capital in general that establishes and consolidates capitalist social relations beyond a simple transfer of physical or financial capital or technology.[14] As a result, theories that capitalize on trade activities or direct foreign investments omit the significance of present transformations.

The advantage of starting with the analysis of capitalist social relations rather than capital as a physical or monetary entity is the recognition of the *internal* (capitalist) transformation of many Third World nations. This is occurring in conjunction with the sweeping changes in the labor processes within the advanced capitalist countries. The context of this conjunction lies in the *global economy,* especially since World War II.[15]

First, a large number of postcolonial states have moved from "primitive accumulation" (centered around the separation of direct producer from means of production) since World War II, to the production of *relative* surplus value, which has facilitated the demise of the *colonial* division of labor. Import-substitution industrialization and its sequel, "export-led growth," were intended to overcome the internal barriers that prevented capitalist development in these countries.[16] This resulted in the *internal* propagation of capitalism and paved the way for embracing the *external* penetration of transnational capital.

Second, from the turn of the century, there has developed a series of organizational and technological transformations that have revolutionized the labor process in the advanced capitalist countries, especially in the United States. These include *Taylorism,* which intensified and regulated the *real* subsumption of labor under capital and which prepared the labor process for a radical transformation toward a continuous system of large-scale mass production.[17] In addition, recent advances in the field of computer technology, applications such as robotics, numerical control (NC), computer-aided design (CAD), etc., in conjunction with the telecommunications revolution, are found in present-day production processes. These technologies confer a new meaning to the devaluation of labor power and grant a new outlook to the spatial control of capital over the global labor process.

As Harley Shaiken elucidates, "Once the machining knowledge is embodied in the numerical control program, it becomes possible to transfer production from a struck plant to shops that are still working, regardless of whether they are across the street or halfway around the world."[18] Here, *scientific management* flourished through the intense application of science and technology for the sake of strengthening the control of *constant* capital over its *variable* counterpart. As Marx maintains, "The principle of developed capital is precisely to make special skills superfluous, and to make manual work, [that is to say] directly physical labor, generally superfluous both as skill and as muscular exertion; to transfer skill, rather, into the dead forces of nature."[19]

The consequence of all this has been the continuous and progressive cheapening of labor power everywhere and the increasing control and domination of capital over labor, following the tendency for proliferation of the most technologically advanced labor processes.[20] Aside from its hegemonic appeal, devaluation of labor power allows for coexistence of the highest level of technology and the lowest possible labor cost, including the training cost of labor, especially in the case of Third World workers. Thus several decades of intense deskilling—that is, devaluation in value terms—and displacement of workers directly affected by technical change in the advanced capitalist countries suddenly finds its cumulative application within the countries of the Third World. As a result, the rising complexity of technology in the production process does not pose a physical limit to raising the rate of exploitation of the working class globally.

The transnationalization of productive capital, unlike merchant and finance capital, provides stimulus for further development of relative surplus value and thereby deepens the real subsumption of labor under capital in LDCs. But the real subsumption of labor under capital may not obtain the status of a *sui generis* mode of production by the introduction of machinery alone. This also requires the *limitation of the working day*. In other words, in the absence of limiting the length of the working day, through working-class struggle supported by the enactment of appropriate legislation, the production based on machinery coexists with the production of absolute surplus value. Here, the further introduction of machinery can be obstructed by *elasticity* of the working day itself.[21]

In nineteenth-century Britain the limitation of the working day was realized by the introduction of legislation on behalf of the working class.[22] In nineteenth-century America the task was accomplished through demand for appropriate legislation and struggle to sustain it, primarily in the northern states.[23] Today, in many Third World societies, more or less, the statutory limitation of the working day has already been achieved. But the length of the average working day is considerably longer than its counterpart in the ACCs. In other LDCs, especially in the more traditional sectors, the length of the working day has yet to be politically defined. This is particularly true in those countries in which the employment of child labor is still prevalent. The transnationalization of capital and proliferation of the labor movement provide the potential for the establishment of a worldwide limitation on the working day. It becomes necessary that, as an initial political step, the international labor movement establish a universally uniform working day, based on what is now in effect in the most advanced capitalist countries.

Gender and the Transnational Labor Process

Despite the debates over the issue of the "new" international division of labor, the fact remains that capitalism has been transcending the guarded boundaries of traditional workplaces, and that it has been forcibly laying the foundation of its contradictory outgrowth, constantly setting up *new barriers* of its own globally. These new barriers must not be confused with impediments external to capitalist production proper. For instance, there are differences between the old colonial division of labor and the present international division of labor, and the decline of patriarchy vis-à-vis the emerging social relations under capitalism. Capitalist relations of production, while undermining the subordination of women to family and patriarchy, expose them more fully to social capital's subordination.

Parallel with the above historical dynamic are the material conditions that surround the participation of women in the global economy. These conditions had their roots in the universal absorption and transformation of the family—as formerly the historical site of production—and its outright subordination to capitalist production proper. The consequence of this has been to reconstitute the modern family in its present "residual" form, and to transform it into a "dual" adjunct of production proper, as a precondition of the proletarianization of women, who having been exposed to the discipline of capitalist *production,* also had, aside from the increasing role of the state, to endure the responsibility of reproduction of the labor power.[24]

In the advanced capitalist countries women were further proletarianized, especially at the bottom of the highly stratified labor markets. Here the rapid decline of family wage, the widespread restructuring of the economy, the rampant plant closings, the general impoverishment of the masses, and the swelling of the reserve armies of the unemployed were among the major contributing factors to increasing the labor force participation rate of women. In the Third World, where abject poverty and massive unemployment are the rule, unbounded flexibility and extraordinary discipline are the *sine qua non* of the labor process. The majority of the female labor force that had traditionally worked in agriculture are driven into urban sweatshops. Given the accelerated pace of transnational activity since the 1970s, women have increasingly shifted toward the manufacturing sector.[25]

The above tendency, however, is more apparent in the so-called newly industrializing countries (NICs), where the role of the export sector is significant. For instance, in the export processing zones (EPZs) and other transnational-led labor processes within the Third World there are more than 2 million women, or nearly "3 percent of total worldwide multinational employment."[26]

Finding the argument of cheap labor inadequate, some writers on the subject have argued that employment of women by transnational capital may also have been motivated by (1) women's alleged characteristics of greater discipline in following orders and their display of work habits that generally imply "docility"; (2) women's possession of "skills" that are normally attributed to their gender socialization—for example, "nimble fingers" and ability to work with delicate objects; and (3) women's condition as a flexible source of labor supply, especially where it comes to the acceptance of temporary assignments, unstable work, and flexible hours, associated with subcontracting in most EPZs.[27]

Arguments such as these that characterize the labor process based on physical features or stereotypical attributes are grossly inadequate and, in many cases, even border on tautology, when considering social capital as a whole. There is the need to emphasize the importance of the socioeconomic preconditions that compelled women of the Third World to accept, tolerate, and continue to perform such dreadful jobs.

Finally, there is a need to confront the controversy concerning the "feminization of employment" in the international sexual division of labor. This debate is largely focused on the apparent shift from import-substitution to export led industrialization within most Third World nations during the 1980s (and also continuing during the 1990s). "Feminization of employment" in the world economy implies that a large portion of Third World manufacturing is supported by the employment of women. A number of studies on this subject do not support such a claim.[28] In fact, women's employment is proportionally higher at the lower tiers of subcontracting than at the top.[29]

The Roots of Working-Class Unity

Today, the continuing globalization of the labor process has provided the material conditions for the unity of the working class across the seemingly insurmountable boundaries of nation-states. The fundamental basis of this contradictory process is the global accumulation of capital in the presence of divided global space among nation-states, and the *objective* conditions for working-class unity—based on local struggles that can no longer remain isolated from the global center stage. The analog of all this is the emergence of a historical stage whose transforming capacity goes well beyond the simple export of capital or the "transfer of technology," or the trade issues anticipated by GATT or NAFTA, from one nation to another. In fact, at the present stage of global transformation, the significance of the above symptomatic activities cannot be adequately understood without a careful study of the manifold character of transnational capital, the crisis of globalization, and the resultant global socioeconomic environment.

Given the past two decades of upheaval in the global economy, the *de facto* global character of capital has already transcended the framework of national boundaries.[30] Here came the mastery of an integrated global territory to perpetuate reproduction of social relations. This territory was also a familiar socioeconomic terrain long known to the pioneer of labor internationalism, the International Working Men's Association (the First International).[31] The primary issue facing labor, then and now, is how to avoid the trap of nationalism and become a formidable force in the struggle against social capital transnationally. To be viable one must be a powerful *match* for one's own adversary. Consequently, if capital knows no nation, so must labor. This is indeed a minimal platform to adopt, and is long overdue.

In his inaugural address to the International Working Men's Association nearly 150 years ago, Marx was wondering, "If the emancipation of the working classes requires their fraternal concurrence, how are they to fulfill that great mission with a foreign policy in pursuit of criminal designs, playing on national prejudices, and squandering in piratical wars the people's blood and treasure?"[32] Marx tried to respond to this necessity by assigning a specific responsibility to the trade unions of his time:

> Apart from their original purpose, [the trade unions] must now learn to act deliberately as organizing centers of the working class in the broad interest of its *complete emancipation*. They must aid every social and political movement tending in that direction. . . .They must look carefully after the interests of the worst paid trade, such as agricultural laborers, rendered powerless by the exceptional circumstances. . . . far from being narrow and selfish, [they must] aim at the emancipation of the downtrodden millions [emphasis in original].[33]

The struggles between labor and capital in the Third World, in many instances, are similar to the ones waged during the early development of the advanced capitalist countries. These struggles are primarily political in nature. The workers in the Third World, even in their daily and immediate struggles, must confront the state as their ultimate adversary. For instance, the micro appearance of an export processing zone, or a discrete structure of an export-platform business, can hardly misdirect the attention of workers from the *political* issues surrounding the workplace. A case in point is the bloody struggle of South Korean workers during the late 1980s. Thus, in such an environment any *economic* issue would immediately become a *political* one, and any local issue, directly a *global* one. Here, direct confrontation of workers with the state is, at the same time, a struggle against capital in general, and by implication a struggle against the hegemony of transnational capital. South Korea is an interesting case because it is known as a showcase of export-led industrialization.

In the advanced capitalist countries the working class (both organized and unorganized) has already lost substantial ground during the past two decades. The economic gains of the past have disappeared through constant global restructuring, which has been accelerated by the present economic crisis, ceaseless devaluation of the workforce, the exploding ranks of working poor, the nearly universal outbreaks of plant closings, and the growing size of the reserve armies of unemployed. Here, the objective conditions present in the global economy provide the basis for working-class unity throughout the world. In other words, the working classes both in the Third World and in the advanced capitalist countries are in the same boat, albeit on different decks, moving in the same direction. As a result, the working classes, particularly those in the advanced capitalist countries, must find a way to free themselves from the shackles of national chauvinism, the narrow limits of *economism,* and, above all, racism and sexism, in order to confront the incessant encroachment of transnational capital with powerful and unified strategies.

Labor Aristocracy or Labor Internationalism?

Since the nineteenth century, segments of the U.S. labor movement have supported strongly the need for international labor solidarity in order to come to grips with the various stages of the internationalization of capital. From the beginning, left-wing socialist, communist, and anarcho-syndicalist sections of the working class have battled with the conservative elements over the *control* of the labor movement and the *meaning* of international labor solidarity. A century-long struggle continues between those elements in the U.S. labor movement that have traditionally pursued strength through increasing international working-class unity, and those who have consistently tied their future to the fortunes of national capital and have allowed themselves to be used as a tool of U.S. imperialism.[34]

Historically seeing itself as part of some all-embracing national interest, the American Federation of Labor (AFL) has found an identity of common global interest with U.S. capital. Recognizing the unique position of U.S. imperialism after World War II, the AFL tied labor's fate to its growing hegemony.[35] The national labor federation intimately embraced the doctrine of *Pax Americana,* which is composed of many subdoctrines, the most significant of which is the "axiom" of Cold War since World War II. This axiom ramifies a complex triad of *containments* whose singular ambition has been the preservation of U.S. global hegemony by all means necessary.[36] The first two containments were intended for the Soviet Union and the Third World. This was motivated by the U.S. postwar position against both Soviet ideology and the independent nationalist movements around the world. The U.S. foreign policy against the Third World, of course, can be exemplified by the notorious CIA coups d'état that were carefully and deliberately conducted against many democratic nationalist movements around the world during the past four decades.[37]

The third containment has been a domestic one. It was designed to circumvent democratic freedoms domestically, and to crush the spirit of resistance in every walk of life in the United States. McCarthyism is only one of many examples in this homegrown tragedy. This, in part, had two important and specific social ramifications for the U.S. labor movement: (1) it dismantled and destroyed the most militant segment of organized labor; and (2) it systematically submitted the workers to a complex set of legitimizing norms imposed by the ideology of the corporate ruling class, thus openly stigmatizing, penalizing, and ultimately terrorizing those who dared to depart from it.[38]

This imperialist rationalization has gone well beyond the workplace itself, steadfastly embracing the whole of American society, from top to bottom. For the persuaded segment in the U.S. labor movement, however, *accommodation* seemed justifiable on the grounds of "American exceptionalism" and the undiminished power of American global hegemony.

The AFL perceived American capital's well-being as part and parcel of American labor's well-being. This led the AFL and later the AFL-CIO (merged in 1955) to adopt a foreign policy based on U.S. nationalism. In the post–World War II era this tendency within the labor movement had openly entered into an explicit alliance with U.S. capital and the state. This conduct is a specific manifestation of *labor aristocracy,* having directly or indirectly to do with extraterritoriality of an imperialist state. In this manner, the nature of the AFL-CIO's involvement in both international labor organizations and the internal affairs of unions of other nations has been guided by the priorities of U.S. foreign policy.[39] Embracing a virulent anticommunism, which saw the world divided into East vs. West, the AFL-CIO in Europe, Africa, Asia, and Latin America has undermined and weakened in a variety of ways the organizational capacity of the international labor movement. It did so by establishing dual unionism—dividing labor movements along Cold War lines by developing procapitalist, anticommunist union structures sympathetic to U.S. capital and subservient to U.S. foreign policy; and by participating with the U.S. government in overt and covert political and military interventions with the purpose of overthrowing democratic, prolabor governments considered too left-wing. The labor federation's involvement in the Cold War on behalf of U.S. imperialism was made possible by purges in the United States of the left-led unions, and of leftists within unions from the labor movement in general. As Mike Davis notes: "By accepting the discipline of the Cold War mobilization, the unions and their liberal allies surrendered independence of action and ratified the subordination of social welfare to global anticommunism."[40]

By weakening international labor solidarity through its divide-and-conquer strategy and, more importantly, through competitive differentiation of wages, employment, and the reserve armies of unemployed, social capital was able to prevent labor from unifying and defending itself on an international basis.[41] The AFL-CIO compromised the organizational capacity of the working class both domestically and internationally in exchange for further material benefits.[42] The benefits of the "social compact," in retrospect, proved transitory after all.

With the new phase of transnationalization of capital beginning in the early 1970s, and accelerating rapidly in the 1970s and 1980s due in part to the worldwide crisis of profitability, the U.S. economy started its decline globally. This marked the onset of the stage of transnational global relations that brought about further integration and worldwide proliferation of capitalist social relations, undermining the existing international system of nation-states and weakening the status of the United States. By the early 1970s capital accumulation had become truly global. This has been also entwined with the onset of global economic crises, beyond the piecemeal (*inter*national) crises of yesteryear. Within the context of attempting to augment surplus value through the global competition of social capital toward cheapening of labor power, the internationalization of capital caused an unprecedented restructuring of industrial production, shifting the concentration of basic industry from its previous centers to newly designated geographical locations. Transnational corporations abandoned the United States as a principal production location, resulting in "captive imports," runaway shops, and outsourcing. The expansion of the United States–based transnationals is now linked to the relative decline of domestic manufacturing. This investment strategy had a negative impact on U.S. workers and contributed significantly to the decline of their status. The ever-present epidemic of plant closings is a case in point.

The decline of U.S. global hegemony during this stage of the transnationalization of capitalist relations has, in the meantime, led to a growing divergence between the material interests of labor and capital. The once-shared interest in the global domination of U.S. capital can now be seen as a source of job loss, demands for concessions, and union busting. The economic conditions underlying the post–World War II accommodation to capital are over. Transnational corporations have shown their determination to play off one group of workers against another in an accelerating process of competition between and within the active and reserve armies of workers worldwide, aiming to drive down the living standards of the international working class to the lowest possible level.

In its periodic restructuring and world economic crisis, global capital strives ceaselessly to extract additional surplus value by lowering the *relative* standard of living of the working class worldwide. Under these conditions, labor unions must either transform themselves into radical organizations acting on behalf of the working class, or continue to operate as hired prizefighters at the service of backward-looking national capital, or join hands as secondary partners with global capital to further subordinate, discipline, and exploit the working classes of all nations.[43]

The weakening and virtual collapse of the labor movement in general and the related decline of the U.S. standard of living in particular will require unions to respond to social capital and the state in fundamentally new ways, creating historic opportunities for both revitalization of the labor movement and formation of a broad-based political movement at home and abroad. The transnationalization of capitalist relations and reorganization of global capitalism create a tendency to divide workers via competition but also provide the potential, through transformed material conditions, for overcoming class collaboration and national chauvinism. The labor movement can no longer survive on economistic objectives alone, without waging a political struggle within an internationalist perspective. This can be detected from the current ideological struggles that are lately beginning to unfold within the U.S. labor movement between a tendency toward accommodation and a zeal for confrontation.[44] These struggles over orientation are also present in the polarized debates over the issues of international trade and investment, and foreign policy; specifically on matters of trade liberalization and regional integration.

Trade Liberalization and Regional Integration: Symptom Not the Cause

The present global restructuring and crisis, and the debates surrounding the adoption of free trade, neoliberalism, monetarism, deregulation, and privatization policies of governments throughout the capitalist world during the 1980s and the first half of 1990s are indeed symptomatic of global integration and the transnationalization of capitalist relations. Given the acceleration of integration of national economies with respect to production, finance, and trade, the adoption of aforementioned policies has been nearly a universal response in both advanced and Third World nations since the early 1970s.

Global labor, however, has been constantly weakened through the globalization of the labor process and the cheapening of labor power throughout the world, especially during the past two decades. While individual capital moved to restore profitability, social capital (as a whole) manifested its very fundamental characteristic through the proliferation of social relations and *competition* for worldwide labor power. Capital has launched a series of offensives that are explicitly designed to weaken or to eliminate the labor movement internationally and to force its capitulation to transnational capital. A consequence of globalization, economic restructuring, and global competition has been the creation of a pool of surplus labor all over the world. Falling real wages; rising unemployment; increasing poverty and income inequality across the board; deteriorating living and working conditions; and increasing violations of worker, human, and civil rights are common problems that are shared by workers throughout both the

Third World and advanced capitalist countries. When it comes to harm, capital is universally dispassionate.

As part of the offensive, global social capital is using international organizations and trade agreements such as the General Agreement on Tariffs and Trade (GATT) and the North American Free Trade Agreement (NAFTA) to formalize and accelerate the process of transnationalization. GATT and NAFTA will assist in the undermining of working and living conditions everywhere for labor and, most importantly, preempt democratic self-government at local, national, regional, and international levels. Global capital and its representatives seek to control attempts by democratic institutions to impose restrictions on transnational corporations by international agreements. Regulation should be in the interests of global capital.[45]

The Mexican Experience

NAFTA, being essentially a response to the globalization process, will tend to formalize and accelerate the process of transnationalization of capital and the global integration of production and exchange that began in Mexico well over twenty years ago. Import-substitution industrialization of the 1950s and 1960s gave way to export-led industrialization in the late 1970s and early 1980s.[46] Attracted by cheap labor and lax enforcement of labor and environmental standards, United States–based transnational corporations began to construct their own integrated production systems (including the export-processing zones) to transfer much of the previously United States–based production activities to Mexico. The intermediate goods and final products produced in the *maquiladoras* would then flow back as imports into the United States.

The IMF and the World Bank have imposed a "structural adjustment policy" on Mexico as a condition for the approval of continued credit. This meant for Mexico to open its markets to foreign products, services and investment; to initiate development based on low-wage export-led industrialization—that is, expansion of the *maquiladoras*; and to reduce public expenditures, especially social expenditures, to further privatize and deregulate industries and to ease their consignment to global capital.[47]

By the late 1980s, limitations on foreign investment had been practically eliminated by further dismantling restrictions on foreign ownership and reducing remaining tariffs and import barriers. This neoliberal model established the unregulated private sector (dominated by foreign-based transnational corporations) as the motor force of economic development based on export-oriented growth.[48] The strategy proved to be an utter disaster for Mexico, as can be seen from the recent crisis; it has failed to fuel national growth or to improve the overall debt situation; and it has further cheapened labor power through accelerating the process of proletarianization. Once a showcase in privatization, Mexico is now grappling with the crisis of worthless currency.[49] For the Mexican working class, it has meant increasing poverty, declining living and working conditions, and intensified state repression of human and workers' rights.

Although the transnationalization of capitalist relations (and the global integration of the labor process) initially improved Mexico's balance of trade partly due to capital inflow and partly through the expansion and modernization of the export sector, it has done so only at the expense of indigenous development and self-reliant industries. Rather than close the development gap between the United States and Mexico, further trade liberalization through NAFTA will enable transnational capital to invest in Mexico virtually without any obstacle, other than the obstacles that are internal to the development of capitalism, including uneven development.

Trade liberalization within the stage of transnationalization of capital means opening the floodgates to the further undermining of working and living conditions of labor everywhere through competition. Workers are joining, albeit unevenly, in opposition to such a downward standardization of global subsistence. To improve the living standard and working conditions of all workers, labor must devise independent and self-reliant global strategies.[50] In the continuing global integration of capitalist labor process, labor unions most affected by this development are beginning to realize that labor solidarity across borders is an essential first step for defending the most tangible interests of their members. Defensive strategies intended to protect the interests of local workers cannot be made effective except through internationally based alliances. The globalization of working-class unity, therefore, is necessary to confront the globalization of capital. However, despite the characteristic of the epoch in which international working class unity is tantamount to labor's material class interest, the anachronistic ideology of national chauvinism still dominates certain sectors of the U.S. labor movement.

Strategic Considerations for Labor

Over the past thirty years, the AFL-CIO has shifted from being the most free-trade–oriented labor movement in the world to being staunchly protectionist. Fighting against free trade in the name of national self-interest, the labor federation embraces a strategy aimed at restoring domestic capital's competitiveness in the world market through protective trade policies. Accommodating national capital industrially and pushing for protectionism politically have constituted the centerpiece of the AFL-CIO's trade policy.[51] At the same time, motivated over the concern for lost jobs and membership, and declining working and living conditions in the United States, the labor federation has demanded fair and balanced trade, and has supported the denial of benefits of specific trade privileges (and aid) to nations in which internationally recognized labor rights are not respected under U.S. trade laws. The AFL-CIO opposes NAFTA and GATT as written. The labor federation's acceptance of multilateral trade agreements is conditioned on the inclusion of enforceable international labor standards and the democratization of trade negotiations themselves. According to the AFL-CIO, the appropriate model in terms of content, structure, and process for NAFTA and GATT has been the European Community's Social Charter, where labor's goal is to regulate the activities of global social capital democratically, in the interests of the majority.[52]

Unfortunately, the labor federation's analysis of international economy has been limited to the sphere of circulation, and the level of the nation-state. By making this restrictive assumption about the nature of social capital, the theory and the public policy recommendations that follow inadequately account for capital's supranational character. There is little recognition of the global integration of production and the transnational character of capitalist social relations. Internationalization of capital is seen primarily as nation-states trading with other nation-states. Analysis is primarily focused on trade surplus/trade deficit, and how it is either good or bad for the "nation." The solution to international economic problems lies in each country playing fair by adhering to the same rules of the so-called competitive game. This, of course, reflects the neoclassical theory of competition based on *harmony* rather than the reality of competitive *struggle* for survival. The labor federation's discussion of NAFTA and GATT begins to address transnational capitalist relations, but only in a very rudimentary and incomplete way. There is mention of transnational corporations, direct foreign investment, and the deleterious effects on *U.S.* industries and *U.S.* jobs. However, as in their discussion of international trade, the prescription for the harmful effects of formal international trade agreements is a fair and equitable trading system between and among nation-states, established through legislation protecting the interests of American workers.[53]

This national chauvinistic response to global social capital supports and intensifies labor's subordination to corporate prerogatives. Raising the specter of "unfair competition," "opposition to free trade," and "support of fair trade" legitimizes the intercapitals' dialogue.[54] Advocating competitive victory for United States–based capital sets workers in the United States against foreign workers and thus severely hampers efforts to achieve international labor solidarity.[55] Capitalism's success in overcoming the growing barriers to accumulation through trade liberalization and economic integration has increased the costs significantly for labor in pursuing a strategy of national autonomy.[56] Continued reliance on nationalism will only further cripple the labor movement in the face of global capital's offensive. Transnationalization of capital has gone too far for protectionism to save domestic jobs. Nationalistic confrontation with the global character of capitalist competition will only continue to demand greater concessions from U.S. workers.

The struggle for labor internationalism is necessary to break down the divisiveness of nationalism and to build solidarity with workers' struggles throughout the world. As Primitivo Rodriquez has so eloquently stated:

Some trade union leaders in the more developed countries seem to be opposing free trade talks out of an outmoded belief that preventing a free trade agreement will save their members' jobs. But blocking such an agreement won't erase the increasing integration among the American economies. Rather, we should look at the free trade agreement debate as an opportunity to develop a vision and an agenda which responds from a people's perspective. . . . What's promising is that today's transnational exchange may lead to the dismantling of barriers imposed by narrow and fragmented interests based on nationalistic perspectives that are increasingly ineffective in enhancing rights and a better life.[57]

There is a growing consensus within the labor movement that recognition of and struggle for international labor standards, as a condition of trade, are *political* acts that have the *potential* to enhance the organizational capacity of the working class internationally, thereby providing legitimacy for international solidarity. The concern for internationally recognized labor rights goes beyond trade and calls attention to the very global relations of capital. Global integration of the capitalist labor process expands the social relations of capital worldwide and, ironically, provides workers with the opportunity to build international solidarity. Labor unions, regardless of their national origin, are finding trade union unity essential in their efforts to defend the interests of their members, and are demanding the enforcement of international labor standards under formal trade agreements. Ending violations of worker rights are increasingly being recognized as mutually beneficial, and as a direct challenge to the prerogatives of U.S. and other transnationals.[58]

While effective enforcement of such labor standards under multilateral trade agreements such as NAFTA and GATT is highly unlikely, their importance for U.S. labor lies in using them along with other measures as a focus for domestic and international political actions in the process of developing international labor solidarity and working-class consciousness. In the struggle to take wages and working and living conditions "out of competition" internationally, workers are building new, and using preexisting transnational structures and coalitions to confront global capital.[59] The task of establishing effective international activity, however, is an extremely difficult one, and often seems impossible given the maze of contradictions between and within national labor movements. A central divisive issue in building international labor solidarity is undoubtedly the attitude of the labor movement toward U.S. foreign policy.[60]

Even in the present post–Cold War era, the labor federation's Department of International Affairs continues to see communism as a central problem for the labor movement in the Third World, where the Third World at present includes the former Soviet Union and former Eastern bloc countries. However, since the late 1970s and early 1980s opposition to the AFL-CIO's support of U.S. foreign policy has been growing within the labor movement. Open conflict has already developed within the house of labor over Central America and U.S. foreign policy in general. For example, more than half the affiliates of the national federation have been actively engaged in an effort to change foreign policy in direct opposition to the labor federation's position on Central America. The AFL-CIO's views of the world are being challenged.[61] This opposition is taking shape within and outside the national labor federation. Some state federations of labor have passed resolutions in opposition to the national AFL-CIO's position regarding U.S. foreign policy on Central America, and their long-standing practice of "shunning" socialist and communist trade unions and federations. Additionally, independent national labor coalitions representing leaders and rank and file, such as the National Labor Committee in Support of Democracy and Human Rights in El Salvador and the Labor Coalition on Central America (LACCA), have emerged opposing AFL-CIO policy and taken an anti-interventionist stance on Central America, thus assisting unions to form mutually reciprocal solidarity ties with relevant "sister unions" in the Third World.

We believe that the *objective* material basis for international working-class action is stronger today than ever before. Plans for international cooperation and mutual aid in support of organizing the unorganized, collective bargaining, strikes, lockouts, etc., in both the Third World and the advanced capitalist countries reflect the increasingly transnational character of the labor movement. Economic integration has led to international solidarity networks of workers within the same corporations, industries, and geographic regions. By working for the same transnational corporation, workers are recognizing that "they have more in common with each other than with their respective national capitals."[62] Rather than just lament job loss to Mexico as a result of trade liberalization, unions are making united working-class action a living reality. According to the United Auto Workers (UAW) Council of Ford Workers, which represents Canadian, U.S., and Mexican workers, "the time has come to prevent Ford from pitting worker against worker, plant against plant, nation against nation."[63] The Cuautitlan Ford workers' democratic union movement in Mexico has pledged to resist work transferred from Canada and the United States if Canadian and U.S. workers assist them in gaining wage and benefit increases and in forming democratic unions. In the fall of 1991, trade union leaders from the Americas met to assess the economic and social effects of free trade in the Western Hemisphere. Shirley Carr, then president of the Canadian Labor Congress (CLC), portrayed the situation as follows: "Either we sit back and let capital divide us one against the other or we try and find ways to cooperate and develop common strategies to tackle the challenges. There is no question that international capital is on the march in this hemisphere and these forces are driving the restructuring of our societies."[64]

In addition, coordination through international trade secretariats (ITSs), a worldwide federation of unions in a particular industry or industries, is increasingly common. The ITSs, through coordinated solidarity campaigns, education, and research, offer the affiliates a vehicle for building trade union unity. Beyond facilitating global trade union activities, ITSs are coordinating campaigns against governments and transnational institutions. For instance, Public Service International (PSI) recently sponsored a campaign to pressure the IMF to revise its structural adjustment formula. The campaign included coordinated protest actions and educational materials/symposia.

A new strategy for labor is emerging in response to the transnationalization of social capital. It includes:

> Transnational solidarity and mutual aid among workers and their allies, making the protection of labor rights a condition of international trade, investment and lending; international corporate campaigns to force TNCs to comply with codes of conduct; challenges to ruinous structural adjustment policies of the World Bank, IMF and other international financial institutions; . . . and the resistance to the use of international "free trade" agreements. . . . All involve transnational coalitions of people's organizations helping themselves by helping each other.[65]

The challenge for labor is to place itself at the center of the global stage and to combine the strength of class politics, the many-sidedness of ideological struggle, and the power of the ongoing social movements into one undivided whole. Building a sustained and viable international working-class solidarity requires many forms of struggle and organizational forms. The issue of regional and global trade, NAFTA and GATT, respectively, has already inaugurated the breaking down of the walls and facilitated the further unity of labor with many social groups (e.g., women, human rights, social justice), thus creating a broader social and class perspective across the boundaries of nation-states. The present trade liberalization, however, must be seen as a polarizing mechanism that not only tends to thrive on the divide-and-rule ideology, but also has its very roots in differentiating and downgrading forces of global competition. The broader the scope of such a polarization, both between and within nations, the greater will be the power of those who are being forced to stand together en masse within the global arena.

While there is a growing objective basis for the unity of the working class worldwide, there are also countertendencies on the part of both global capital and labor. For instance, the intensification of labor process will be frequently tied to the divide-and-rule strategy of social capital as well as the competition of workers worldwide. Hence there is no *automatic* remedy for the unification of workers' struggles at the global level, for the *necessity* of material condition must meet the *sufficiency* of conscious activities of workers as a universal class. We are thus confronted with a classic Marxian dilemma posed by the master himself: people make their own history but they do not make it as they wish. This precludes any predetermined and general conclusions on the future of the global labor movement.

It is worth noting that the effects of capital as a social relation go well beyond the walls of the factory. Capitalism, as a social system, creates its own histori-cally specific social categories and questions, such as the questions of gender, race, environment, social justice, human and worker rights, and freedom. The answers to all these questions, however, are already measured in terms of the immutable yardstick of wage labor. But such a measurement, like all other phenomena in capitalism, is contradictory. Any measure entails its own counter-measure. The primary challenge of labor is not to succumb to the dominant ideology of capital. This can be accomplished by recognizing the transitory and limited nature of wage labor as an economic and social category of exploitation. The immediate task of survival for labor must not be carried out without ade-quate recognition of the long-term considerations.

Conclusions

Considering *capital* as a social relation, not a fetishized object of exchange, we have argued that essentially any contemporary labor process would exhibit two broadly recognized historical tendencies: (1) a progressive cheapening of labor power through the everlasting subjugation of living labor by capital, thus raising the rate of exploitation; and (2) a global *victory* of capital over the remaining vestiges of old and disintegrating social formations, beyond the boundaries of the nation-state.

Competition is a *permanent* feature of capitalism, and, contrary to both the neoclassical and monopoly capital theories, its manifold effects have been fur-ther intensified during the present stage of global capitalism. The primary mani-festation of this heightened competition of social capital for labor power is embodied in the tendency for the *cheapening* of labor power in general, and the *real* subsumption of labor under capital on a gigantic scale. This is contrary to the *thesis* of cheap labor, whose very premise predicates cheap labor as a *cause* of the globalization of labor process, and, as a subject of investigation, consti-tutes circularity by presuming, as a theoretical point of departure, capitalist pro-duction proper. We do not deny that there is a strong motivation for appropriation of cheap labor by individual capital. Yet we maintain that the notion of cheap labor succumbs to tautology where it comes to the analysis of social capital as a whole.

Hand in hand with the above processes is the spatial mobility of capital based on the global victory of capitalist mode of production. The result has been the formation of an integrated network of transnationalized labor processes that are subject to the constant devaluation of labor power globally. This global process of socialization, in turn, demands all-embracing and unified action by interna-tional labor, on a par with the scope and magnitude exhibited by capital itself. The erosion of Pax Americana by the internationalization of capital has resulted in the fall of U.S. labor aristocracy. The concept of international solidarity is indeed a minimal platform on which labor can stand, especially in view of today's world, in which the very livelihood of workers is threatened, in both the advanced capitalist countries and their counterparts in the Third World.

The issue of trade liberalization and formalization of multilateral trade agreements cannot be fully understood outside the context of transnationalization of the labor process. Within the same contextual framework, many labor unions in both the Third World and the advanced capitalist countries are beginning to view themselves as constituent parts of a larger economic and political picture. There is a growing agreement on the nature of the problems facing labor and the commonality of interests beyond national borders, as the issues are increasingly demanding universal struggle.

Notes

1. The literature on the globalization of capital is vast, varied, and uneven. There are several major strands within this literature, from viewing the global transformation along the neo-Smithian division of labor, the Monthly Review school of monopoly capitalism, the Regulation school, to the classical Marxian social relation school, all in one way or the other having to do with the nature of the labor process and global competition. This chapter follows Marx's lead in the latter framework, explaining the emergence of global labor processes that are at present proliferating, albeit unevenly, beyond the boundaries of nation-states. See Cyrus Bina and Behzad Yaghmaian, "Postwar Global Accumulation and the Transnationalization of Capital," *Capital & Class* 43 (Spring 1991): 107–30; Sol Picciotto, "The Internationalization of the State," *Capital & Class* 43 (Spring 1991): 43–63; Nicos Poulantzas, "Internationalization of Capitalist Relations and the Nation-State," *Economy and Society* (1975); Alain Lipietz, "Toward Global Fordism," *New Left Review* 132 (1982); N. Haworth and H. Ramsay, "Grasping the Nettle: Problems in the Theory of International Labor Solidarity," in P. Waterman, ed., *For a New Labor Internationalism* (The Hague: ILERI); R. Bryan, "Monopoly in Marxist Method," *Capital & Class* 26 (1985); Paul Burkett, "A Note on Competition Under Capitalism," *Capital & Class* 30 (1986); Cyrus Bina, "Competition, Control, and Price Formation in the International Energy Industry," *Energy Economics* 11, no. 3 (July 1989): 162–68; Cyrus Bina, "Oil, Japan, and Globalization," *Challenge* 37, no. 3 (May–June 1994): 41–48; Cyrus Bina and Behzad Yaghmaian, "Import Substitution and Export Promotion Within the Context of the Internationalization of Capital," *Review of Radical Political Economics* 20, nos. 2 and 3 (1988): 234–40; Anwar Shaikh, "Foreign Trade and the Law of Value: Part I & II," *Science & Society* 63 and 64, nos. 3 and 1 (Fall 1979 and Spring 1980): 281–302 and 27–57; Berch Berberoglu, *The Internationalization of Capital* (New York: Praeger, 1987); Jerry Lembcke, *Capitalist Development and Class Capacities* (Westport, CT: Greenwood Press, 1988); James Cypher, "The Internationalization of Capital and the Transformation of Social Formations: A Critique of the Monthly Review School," *Review of Radical Political Economics* 11, no. 4 (1979); Mike Davis, *Prisoners of the American Dream* (New York: Verso, 1986); Rhys Jenkins, *Transnational Corporations and Uneven Development* (New York: Methuen, 1987); Kim Moody, *An Injury to All: The Decline of American Unionism* (New York: Verso, 1988); Hugo Radice, "The National Economy: A Keynesian Myth?" *Capital and Class* 22 (1984); William K. Tabb, "Capital Mobility, the Restructuring of Production, and the Politics of Labor," in Arthur MacEwan and William K. Tabb, eds., *Instability and Change in the World Economy* (New York: Monthly Review Press, 1989); John Willoughby, *Capitalist Imperialism, Crisis and State* (New York: Harwood Press, 1986); *Capital & Class* (Autumn 1991), in which a substantial part is

devoted to discussing the fate of unions in the transnational economy; Robert Brenner, "The Origins of Capitalist Development: A Critique of Neo-Smithian Marxism," *New Left Review* 104 (July–August 1977): 25–92; Ben Fine's rejoinder, "On the Origin of Capitalist Development," *New Left Review* 109 (May–June 1978): 88–91; Jeremy Brecher and Tim Costello, *Global Village vs.*

Global Pillage: A One-World Strategy for Labor (Washington, DC: International Labor Rights Education and Research Fund, 1991); Cyrus Bina and Chuck Davis, "Transnational Capital, the Global Labor Process, and the International Labor Movement," in Berch Berberoglu, ed., *The Labor Process and Control of Labor* (Westport, CT: Praeger, 1993); and Cyrus Bina and Chuck Davis, "Labor and the World of Coercive Competition," paper presented at the Allied Social Science Associations (ASSA) meeting (January 5–7, 1993), Anaheim, CA.

2. The integrated circuits of capital in all its forms—commodity, money, and productive capital—manifest the organic unity of social capital globally with the last phase of the globalization of productive capital. For a more detailed study see Karl Marx, *Capital*, vol. II (New York: Vintage, 1981). See also Ben Fine, *Economic Theory and Ideology*, ch. 2 (London: Edward Arnold, 1980); and C. Palloix, "The Internationalization of Capital and the Circuit of Social Capital," in Hugo Radice, ed., *International Firms and Modern Imperialism* (Harmondsworth, Eng.: Penguin, 1975).

3. See, for instance, David Gordon, "The Global Economy: New Edifice or Crumbling Foundations?" *New Left Review* 168 (1988). This paper is written by a leading figure in the paradigm of Social Structure of Accumulation (SSA) and, as expected, denies that the world economy has entered into a new phase since the 1970s. Although there is no intention here on our part to present a critique of the SSA, in the view of Michele Naples' contribution in this volume, we simply need to point out that (1) despite its name, one can neither see a structural determination nor a specified accumulation process associated with it; (2) to the extent that it does, it tends to conflate all aspects of social accumulation on the same footing; (3) the theory does not seem to know its own limits; and (4) the SSA is a nationalist conjecture whose application is limited, particularly in the view of the present decline of nation-states. For an application of the SSA framework to the United States in the postwar period, see Samuel Bowles, David M. Gordon, and Thomas E. Weisskopf, *Beyond the Waste Land* (Garden City, NY: Anchor/Doubleday, 1983); Samuel Bowles, David M. Gordon, and Thomas E. Weisskopf, *After the Waste Land: A Democratic Economics for the Year 2000* (Armonk, NY: M.E. Sharpe, 1990). For a critique of the SSA see P. Nolan and P.K. Edwards, "Homogenized, Divide and Rule: An Essay on *Segmented Work, Divided Workers,*" *Cambridge Journal of Economics* 8 (1984): 197–215; C. Lever-Tracy, "The Paradigm Crisis of Dualism: Decay or Degeneration?" *Politics and Society* 13, no. 1 (1984); Howard Botwinick, *Persistent Inequalities: Wage Disparity Under Capitalist Competition* (Princeton, NJ: Princeton University Press, 1993), 46–52, and ch. 4; and John Willoughby, "Is Global Capitalism in Crisis? A Critique of Postwar Crisis Theories," *Rethinking Marxism* 2, no. 2 (Summer 1989): 83–102.

4. See Tabb, "Capital Mobility, the Restructuring of Production, and the Politics of Labor," in MacEwan and Tabb, eds., *Instability and Change in the World Economy*. Here in this essay the author's position is one of international solidarity. Unfortunately, he offers no specific analytical framework concerning the transnationalization of the labor process.

5. See Anwar Shaikh, "Neo-Ricardian Economics: A Wealth of Algebra, a Poverty of Theory," *Review of Radical Political Economics* 14 (Summer 1982), for a critique of the neo-Ricardian school, whose theory of competition is borrowed straight from neoclassical orthodoxy. See also Shaikh, "Foreign Trade and the Law of Value"; John Weeks, *Capital and Exploitation*, ch. 6 (Princeton, NJ: Princeton University Press, 1981); James Clifton,

"Competition and the Evolution of the Capitalist Mode of Production," *Cambridge Journal of Economics* 1, no. 2 (1977): 137–52; Willi Semmler, *Competition, Monopoly, and Differential Profit Rates* (New York: Columbia University Press, 1984); Anwar Shaikh, "Marxian Competition Versus Perfect Competition: Further Comments on the So-called Choice of Technique," *Cambridge Journal of Economics* 4, no. 1 (1980): 75–83; Mark Glick and Hans Ehrbar, "Long-Run Equilibrium in the Empirical Study of Monopoly and Competition," *Economic Inquiry* 28 (January 1990): 151–62; Rhonda M. Williams, "Capital, Competition, and Discrimination: A Reconsideration of Racial Earnings Inequality," *Review of Radical Political Economics* (Summer 1987); Patrick L. Mason, "The Divide and Conquer and Employer/Employee Models of Discrimination: Neoclassical Competition as a Familial Defect," *Review of Black Political Economy* 21, no. 2 (1992); Patrick L. Mason, "Race, Competition, and Differential Wages," *Cambridge Journal of Economics* 19, no. 4 (August 1995): 545-65; and, particularly, the important work by Howard Botwinick, *Persistent Inequalities.* On the issue of the antithetical question of monopoly and competition in capitalism see Karl Marx, *The Poverty of Philosophy* (Moscow: Progress, 1955): 126–34.

6. For an exposition of dominant theory of market structure and its critique see Cyrus Bina, *The Economics of the Oil Crisis,* ch. 6 (New York: St. Martin's Press, 1985). Here the author explains how the school of monopoly capitalism has a lot in common with the neoclassical theory of market structure on the subject of competition. See Paul Sweezy, "On the Definition of Monopoly," *Quarterly Journal of Economics* (1937), and Paul Sweezy, "Demand Under Conditions of Oligopoly," *Journal of Political Economy* (1939); Paul Baran and Paul M. Sweezy, *Monopoly Capital* (New York: Monthly Review Press, 1966). It is also appropriate to recognize the role of Hilferding's *Finance Capital* in shaping the above theory. See Jonas Zoninsein, *Monopoly Capital Theory: Hilferding and Twentieth-Century Capitalism* (New York: Greenwood Press, 1990).

7. Karl Marx, *Grundrisse* (New York: Vintage, 1973), 651.

8. Ibid., 729–30.

9. Bina, *The Economics of the Oil Crisis,* 57.

10. This simply prevents us from falling into the trap of the "fallacy of composition," a problem that is plaguing mainstream macroeconomics. See Kenneth J. Arrow's Richard T. Ely Lecture, "Methodological Individualism and Social Knowledge," *American Economic Review* 84, no. 2 (May 1994): 1–9. For an excellent exposition of Marx's method, particularly in the matter of overcoming the above problem, see Ben Fine, *Economic Theory and Ideology,* ch. 1; and Ben Fine, *Theories of the Capitalist Economy,* ch. 1 (New York: Holmes & Meier, 1982).

11. See Marx, *Grundrisse,* 414–15. Bina, in *The Economics of the Oil Crisis,* summarizes the assertion of the laws of competition in capitalism, in both its nineteenth- and twentieth-century developments, in the following manner:

> (1) The accumulation process under the rule of capital is a contradictory process. (2) Competition is the external manifestation of this contradiction, and not the result of an arbitrary force or motivation. (3) Competition does not originate in the sphere of circulation, i.e., from the level of many capitals. Thus, it cannot be eliminated through the elimination of competing capitals. (4) Competition is specific to the period of history under capitalism alone. (5) Competition, as the external manifestation of the motion of capital (in general), is necessarily relevant to both *laissez-faire* and *monopoly* phases of capitalism. (6) "The coercive law of competition" leads to a merciless war of capital against capital for survival. (pp. 57–58; emphases in original)

12. Karl Marx and Friedrich Engels, *Selected Correspondence,* 3d rev. ed. (Moscow: Progress Publishers, 1975), 254–55. The real emancipation of the working class runs

counter to the very idea of wage slavery and the system of wage labor itself. But no viable political movement will be able to take upon itself to engage in a qualitative transformation of society without turning all the existing economic movements into a political one with a unified class-based vision that recognizes the transitory nature of global capitalism. Collective struggle of labor under an independent, worldwide unionist movement provides the necessary first step toward the above objective. As Engels wrote more than a century ago, "the working class will have understood that the struggle for high wages and short hours, and the whole action of trade unions as now carried on, is not an end in itself, but a means, a very necessary and effective means, but only one of several means toward a higher end: the abolition of the wage system altogether" ("Trade Unions II," *Articles from the Labor Standard* [1881] [Moscow: Progress Publishers, 1965], 17). By accepting that capitalism is a historically transitory social system, one cannot but also accept that putting a human face on wage slavery (similar to the efforts toward "humanizing" the effect of chattel slavery by the benevolent gentlemen of Confederate slavery in the nineteenth-century United States) will have its own limits that would certainly run up against the limitations of this mode of production sooner or later. Despite the present social atmosphere of hype, demagoguery, and self-congratulation, triggered by the demise of Soviet-style (so-called) socialism, we wish to remind the reader that we do not claim to know what is in store for distant future societies. But we know that global capitalism, as we know it, will never be able to sustain itself beyond its transitory mold.

13. For the lack of better terms we use LDCs for those countries that are not yet at the advanced stage of capitalist development. This distinction does not indicate superiority of one group over the other. It is only recognition of material transformation. The role of foreign capital and imperialist penetration has many interpretations in international development literature. The theory of "unequal exchange" and the dependency school, for instance, are among such approaches that are to a lesser extent concerned about the pivotal role of social relations, and thus less interested in the internal development of the so-called peripheral societies, via "primitive accumulation." For critical analysis of the subject, including the treatment of Dependency Theory and World Systems Theory, see Brenner, "The Origins of Capitalist Development"; John Weeks, *Limits to Capitalist Development* (Boulder, CO: Westview Press, 1985); Bina and Yaghmaian, "Import Substitution and Export Promotion," and "Postwar Global Accumulation."

14. Here we try to distinguish between the transfer of means of production and the establishment of social relations that would utilize these means.

15. For the internal transformation of the Third World see Bina and Yaghmaian, "Import Substitution and Export Promotion" and "Postwar Global Accumulation." For lack of better term, we are referring to the less (capitalistically) developed countries as the Third World. Now that the Second World has gone under and the First World has developed substantial internal zones identical to the Third World, what is the significance of utilizing such world divisions anymore?

16. A careful examination of post–World War II land reform programs in the Third World would point to the massive separation of the immediate producer from the means of production globally. This resulted in an enormous supply of potential wage labor for the import-substitution and, subsequently, the export-led industries in the above countries. This was somewhat the same story, *mutatis mutandis,* during the early days of industrial revolution, as Marx explains: "Thus were the agricultural folk first forcibly expropriated from the soil, driven from their homes, turned into vagabonds, and then whipped, branded and tortured by grotesquely terroristic laws into accepting the discipline necessary for the system of wage labor" (*Capital* 1, ch. 28, 899). This is none other than the conditions for "victory" of capital's mode of production, and its associated labor process, in one of the most civilized nations of the world. Elsewhere in the same volume, Marx emphasizes that

"The expropriation and eviction of a part of the agricultural population not only set free for industrial capital the workers, their means of subsistence and materials of their labor; [these factors] also created the home market" (*ibid.*, ch. 30, 910). Here, in their twentieth-century scenario, the land reform programs of the postwar period have led to the creation of a home market, hand in hand with the world market.

17. See Frederick W. Taylor, *Scientific Management* (New York: Harper & Brothers, 1947). From the standpoint of the institutional changes, the corporate revolution—that is, the separation of ownership from control—is also of chief importance. See A.A. Berle and G.C. Means, *The Modern Corporation and Private Property* (New York: Macmillan, 1932).

18. Harley Shaiken, *Work Transformed: Automation and Labor in the Computer Age* (Lexington, MA: Lexington Books, 1986), 260.

19. Marx, *Grundrisse*, 587. The most basic law of developed capitalism is not the usage of readily available cheap labor, but rather the cheapening of labor power through constant improvements in the means of production. A by-product of this is a massive surplus population at the global level. The outcome will be the downgrading of working-class living standards everywhere. Thus relying on the argument of *cheap labor* will not sufficiently reveal the secret of capital's global accumulation. Here one must rely on Marx's theory of competition—that is, competition at the level of capital as a whole.

In connection with David Ranney's singular emphasis on the devalorization of capital (in this volume), we have no choice other than to caution the reader. Contrary to Ranney, we maintain that valorization and devalorization are part and parcel of a single and inseparable process aiming at the expanded accumulation and periodic restructuring of social capital. This sort of restructuring is commonly known as economic crisis in Marxian political economy. Hence, speaking of devalorization alone would not make any sense at all. Neither does its usage in relation to valorization in terms of an accounting approach to the calculations of values. Technical change in capitalism requires a three-way distinction among technical composition of capital (TCC), organic composition of capital (OCC), and value composition of capital (VCC). This denotes the incommensurability of values, before and after technical change. Arguments based on devalorization alone also obtain a residue of circularity; rather than focus on the cause, they center on the effect of value formation. This position is consistent with our interpretation of Marx, having to do with centrality of the cheapening of labor power in capitalism. Thus the genesis of valorization and devalorization lies in the labor power itself. In this manner, the effects of capital's restructuring, such as the destruction of capital, property, and human lives, are all rendered "incidental" in this mode of production. See Cyrus Bina, "Competition, Control and Price Formation in the International Energy Industry," *Energy Economics* 11, no. 3 (July 1989): 162–68.

20. Harry Braverman, *Labor and Monopoly Capital: The Degradation of Work in the Twentieth Century* (New York: Monthly Review Press, 1974). Here Braverman defines deskilling in terms of (1) "the dissociation of the labor process from the skills of the workers" (113); (2) "the separation of conception from execution" (114); and (3) "monopoly over knowledge to control each step of the labor process and its mode of execution" (119). While these and many other points in this seminal volume present new insights in the analysis of the labor process, we believe that the author's undue attachment to the school of monopoly capitalism and failure to incorporate the historical importance of class analysis diminish his argument. Additional sources on the issue of the labor process are Stephen A. Marglin, "What Do Bosses Do? The Origins and Functions of Hierarchy in Capitalist Production," *Review of Radical Political Economics* 6 (Summer 1974): 60–112; and Stephen A. Marglin's "Losing Touch: The Cultural Conditions of Worker Accommodation and Resistance," in F.A. Marglin and S.A. Marglin, eds., *Dominating Knowledge*

(Oxford: Clarendon Press, 1990), 217–82. See also the section "Competition, Globalization, and the Labor Process" in this chapter. For criticism of the monopoly school see John Weeks, *Capital and Exploitation,* ch. 6; Anwar Shaikh, "Marxian Competition Versus Perfect Competition"; and Bina, *The Economics of the Oil Crisis,* ch. 6.

21. Marx, *Capital* I, chs. 10, 16, and 17. See also Fine, "On the Origin of Capitalist Development," for an excellent exposition on the role of limitation of the working day and its relationship with the real subsumption of labor under capital.

22. See Marx, *Capital* I, ch. 10, for the British experience.

23. See David R. Roediger and Philip S. Foner, *Our Own Time: A History of American Labor and the Working Day* (New York: Verso, 1989), for the American experience. See also Juliet B. Schor, *The Overworked American: The Unexpected Decline of Leisure* (New York: Basic Books, 1992), for recent changes in the length of working hours in the United States.

24. For an outstanding analysis on dualism of sex and class see Susan Himmelweit, "The Real Dualism of Sex and Class," *Review of Radical Political Economics* (Special Issue: The Political Economy of Women) 16, no. 4 (Spring 1984): 167–83. Here Himmelweit offers a compelling critique of patriarchy, domestic wage theory, and the reductionist labor theory of value. The following passage clarifies the notion of family wage:

> In the initial stage of industrialization, it was often women and children who were taken into the factories, whilst their men-folk failed to eke out a living as the prices for the products of their traditional labor were undercut by those of the products of the new factories. But later, as household production became no longer viable, men entered the factories too, replacing or working besides women and children. Eventually men fought for, and in some industries won, the right to be the sole breadwinner; to be paid a wage adequate to support a non-earning family. (178)

For a comprehensive and critical review of gender, family, and employment, see also Ben Fine, *Women's Employment and the Capitalist Family* (New York: Routledge, 1992). This book is particularly important in connection with the periodization of the family and the role of the modern welfare state and the reproduction of the labor force in capitalism.

25. Lourdes Beneria, "Gender and the Global Economy," in MacEwan and Tabb, eds., *Instability and Change in the World Economy,* 246–47.

26. Ibid., 246. See also Kumudhini Rosa, "Strategies of Organization and Resistance: Women Workers in Sri Lankan Free Trade Zone," *Capital & Class* 45 (Autumn 1991): 27–34.

27. Beneria, "Gender and the Global Economy," 250–51. See also Diane Elson and Ruth Pearson, "Nimble Fingers Make Cheap Workers: An Analysis of Workers in Employment in Third World Export Processing," *Feminist Review* 33 (1981).

28. See, for example, Nilufer Cagatay and Gunseli Berik, "Transition to Export-Led Growth in Turkey: Is There Feminization of Employment?" *Capital & Class* 43 (Spring 1991): 153–77. Here the authors did not find any evidence, in either the private or public sectors, in support of the "feminization of employment" in Turkey.

29. Beneria, "Gender and the Global Economy," 247. This relates to a subcontracting case in Mexico City in the early 1980s. See Lourdes Beneria and Martha Roldan, *The Crossroads of Class and Gender: Homework, Subcontracting and Household Dynamics in Mexico City* (Chicago: University of Chicago Press, 1987).

30. See Bina and Yaghmaian, "Postwar Global Accumulation."

31. See L.E. Mins, ed., *Founding of the First International: A Documentary Record* (New York: International Publishers, 1937).

32. Ibid., 38.

33. Karl Marx, "Trades' Unions, Their Past, Present, and Future," in Simeon Larson and Bruce Nissen, eds., *Theories of the Labor Movement* (Detroit: Wayne State University Press, 1987), 36–37.

34. See Lembcke, *Capitalist Development and Class Capacities.* Here we simply reject David Ranney's (see p. 57) dismissal of the emergence of postwar U.S. Labor aristocracy.

35. Stanley Aronowitz, *Working Class Hero: A New Strategy for Labor* (New York: Adama Books, 1983).

36. For an analysis of containments and decline of the U.S. global hegemony since the early 1970s see Cyrus Bina, "The Rhetoric of Oil and the Dilemma of War and American Hegemony," *Arab Studies Quarterly* 15, no. 3 (Summer 1993): 1–20; Cyrus Bina, "Global Oil and Inviability of Pax Americana," *Economic and Political Weekly* (July 11, 1992), 1467–69; Cyrus Bina, "Farewell to the Pax Americana," in H. Zangeneh, ed., *Islam, Iran, and World Stability* (New York: St. Martin's Press, 1994), 41–74; and Cyrus Bina, "Towards a New World Order," in H. Mutalib and T. Hashmi, eds., *Islam, Muslims, and the Modern State* (New York: St. Martin's Press, 1994) 3–30.

37. See, for instance, Noam Chomsky and Edward Herman's two-volume set, *The Washington Connection and Third World Fascism* and *After the Cataclysm: Postwar Indochina and the Reconstruction of Imperial Ideology* (Boston: South End Press, 1979). Also, Philip Agee's *Inside the Company: CIA Diary* (Baltimore: Penguin, 1975), in which a detailed and firsthand account of America's outward character is masterfully documented.

38. At the more general level, we find Noam Chomsky's *Necessary Illusions: Thought Control in Democratic Societies* (Boston: South End Press, 1989), especially appealing. At the specialized level see Roger Keeran, *The Communist Party and the Auto Workers' Unions* (Bloomington, IN: Indiana University Press, 1980); and Harvey Levenstein, *Communism, Anticommunism, and the CIO* (Westport, CT: Greenwood Press, 1981).

39. See Kim Moody, *An Injury to All: The Decline of American Unionism* (New York: Verso, 1988). See also Sheila Cohr's review of Moody's book, "Us and Them: Business Unionism in America and Some Implications for the U.K.," *Capital and Class* 45 (Autumn 1991): 95–127.

40. Davis, *Prisoners of the American Dream,* 96.

41. Carolyn Howe, "The Politics of Class Compromise in an International Context: Considerations for a New Strategy for Labor," *Review of Radical Political Economics* 18, no. 3 (1986): 1–22. Botwinick, *Persistent Inequalities,* chs. 5 and 6.

42. See Botwinick, *Persistent Inequalities,* chs. 5 and 6.

43. See Moody, *An Inquiry to All;* Howe, "The Politics of Class Compromise."

44. Howe, "The Politics of Class Compromise"; Tabb, "Capital Mobility."

45. We have to also recognize that the traditional view of *block formation,* which had its origin in the globalization of *finance capital,* is not entirely in accord with the present-day transnational economy and its corresponding labor process. Regional block formation is but a transitory phenomenon. Competition leads to further integration of capital, but this will increase capital's competitiveness. As a result, popular but simplistic characterization of the European Community (EC) as "fortress Europe" is a contradiction in terms. See, for instance, David McNally, "Beyond Nationalism, Beyond Protectionism: Labor and Canada-U.S. Free Trade Agreement," *Capital & Class* 43 (Spring 1991: 236–38, where the author erroneously emphasizes the global block formation, a code phrase for monopoly, rather than global competition.

46. For further study of import-substitution and export-led industrialization, see Bina and Yaghmaian, "Import Substitution and Export Promotion" and "Postwar Global Accumulation."

47. Brecher and Costello, "Global Village."

48. See Bina and Yaghmaian, "Import Substitution and Export Promotion," for theoretical connection of export-led industrialization and the transnationalization of capital.

49. Jack Sheinkman, "Preface: Worker Rights in Central America," in *Worker Rights in the New World Order* (New York: The National Labor Committee in Support of Democracy and Human Rights in El Salvador, 1991). For the recent currency crisis in Mexico see James M. Cypher, "NAFTA Shock: Mexico's Free Market Meltdown," *Dollars and Sense* 198 (March–April 1995): 22–25, 39.

50. For the example of double standard practice by enterprise unions associated with Japanese TNCs see Hugh Williamson, "Japanese Enterprise Unions in Transnational Companies: Prospects for International Cooperation," *Capital & Class* 45 (Autumn 1991): 17–26.

51. John Willoughby, "The Promise and Pitfalls of Protectionist Politics," in Robert Cherry et al., eds., *The Imperiled Economy, Book I* (New York: Union for Radical Political Economics, 1987), 215–23; see also Michael Perelman, *The Pathology of the U.S. Economy: The Cost of a Low Wage System* (New York: St. Martin's Press, 1993).

52. For a critical analysis of the Social Charter, see John Stirling, "This Great Europe of Our Trade Unions and 1992," *Capital & Class* 45 (Autumn 1991): 7–16.

53. See AFL-CIO Economic Research Department, *The Trade Picture: Year End 1993* (Washington, DC, April 1994).

54. Tabb, "Capital Mobility," 264.

55. See Picciotto, "The Internationalization of the State."

56. David McNally, "Beyond Nationalism."

57. Quoted in Brecher and Costello, *Global Village,* 33–34.

58. See Tabb, "Capital Mobility," 268.

59. *The Union Advocate* (June 3, 1991).

60. See "Solidarity Across Borders: U.S. Labor in a Global Economy," *Labor Research Review* 8, no. 1 (Spring 1989).

61. Moody, *An Injury to All,* 247.

62. Howe, "The Politics of Class Compromise," 18.

63. Elaine Burns, "Free Trade Era Looms Over Mexico," *Guardian* (January 8, 1991): 16.

64. Quoted in *The Union Advocate* (August 5, 1991).

65. Brecher and Costello, *Global Village,* 19.

2

Labor and Today's Global Economic Crisis: A Historical View

David C. Ranney

In facing the 1990s, labor must come to terms with nearly two decades of declining organization and declining jobs—especially manufacturing jobs. The 1980s, particularly, represented the beginning of an ongoing worldwide decline in living standards. Much of the literature on labor discussing these problems treat these issues as if they could be resolved by more effective management and more clever marketing techniques within the borders of the nation-states concerned. To the extent that the global dimension of these problems is recognized at all, it is generally confined to the difficulty of coping with competition in a narrow sense, capitalizing on the entry of foreign firms into the international markets. Policy instruments such as tax abatements, loans with below-market interest rates, planned manufacturing districts, tax increment financing, infrastructure improvements, research and development in specified sectors, and various flexible manufacturing arrangements and employee ownership are often supported by the labor-oriented organizations. Such policy instruments and proposals have common origin in the view that the problems faced by labor can be resolved through better planning and management and, more importantly, within the borders of the nations concerned.

This chapter presents an alternative explanation concerning the loss of manufacturing jobs and the declining living standards of workers throughout the world. In the following pages I argue that deindustrialization and capital flight, far from being particular to U.S. economic restructuring, are a global response to the deepening contradictions in the world capitalist economy. In this context, management decisions to close factories are a very "reasonable" response to the capitalist decline and, in fact, fit in with a rational global strategy for capital as a collective entity. I argue further that nation-states that allied themselves with major segments of capital have an "industrial policy" of saving capital through the process of "devalorization," having to do with the restructuring and/or destruction of firms, infrastructure, industrial capital, and driving down wages and living standards worldwide. These propositions have important implications for the way in which labor should organize itself. This suggests that while efforts toward defending the communities and living standards of people are vital, such struggles must be pursued within a broader context of class interest and class organization. Finally, I discuss the sort of labor agenda that follows from this analysis.

Policy and Analysis

Several divergent analyses of the state of the economy have resulted in varied public policies that have gained the support of organized labor leadership and many labor-oriented community groups. Throughout the 1960s and 1970s, local economic development strategies were dominated by efforts known as "smokestack chasing." Cities or states sought out the entrance of new firms and offered them incentives to locate in their jurisdiction. While such efforts continue to this day, their intensity subsided with the close of the 1970s.[1] A change to a "second wave" of economic development strategy, stressing local capacity building rather than smokestack chasing, was closely related to the emerging trend of deindustrialization, with massive losses in manufacturing jobs during the 1980s.

Capacity building strategies of the 1980s, however, had different emphases reflecting the divergent views on the cause of manufacturing job loss. Many policymakers in the cities and states have adopted a point of view that deindustrialization was a good thing. Manufacturing job loss was seen as part of a transition to the "postindustrial" society, where service- and information-centered industries would dominate.[2] Capacity building in this context has focused on the service sector and "bowed out" of manufacturing.[3]

A second point of view also saw deindustrialization as generally positive, but held that the world economy is in transition to a new system of production, organized in terms of "flexible specialized units."[4] More recently this idea has been extended to forge a national industrial policy capable of countering deindustrialization, thus giving stimulus to a new stage of capitalist development that can improve conditions of the workers.[5] Capacity building in these terms means the stimulation of new "third wave" organizational mechanisms that would promote flexible manufacturing, such as industrial parks devoted to interdependent manufacturing activities.[6] Others who accepted the primacy of market forces, nevertheless, argued that interference by government and "big labor" had set the costs of doing business at extremely high levels. Capacity building from this perspective involved "bidding down" the cost of doing business through antilabor and antitax campaigns, while encouraging business incentives, such as tax abatements, below-market interest rate loans, and enterprise zones.[7]

Yet, another view of deindustrialization, which rejects the notion that manufacturing job loss is "natural" or inevitable, finds expression in the work of Bluestone and Harrison.[8] According to this view, the "profit squeeze" of the mid-1970s was the result of the decline in productivity and increased foreign competition. In response, American management embarked on a strategy of cost containment that led to a complete elimination of certain product lines or encouraged the transfer of production to lower-cost regions.[9] Ann Markusen presents a related but somewhat dissimilar point of view when she argues that the firms' response to the profit squeeze generally depends on where they have completed their historical "profit cycle." As an industry ages and oligopolizes, its constituent firms tend to lose an incentive to develop new technologies and management techniques, thus causing stagnation and declining profits.[10] Accordingly, decline attributed to the profit cycles can be offset by a national industrial policy that would stimulate productivity-enhancing innovation and help the development of new markets.

The notion that manufacturing can operate competitively in a domestic setting has given rise to a variety of policy initiatives. A general policy perspective that encompasses these strategies is known as "betting on the basics." This approach focuses on strengthening traditional industries.[11] A national industrial policy that would focus on specific industrial sectors toward subsidizing research and development, and enhancing job training, has been recommended widely. At a regional level, there have been institutional initiatives such as the Tri-State Conference on Steel/Steel Valley Authority.[12] In Chicago, for instance, the idea of setting development priorities based on the labor force characteristics of targeted groups has been attempted.[13] Other local policy initiatives include the use of planned manufacturing districts and flexible manufacturing. President Clinton's "empowerment zone" initiative falls in this category.[14]

Accompanying these policy ideas have been a host of local activities.[15] Efforts to resist plant closings, for example, are well documented.[16] The move for strong plant closing legislation, the use of early warning systems, worker buyouts, corporate campaigns, and lawsuits have all been utilized to stop closings at the local level. Such tactics have often been combined with the use of financial incentives and targeted job training as well as flexible manufacturing proposals.[17] Notwithstanding these efforts, the problem of worker displacement is not fully explicable in terms of deindustrialization or "worker adaptation."[18]

What is lacking in all these discussions, however, is the critical centrality of deindustrialization in connection with the growth and development of transnational corporations toward a unified global production strategy. Guile and Brooks explain the nature of transnational production:

> For a variety of products, fabrication, assembly, distribution, and maintenance activities are organized in such a manner that information, funds, materials, components, final products, and people cross national boundaries as part of everyday commerce.[19]

While there is some recognition that the globalization of manufacturing is connected to domestic problems, this has not been systematically articulated in conjunction with appropriate policy initiatives. Furthermore there is certain disagreement over the relative importance of transnational strategies in explaining domestic deindustrialization.[20]

A Theoretical Perspective

Against the above arguments, I present an alternative view that is intimately connected to the primary cause of deindustrialization itself. Because of capital's global reach, labor must face today's realities by considering the matters on a global scale. Following Bina and Yaghmaian, I would argue that adoption of any unit of analysis other than the globe itself will fail to produce any meaningful analysis. In other words, global social capital is more than the sum of its parts.[21]

As Marx argued, the basic problem of a capitalist economy is to create sufficient surplus value so that capital can reproduce itself and grow.[22] The process through which it finds resolution is called the valorization process; it starts with a sum of money capital and ends up with additional money capital—as surplus value. The production of surplus value is contingent on the productivity of labor. Thus more and more surplus value is required for the continuity of the valorization process.

Marx demonstrated that only living labor engaged in productive activity can support the valorization process.[23] Machines merely transfer the value created by workers in the prior stage of production. Labor power, however, is a kind of commodity that creates more value than the value of its own reproduction. In other words, workers by necessity work more hours than required for their own daily sustenance. From the standpoint of capital, workers in economic sectors that are dealing with finance and distribution of commodities are not considered productive. They do not create value in conjunction with the valorization process. While their work is important and critical to the functioning of a capitalist economy, they are, nevertheless, paid from the surplus value produced by those engaged in the production process. Thus, the valorization process is prone to economic crisis.

An early manifestation of such crises is a decline in the average rate of profit. Shaikh presents the empirical evidence of such a decline in the United States since 1947.[24] He argues that competition among the blocs of capital requires increased productivity at decreased cost. This necessity further necessitates the introduction of machinery, which, in turn, lowers prices to the extent that most blocs of capital have to face falling profits. This causes the average rate of profit to decline. Eventually falling profit rates truncate the valorization process, because the needed expansion of values is greater than the value-producing ability of the system. At this point there must be either a rapid expansion of surplus value or devalorization in which the claims on existing values can be eliminated. I would argue that the action of most influential blocs of capital today accords with devalorization on a world scale.

A Historical Perspective of Today's Crisis

Historically, the mode of accumulation of values has varied at different periods. The modes of accumulation have also shaped and been shaped by the nature of the response/resistance of the labor movement. Thus an analysis of capital must recognize different periods defined in terms of both the dominant mode of accumulation and the nature of human activity.[25] Below I present a brief summary of the relationship of capitalist strategies to the various social movements.

Primitive Accumulation

To get started, the capitalist system had to employ a means to accumulate capital without full-blown capitalism. This is "primitive accumulation" that has emerged primarily through the ruthless activities of the rising capitalist class. As Marx noted:

> The capitalist system presupposes the complete separation of the laborers from all property in the means by which they can realize their labor. . . . The process, therefore, that clears the way for the capitalist system can be none other than the process which takes away from the laborer the possession of his means of production; a process that transforms, on the one hand, the social means of subsistence and of production into capital [and], on the other, the immediate producers into wage-laborers.[26]

In Europe, a key to primitive accumulation was the enclosures movement in which the declining feudal class of nobility, strapped for cash, fenced off communal lands that had been used by peasants for subsistence farming and restricted their use to sheep grazing. Between the thirteenth and sixteenth centuries, nearly 90 percent of former tenants of these lands were forced off the land and into the city to become wage laborers.[27] Another method of primitive accumulation was the use of force by the rising capitalist class to lower real wages through massive price inflation. During the sixteenth century, prices in Europe increased between 150 and 400 percent.[28] There was also the growth of trade and commerce, which was stimulated, in part, by colonialism. The power of colonial nations was used simply to appropriate the wealth of underdeveloped nations through agencies such as the British East India Company, with the full might of the British military behind them. Finally, there was slavery and the slave trade, which has been compounded by outright extermination of indigenous peoples. And when they resisted the efforts of capitalist powers to take and exploit their lands, there was genocide. Marx describes the process of primitive accumulation in the United States:

> The discovery of gold and silver in America, the extirpation, enslavement and entombment in mines of the aboriginal population, the beginning of the conquest and looting of the East Indies, the turning of Africa into a warren for the commercial hunting of Black skins, signalized the rosy dawn of the era of capitalist production.[29]

Primitive accumulation in all its forms was the dominant mode of accumulation from the beginnings of capitalism until about 1815.[30] During this period the dominant forms of resistance were necessarily violent, as people resisted efforts to separate them from property necessary for their survival. Such resistance included the wave of peasant revolts that swept Europe between the fourteenth and sixteenth centuries. In England and America there were rebellions of indigenous peoples; in the United States there were also slave revolts. The ferocity of these revolts matched the ferocity of the displacement, forced poverty, and repression that accompanied the "rosy dawn" of early capitalism. It is estimated, for example, that more than 100,000 peasants were killed in the suppression of the peasant revolts in Germany alone.[31]

Expanding Working Hours

The period between 1815 and 1914 was marked by the dominance of a different mode of accumulation. It involved expanding working hours through growing production and longer working days. The early part of this period was one of a rapid expansion of capitalist production in Europe and the United States. But the expansion was accompanied by brutal working conditions for the new proletariat. Families were destroyed as men, women, and children were forced to work long hours in dangerous and unhealthy factories. Living conditions were equally bad.

Despite the rapid accumulation of surplus value resulting from the high rate of exploitation, the contradiction between the produced value and the claim on that value manifested itself. Throughout the period there were a series of economic crises. Between 1850 and 1859 there were two major financial panics that led to mass emigration from Europe to the United States. But there were also crises in the 1860s, 1870s, 1880s, and 1890s. Efforts to deal with these crises through an expansion of surplus values took two forms. Capitalist power was to be concentrated through the emergence of huge corporations. In addition, there was export of capital through the rise of imperialism. The new power of capital was backed by the capitalist state, which used all means at its disposal to hold workers to subsistence wages. State actions on behalf of workers such as child labor and health and safety laws became necessary to ensure the workers' survival. But conditions and wages remained poor. Furthermore, the military power of the state was used to promote the expansion of markets abroad.

Labor's activity in its own behalf during this period was directly related to the mode of accumulation itself. The early expansion of production and the accompanying destruction of working-class living standards were met by a series of largely spontaneous revolts. Between 1815 and 1845 there were eight major worker rebellions over working and living conditions. These occurred in the years 1811–13, 1815–17, 1819, 1826, 1829–35, 1838–42, 1843–44, and 1846–48.[32] These culminated in the 1848 revolutions. In addition, between 1850 and 1886 there were waves of worker movements for shorter workdays. In the 1850s there were the ten-hour–day movements. By 1860 the demand was an eight-hour day. These movements continued for thirty years. Their high point was between 1878 and 1886, culminating in serious repressions, including the executions of the U.S. activists around the Haymarket incident.[33]

Transition

The period beginning with World War I and ending with World War II saw a transition to the modern era. The labor movement had seriously restricted the ability of capital to extend the workday. Capital responded by significant changes in the organization of production, which paved the way for major innovations and which replaced workers with machines. During this period mass production technologies enabled firms to engage in considerable vertical integration. Ford Rouge, which produced automobiles in Detroit in a complex factory accommodated for the combined production of steel and glass, and practically everything that went into the final product, became a symbol of the new "Fordist" production technique. In addition, the principles of scientific management, reducing workers to appendages of the machinery, were introduced by Frederick Taylor.

Furthermore, colonialism had given way to imperialism as powerful capitalist nations began to export capital, creating spheres of economic and military influence. These efforts to extend the influence of specific national groupings of capital led to clashes between blocs of capital. However, neither the innovations in production technique nor the imperialist expansions did much to ease the contradiction between the amount of value produced and the claims on that value. As a result, there were severe economic crises. The wars and the Great Depression eased the contradiction between claims on value and its existing sum by destroying both labor and capital. Wars and depression involve a very costly process of devalorization that would wipe out claims on value and enable the accumulation process to begin anew.

During this crisis-ridden period, labor organizations grew. Labor organized itself according to major industries in response to capital's demand for greater hegemony over the labor process through large-scale production. This organizing task in the United States began with the formation of the Industrial Workers of the World. It continued and succeeded in the 1930s with the birth of the CIO.

Yet, despite the militancy and determination of organized labor, its efforts ended up assisting capital in the development of a new stage of accumulation that would replace the human worker with the machine. The Taft-Hartley Act (1947) was both a culmination and a starting point for this process. Better wages and working conditions were traded for the guarantee of production continuity, thus setting the stage for what was to come.[34]

Labor Intensification and Automation

Since World War II we have witnessed the establishment of yet another stage of accumulation. The need for continuously increasing surplus value demanded by the valorization process has been dealt with not by extending the workday, but by increasing productivity through automation and greater work intensity. Both because of militant worker resistance and the relationship between automation and the falling rate of profit, this mode of accumulation provided only temporary relief to the contradictory process of valorization. Thus there was an impetus to develop massive credit mechanisms, both domestic and international, through which money could be exchanged for commodities even when there was insufficient value to be traded.

Because of its relative economic and military strength following World War II, the United States was able to develop mechanisms of international trade and finance that would be most favorable to American capital. At Bretton Woods in 1944, the United States used its position to establish a system that would provide a seemingly limitless demand for its products. The U.S. dollar was established as the international medium of exchange. Necessary institutions were created (the International Monetary Fund [IMF], the World Bank, and the General Agreement on Tariffs and Trade [GATT]) to facilitate the rebuilding of the capitalist world on terms most favorable to the United States and its major corporations.

At the time of the signing of the Bretton Woods agreement, the IMF and the World Bank had well-defined roles in the rebuilding of Western Europe after World War II. The IMF's purpose was to maintain stable values for currencies to facilitate international trade. The World Bank was established as a financial intermediary between U.S. lenders, on the one hand, and the countries of Europe and Great Britain, on the other, who needed dollars to finance exports. In addition, the World Bank helped implement programs for long-term economic development.

These arrangements enabled U.S. corporations to expand their profitability and blunt the effects of cyclical crisis. These international mechanisms found their U.S. domestic counterpart in government fiscal and monetary policies that used government powers to spend, tax, print money, and establish the terms of borrowing and credit extension to continue a valorization process in the face of capital's historic contradiction. The new mode of accumulation, with its supportive trade and financial institutions, enabled the United States to generate boom conditions from the end of World War II to the early 1970s. The boom conditions enabled organized labor to readily agree to ensure continuity of production in return for a cut in prosperity.

The boom also generated long-standing contradictions within labor's rank and file. The disparity in pay and working conditions between U.S. workers of color and whites, as well as between women and men, resulted in struggles aimed at the elimination of white male privileges within the working class. While resistance by workers of color to discrimination was not new, the combination of the postwar boom and the movements by African Americans, Latinos, Native Americans, and women initiated a greatly intensified workers' effort to end white male privileges at the workplace. The manifestations of these efforts were outside the framework of trade unionism, typified by shop floor caucuses and the Revolutionary Union Movements (RUMs).[35] While the most liberal wing of organized labor supported equal rights as a general proposition, they were often in direct opposition to its most militant expression against union leadership.

It is in this context that the alliance between organized labor leadership and the U.S. capitalist class can be explained. Needless to say, such an alliance has often been at odds with rank-and-file labor. What held the alliance together, moreover, was the U.S. prosperity associated with a new mode of accumulation based on capital mobility and increased labor productivity via automation and labor intensity.

The basis for this prosperity still embodied a contradiction of its own, which in turn continued to undermine the postwar boom. Once other economies around the world began to develop, U.S. corporations could no longer expand their international operations with impunity. By the 1970s we witnessed not only stronger European economies, the beginnings of the European Economic Community (EEC), and a mighty Japan, but also the rise of the so-called newly industrialized countries (NICs).

The continuous export of capital that destroyed indigenous economies in developing nations also began to cut deep into the workers' standard of living in advanced capitalist nations. Imperialism, far from being a means to create an aristocracy of labor, was in fact beginning to do just the opposite. The resulting demise of industrial areas in major U.S. and European cities known as deindustrialization was in fact a form of devalorization. This devalorization was intended to destroy claims on surplus value without resorting to war or deep depression.

Capital and Labor Today: Global Devalorization

In the light of what has been discussed above, capitalism is entering a new phase in its development. I refer to this as the era of global devalorization. This conceptualization rests on several global transformations, including the fact that the United States is no longer the center of world capitalism. In addition, we have seen the rise of global supranational corporations and a globalized economy. Finally, the present era is exemplified by the development of new political institutions beyond nation-states.

Supranational Capital's Social Agenda

In the mid-1960s the French responded to the loss of U.S. global hegemony by trying to cash in their dollars for gold. In 1971 President Nixon staved off an impending world financial crisis by refusing to honor the gold demand for U.S. dollars. By 1973 the United States officially went off the gold standard, and the value of all national currencies was allowed to float. This was the end of the Bretton Woods agreement.

The supranational corporate agenda, while not a fully cohesive concept, has a number of discernible ingredients. First, it is necessary to cheapen the costs of production in order to halt falling profit rates and remedy the contradiction in which the claims on the value of what is being produced are greater than the value produced globally. Part of this agenda was stated starkly by Jacques de Larosiere, a former chairman of the International Monetary Fund:

> Over the past four years [1980–83] . . . a clear pattern [has emerged] of substantial and progressive long-term decline in rates of return to capital. There may be many reasons for this. But there is no doubt that an important contributing factor is to be found in the significant increase over the past twenty years or so in the share of income being absorbed by employees. . . . This points to the need for a gradual reduction in the rate of increase in real wages over the medium term if we are to restore adequate investment incentives.[36]

The vehicle for cheapening the costs of production is capital mobility. Mobile capital, in turn, requires technologies and institutions that would make it cost-effective. In the institutional realm there is a need for supranational entities that can facilitate capital mobility and combat institutional and human impediments to the dominant corporate agenda. Thus the emerging supranational corporate agenda has four interrelated elements: cheapening production costs, capital mobility, technological developments, and institutional developments. There is a strong interconnection between capital mobility and the cheapening of the costs of production. Not only does mobility provide an opportunity for relocating to low-cost areas and pit the peoples of different nations against one another, it also requires the destruction of claims on value. It requires, for instance, destruction through the elimination of "nontariff barriers" to trade and investment flows. Health care, welfare, and subsidized housing programs; worker and consumer safety standards; and environmental regulations all can be (and have been) viewed as barriers to trade in that they raise the costs of production and investment. Capital mobility also destroys claims on value in another way. By using the very real threat of moving en masse, corporations can extract wage and work rule concessions from workers in their home country.

From Transnational to Supranational

Going hand in hand with a supranational corporate agenda has been the transformation of the corporations themselves. Transnational corporations based in one country have established majority-owned foreign affiliates (MOFAs) in others. In addition, there has been a growth of collaborative arrangements among transnational corporations based in many countries. These developments show that many transnational corporations are becoming supranational, with their home base having a declining significance.

These supranational corporations (SNCs) make up an increasing share of total global economic activity. In 1990 there were 35,000 SNCs with 150,000 foreign affiliates.[37] It is estimated that the largest of these corporations account for approximately one-quarter of the value added in production of goods in the world economy.[38] Nearly 80 percent of U.S. external trade (both exports and imports) is currently undertaken by supranational corporations.[39] Between 1985 and 1990, global foreign direct investments grew four times faster than domestic investments.[40] United States–based SNCs devoted an increasing portion of their capital expenditures to their foreign affiliates (MOFAs) during the past decade. These MOFAs increased their share of corporate net income from 20 percent in 1982 to 35 percent by 1990.[41]

Increasingly, globalization of the economy is taking the form of collaborative arrangements—often nonequity arrangements—among SNCs based in different nations. These arrangements include outsourcing, cross-licensing of new technologies, joint ventures, joint research and development programs, and mutual ownership. U.S. secretary of labor Robert Reich believes that the global economy is predominantly characterized by production through "global webs" that involve many different companies based in a variety of nations. Corporations, according to Reich, are "facades" behind which "teems an array of decentralized groups and subgroups continuously contracting with similarly diffuse working units all over the world."[42] He further contends that American (or British or Japanese, etc.) corporations are ceasing to exist in any sense that would distinguish them as unique components of a global economy.

Overall, the post–Bretton Woods period allowed United States–based banks to transform their international activities into supranational operations beyond the control of nation-states. Their lending to United States–based corporations led to the expansion of U.S. investment and production abroad. The rapid development of supranational banking and industrial production gave rise to similar activities by corporations throughout the developed world. Between 1974 and 1988, Japanese commercial banks enjoyed a rapid growth in assets. In 1991 the top ten commercial banks (in terms of assets) were all based in Japan.[43]

Evolving Supranational Institutions

In the wake of the collapse of the Bretton Woods agreement, some of the old Bretton Woods institutions transformed themselves, while new supranational institutions were and are being created. The creation of supranational institutions has closely followed the evolution of the supranational agenda on social policy. In this context, while stabilization and structural adjustment programs vary from nation to nation, they hold some common elements that neatly coincide with the agenda of mobile capital and the cheapening of the costs of production for SNCs. These include:

> Devaluation of the currency; curtailment of government expenditure . . . in-cluding the dismissal of public employees and drastic cuts in social service programs; . . . elimination of subsidies and price controls; compression of real earnings . . . ; liberalization of trade and the elimination of protective barriers; privatization of state-controlled commercial, financial and industrial enter-prises, often through the sale of assets to foreign capital . . . ; [privatization] of social sector programs like education, health and nutrition. . . .[44]

There is an extensive literature on the impact of these programs on developing countries. Most researchers agree that the stabilization and structural adjustment programs have been very costly to the poor and have redistributed income upward. There is evidence that IMF programs lead to serious reductions in labor's share of income.[45] Social upheavals due to IMF conditionality programs have been widespread. Recently, in a meeting of forty-six nations in Washington, D.C., there emerged an organization and a campaign against these programs.[46]

Another Bretton Woods institution that has undergone a significant change since its founding is the General Agreement on Tariffs and Trade (GATT). It is an important component of the evolving supranational policy arena. In fact, the most recent Uruguay Round GATT proposal has served as a model for regional trade agreements such as the North American Free Trade Agreement (NAFTA).

If emerging supranational policy is to facilitate capital mobility to cheapen the costs of production, the means for implementing the expanded functions of GATT in the Uruguay Round proposal suit this agenda quite well. There are several additional provisions in the Uruguay Round agreement that significantly expend GATT's jurisdiction: (1) addition of new commodities, (2) addition of services, (3) addition of trade-related investment measures (TRIMs), (4) addition of trade-related intellectual property rights (TRIPs), and finally (5) changing GATT to a world trade organization (WTO).

Before the Uruguay Round, disputes were settled by a panel of three trade officials (often international trade lawyers representing SNCs). Hearings are secret and void of testimony from interested consumer, health, labor, or environmental groups. No one from the public or media is allowed to attend. The Uruguay Round extends this process in two ways. First, by enlarging the scope of GATT's activity, it effectively increases the terrain of potential disputes that could be subject to such a process. Second, the creation of a WTO with extraordinary global powers gives supranational capital a powerful institution to implement its policy of global devalorization. In many ways the WTO is a return to the thinking behind the ITO, which was rejected by the U.S. Congress in 1945. This time, however, the new agency will be independent of the United Nations and have far broader powers than the relatively egalitarian ITO. All nations under the WTO are obliged to reconsider their own laws in order to comply with the content of the WTO.

Finally, these institutional developments obtain no objective other than serving the interests of the supranational policy agenda in the years to come. This may have significant implications for the multitude of humanity, including workers organizing for social justice. The emerging supranational policy agenda and arena tend to undermine efforts of such groups by eliminating the efficacy of national, regional, or local government policy and by isolating groups that are organized on a national basis. NAFTA and GATT, for example, threaten local efforts to enhance the economic welfare of African Americans, Latinos, Native Americans, and women by challenging regulations that require the use of minority- or women-owned businesses or "first source hiring" as "unfair barriers to trade." Environmental and food safety regulations that are more stringent than the ones prevailing elsewhere in the world are similarly threatened. Human and civil rights standards, including universal health care, are threatened by the "whipsaw" effect of firms moving to areas with the lowest standards. The ability to implement governmental policies in virtually every nation in the world is hampered by the trade agreements and the structural adjustment policies of the IMF and the World Bank.

Conclusions

I have argued that the supranational policy agenda, and the institutional arena associated with it, is designed to meet the contemporary form of capital's historic contradiction. Structural adjustment on a world scale destroys claims on value by driving down living standards and dismantling the protective regulations designed for the health, safety, and social security of working people throughout the world. These policies also have an adverse effect on regulations designed to protect the environment. Highly mobile supranational corporations backed by the policies of the IMF/World Bank (and the transformed GATT) are in fact implementing a program of global devalorization.

I have pointed out that historically the efforts by working people aiming to improve their social conditions are closely related to the dominant mode of capitalist accumulation. What we face today, in conjunction with global devalorization, is reminiscent of the enclosures movement during the period of primitive accumulation. People throughout the world must face the *common* realities that are undermining their capacity to maintain a decent standard of living.

Under the increasingly harsh economic conditions, it is natural to turn to government for some relief. But all government policies that support a declining standard of living—even the so-called safety net programs—contribute to the devalorization process. When the labor movement turns to support productivity-enhancing work rules, two-tiered wage structures, wage concessions, and "worker-ownership" schemes that result in layoffs, it, too, contributes to the destruction of its own base by promoting devalorization.

Historically it is important to note that significant people's movements such as the movement to limit the workday, industrial unionism, and battles against automation were all human responses to capital's strategy saving the system with antihuman means. However, the efforts of working people, who tend to organize themselves by responding to the realities of capital's strategy, can be truncated by various false visions of what is possible. The contribution of intellectuals and activists is to clarify the nature of the present situation and to stimulate discussion among ordinary people about the dangers of false hope.

One implication of this analysis for labor organizers is pointing to the illusion that people can live a good life if the wealth generated by capital is distributed in a just manner. As the actual size of the pie shrinks through the process of devalorization, however, workers acting under such assumptions can become demoralized and may resort to various forms of chauvinism, fascism, or war to get "their" share. The display of national chauvinism in response to the Persian Gulf War, the passage of Proposition 187 in California, and similar anti-immigrant measures in other countries offer a chilling preview of the possibilities. Thus clarity about the limits of capitalism rather than illusions, such as faith in government policies or enthusiasm about labor-controlled enterprises, must be the guide. Similarly, it is critical to prevent particular segments of the working class from gaining benefits at the expense of the remaining segments. This is the thorniest question of all, especially in an era of declining capitalism. A labor movement based on the elimination of relative privilege of segments of the working class also requires an international dimension to all organizing efforts.

On the North American continent, the coalitions that formed to oppose NAFTA demonstrated the viability of such a movement. In the United States the Alliance for Responsible Trade and the Citizens' Trade Campaign brought together labor unions, community organizations, environmental organizations, religious associations, women's groups, and people of color into a common movement for economic and environmental justice. In Canada, Action Canada

(AC) and Common Frontiers, experienced through their struggle against the Free Trade Agreement (FTA) with the United States, brought a similar coalition together. And in Mexico, the Mexican Network on Free Trade (RMALC) launched a struggle against an entrenched government that was committed to the program of supranational capital. RMALC represented virtually all sectors of Mexican society. In the aftermath of the NAFTA struggle, new cross-border organizing efforts involving U.S. and independent Mexican trade unions have been launched. International conferences on education, women's rights, the rights of indigenous people, and the environment have been planned and held. A document, "A Just and Sustainable Trade and Development Initiative for the Western Hemisphere," which details an alternative development model to NAFTA, has evolved out of several years of exchange among activists from the United States, Canada, Mexico, Chile, and a growing list of countries in the Western Hemisphere.[47]

As hopeful as these signs are, there is a long way to go. The U.S. coalitions contain numerous dualities that, for instance, can be detected from the action of California's anti-NAFTA/anti-GATT coalition that supported Proposition 187—a fascistic anti-immigrant law. Therefore, greater clarity about the nature of the crisis, and its universal effect on all working people, is essential.

Notes

1. Douglas Ross and Robert Friedman, "The Emerging Third Wave: New Economic Development Strategies of the 90s," *The Entrepreneurial Economy Review of the Corporation for Enterprise Development* 9, no. 1 (Autumn 1990).
2. Daniel Bell, *The Coming of Post-Industrial Society* (New York: Basic Books, 1974).
3. Ann Markusen, "Planning for Industrial Decline: Lessons from Steel Communities," *Journal of Planning Education and Research* (Spring 1988): 2–12.
4. Michael Piore and Charles Sabel, *The Second Industrial Divide* (New York: Basic Books, 1984).
5. David M. Gordon, "The Global Economy: New Edifice or Crumbling Foundation?" *New Left Review* 2 (1988); Bennett Harrison, *Lean and Mean: The Changing Landscape of Corporate Power in an Age of Flexibility* (New York: Basic Books, 1994).
6. C. Richard Hatch, "Manufacturing Modernization: Strategies That Don't Work, Strategies That Do," *The Entrepreneurial Economy Review of the Corporation For Enterprise Development* 9, no. 1 (Autumn 1990).
7. Markusen, "Planning for Industrial Decline."
8. Barry Bluestone and Bennett Harrison, *The Deindustrialization of America: Plant Closings, Community Abandonment and the Dismantling of Basic Industry* (New York: Basic Books, 1982); Bennett Harrison and Barry Bluestone, *The Great U-Turn: Corporate Restructuring and the Polarizing of America* (New York: Basic Books, 1988).
9. Harrison, *Lean and Mean.*
10. Ann Markusen, *Profit Cycles, Oligopoly and Regional Development* (Cambridge, MA: MIT Press, 1985).
11. Markusen, "Planning for Industrial Decline."
12. Mike Stout, "Reindustrialization From Below: The Steel Valley Authority," *Labor Research Review* V, no. 2 (Fall 1986): 19–34.

13. David C. Ranney and John J. Betancur, "Labor Force Based Development: A Community Oriented Approach to Targeting Job Training and Industrial Development," *Economic Development Quarterly* 6, no. 3 (August 1992): 286–96.

14. Bennett Harrison has presented a similar strategic perspective in Harrison, *Lean and Mean.*

15. Wim Wiewel et al., "Community Economic Development Strategies: A Manual for Local Action," University of Illinois at Chicago: Center for Urban Economic Development, 1987.

16. David C. Ranney, "Plant Closings and Early Warning Indicators," *Journal of Planning Literature* (Winter 1988): 22–35.

17. The work of the affiliates of the Federation of Industrial Retention and Renewal (FIRR), a national coalition of labor/community organizations, provides noteworthy examples of these tactics. Their efforts are reported in *FIRR News,* 3411 Diversey Avenue, No. 10, Chicago, IL 60647.

18. Mayor's Task Force on Steel and Southeast Chicago, "Building on the Basics: The Final Report of the Mayor's Task Force" (City of Chicago, 1988).

19. Bruce R. Guile and Harvey Brooks, *Technology and Global Industry: Companies and Nations in the World Economy* (Washington, DC: National Academy Press, 1987), p. 1. More recent descriptions are developed in Robert Reich, *Work of Nations: Preparing Ourselves for 21st Century Capitalism* (New York: Vintage Books, 1992); Harrison, *Lean and Mean;* and Richard J. Barnet and John Cavanagh, *Global Dreams: Imperial Corporations and the New World Order* (New York: Simon & Schuster, 1994).

20. Folker Frobel, Jurgen Heinrichs, and Otto Kreve, *The New International Division of Labor: Structural Unemployment in Industrialized Countries and Industrialization in Developing Countries* (New York: Cambridge University Press, 1977); David M. Gordon, "The Global Economy: New Edifice or Crumbling Foundations?" *New Left Review* 2 (1988): 24–64; and Cyrus Bina and Behzad Yaghmaian, "Postwar Global Accumulation and the Transnationalization of Capital," *Capital and Class* 43 (Spring 1991): 107–30.

21. Bina and Yaghmaian, "Postwar Global Accumulation": 110–11.

22. Marx, *Capital: The Process of Capitalist Production as a Whole* 3, ed. Friedrich Engels (New York: International Publishers, 1973), 241–66.

23. Ibid., I.

24. Anwar Shaikh, "The Falling Rate of Profit and the Economic Crisis in the U.S." In Robert Cherry et al., eds., *The Imperiled Economy: Macroeconomics from a Left Perspective, Book I* (New York: Union for Radical Political Economics, 1987), 118–23.

25. Bina and Yaghmaian have developed a similar periodization based on circuits of capital that represent the unity of spheres of production and exchange. They recognize that these periods correspond with the dominant mode of accumulation emphasized in the present analysis, "Postwar Global Accumulation": 111. Also see Cyrus Bina and Chuck Davis, "The Transnationalization of Capital and the Decline of the U.S. Labor Movement," paper presented at the ASSA convention, Washington, DC, December 1990.

26. Marx, *Capital* I, 714.

27. E.K. Hunt, *Property and Prophets: The Evolution of Economic Institutions and Ideologies,* 2d ed. (New York: Harper & Row, 1975), 23.

28. Ibid., 24.

29. Marx, *Capital* I, 751.

30. Hunt, *Property and Prophets,* 24.

31. Ibid., 22.

32. Ibid., 60.

33. Marx's ideas and activity around the workday movements are discussed in detail

by Raya Dunayevskaya, *Rosa Luxemburg, Women's Liberation and Marx's Philosophy of Revolution* (Atlantic Heights, NJ: Humanities Press, 1981), 145–56.

34. This point is developed in detail by Kim Moody, *An Injury to All: The Decline of American Unionism* (New York: Verso Press, 1988).

35. Charles Denby, *Indignant Heart: A Black Worker's Journal* (Detroit: Wayne State University Press, 1989), 245–94; David C. Ranney, "Combating Plant Closings," *Journal of Ideology* (Winter 1987); Andy Phillips and Raya Dunayevskaya, *The Coal Miners' General Strike of 1949–50 and the Birth of Marxist-Humanism in the U.S.: A 1980s View* (Chicago: News & Letters, 1984).

36. From an address to the Economic and Social Council of the United Nations in Geneva in 1984. Cited in Howard Wachtel, *Money Mandarins: The Making of a New Supranational Economic Order* (New York: Pantheon, 1986), 137.

37. UNCTC, *World Investment Report 1992: Transnational Corporation as Engines of Growth* (New York: United Nations, E.92.II.A.19), 11.

38. UNCTC, *World Investment Report 1991: The Triad in Foreign Direct Investment* (New York: United Nations, E.91.II.A-a–12), 47.

39. UNCTC, *World Investment Report 1992*, 200.

40. Ibid.

41. *Survey of Current Business* (August 1992).

42. Robert E. Reich, *The Work of Nations: Preparing Ourselves for 21st Century Capitalism* (New York: Alfred A. Knopf, 1991), 81.

43. Berch Berberoglu, *The Legacy of Empire: Economic Decline and Class Polarization in the U.S.* (New York: Praeger, 1992), 43.

44. Public Interest Research Group, "Structural Adjustment: Who Really Pays?" Public Interest Research Group, 142 Maitri Apartments, Plot no. 28, Indraprastha Extension, Delhi, 110092 India (March 1992), 8.

45. Manuel Pastore, "The Effects of IMF Programs in the Third World: Debate and Evidence from Latin America," *World Development* 15, no. 2 (1987): 249–62.

46. NGO CASA may be contacted c/o Development GAP, 1400 I Street, NW, Suite 520, Washington, DC 20005. Papers from the 1992 forum tracing the impacts of structural adjustment on NGO CASA members are available. In addition there is a quarterly newsletter, *Bankcheck,* which publishes news of antistructural adjustment campaigns and impacts. *Bankcheck* is available from The Tides Foundation, International Rivers Network, 1847 Berkeley Way, Berkeley, CA 94703. Other recent works assessing the impacts of IMF and World Bank adjustment programs on the developing world include the following: Dharam Gai, ed., *The IMF and the South: The Social Impact of Crisis and Adjustment* (London: Zed Books, 1991); Kathy McAfee, *Storm Signals: Structural Adjustment and Development Alternatives in the Caribbean* (Boston: South End Press, 1991); Ramesh F. Ramsaran, *The Challenge of Structural Adjustment in the Commonwealth Caribbean* (New York: Praeger, 1992); Ved Nanda, George W. Shepherd, Jr., and Eileen McCarthy-Arnolds, eds., *World Debt and the Human Condition: Structural Adjustment and the Right to Development* (London: Greenwood Press, 1993).

47. Alliance for Responsible Trade, Citizens Trade Campaign, the Mexican Action Network on Free Trade, "A Just and Sustainable Trade and Development Initiative for the Western Hemisphere," November 1994, ARTm, 100 Maryland Avenue, NE, P.O. Box 74, Washington, DC 20002.

3

Political Entrepreneurialism: Deregulation, Privatization, and the "Reinvention of Government"

Laurie Clements

Introduction

The 1980s was a decade in which conservative philosophy and dogma were reasserted in the United States and the power of the state was openly and conspicuously used to support the interests of corporate America. Deregulation, the clarion call of conservatives, led to a reduction in government regulations in many parts of the economy and a moratorium on the introduction of new regulations.[1] The rhetoric of deregulation was laced with calls to "reduce government influence" and "let the market take care of business." Prior to adopting or issuing major rules, agencies were also required to submit a cost impact study to the Office of Management and Budget (OMB). This had the effect of reducing the level of open discussion about the impact of proposed regulations on business, which primarily benefited the sectors subject to government regulation.[2] There also occurred a relaxation of rules on corporate mergers and acquisitions that encouraged a level of speculative investment not seen in sixty years.[3]

In the same decade, corporate America, with the support of the Reagan administration, developed strategies to undermine the power of organized labor. Whereas union busting is not new, it came to rely more heavily on psychological and legal manipulation. Changes in the economic, political, and legal environment made the everyday operations of unions more difficult. Domestic economic instability, the restructuring of capital, and the increasing pressure of foreign competition all contributed to this antiunion hostility. Within this framework unions were portrayed as fetters on economic development and a hindrance to the rationalization of American capitalism.

The deregulation of the economy, the growth of antiunion hostility, and the intensification of international competition have all influenced governmental economic management. Since 1945 economic policy making has expanded dramatically in all capitalist countries.[4] In the United States all levels of government, while less involved in direct production or the tripartite indicative planning found in Europe and Japan, expanded the scope of their activities. The interpenetration of international capital, however, increased the pressure on the federal government to protect and enhance national economic interests. During the 1980s, the federal government responded to these pressures by shifting toward a less interventionist approach in the domestic economy, while becoming increasingly aggressive in advocating free market policies abroad. As American corporate hegemony was challenged, the government, operating through the World Bank and the International Monetary Fund, increased pressure on economically weaker countries to accept both a structural and an ideological commitment to free markets.

In this dynamic situation the concept of privatization emerged in the political debate. Privatization, while not a new concept, became an imperative affecting economic and political relations on a global scale. Privatization, it seems, was sweeping the world.[5] The term "privatization" means to make private or to change from public to private ownership and control. It focuses on the hegemony of "free" market forces, is committed to a reduction in the size, scope, and role of government, and has influenced public policy making in economies at all levels of development across a broad ideological spectrum. The globalization of privatization is an integral element of the international restructuring of capital and the new world division of labor. Global developments in privatization provided a mechanism that allowed multinational capital to acquire resources around the world as less developed states explored the "privatization solution."

Privatization assumes that the market will cure all economic and political problems. Faith in the market became a national myopia.[6] Deregulation and privatization are designed to expand markets and isolate private property rights from broader-based accountability. Such governmental policies are value-laden and ideologically focused and directly benefit the interests of private capital. Both reduce government influence over commercial markets and promote the downsizing and restructuring of government.

But weak states do not change in a few years what had taken decades to create, and it is a mistake to regard such policies as a dilution of government economic intervention. In examining the British privatization program Fine argues that "the ability to privatize represents the culmination of the process of reorganizing the industries concerned, a process often beginning with the first days of public ownership."[7] He suggests that privatization, rather than being a radical change, is an example of government adjusting its policies in the face of global competition. Privatization and deregulation offer a deconstructionist illusion of government that is more ideological than real. In the United States the ideological battleground, as manifested in the Republican party's "Contract with

America," reflects a continuation of the conservativism that has dominated public policy making for the past twenty years. The fundamental shift occurred in the late 1970s, suggesting that the contemporary discussion regarding the appropriate role of government is not a radical departure from the past but an extension of governmental attempts to downsize and transfer service delivery to the private sector. Both deregulation and privatization highlight government as the facilitator of policies closely attuned to meet the needs of private capital. They do not weaken the state but modify and restructure its role, which has led to a questioning of American public policy in the post–New Deal and especially post–Great Society eras. "Reaganomics" subjected these earlier periods to historical revisionism by fusing the "free market" with a populist libertarianism that redefined earlier government initiatives as misguided. Any analysis of deregulation and privatization therefore must be located in the context of the resurgence of free market economics and the challenge to Keynesian economic policy making.

The Ideological Retreat from Keynesianism in America

The state is a complex organizational structure rooted in a political economy. Governments therefore can never be neutral agents in the process of economic management, particularly in times of economic instability. Deregulation and privatization are as much a part of crisis management as were earlier Keynesian policies. But whereas the New Deal philosophy was based on increasing government intervention to counter unemployment and the massive social dislocations of the 1930s, the Reagan-Bush era was marked by a philosophy of general disengagement from government intervention, especially corporate regulation. In the 1980s fiscal policy also promoted the most dramatic redistribution of wealth in the past half century. The New Deal liberalism had sought to reconcile capital-labor relations in order to stabilize capitalism. Government's role was to maintain a basic social wage and control the level of unemployment. This provided political stability, a safety net for workers, and helped sustain private capital. After a quarter century of government intervention some commentators suggested the emergence of a post-capitalistic society,[8] but the prematurity of this proposition was confirmed in the 1970s and 1980s when policies designed to support those in need gave way to policies that bolstered private capital. High levels of both inflation and unemployment undermined the faith in Keynesian countercyclical policy, and by the late 1970s, government was rapidly being redefined as part of the problem not the solution. The challenge to Keynesian economics took a number of guises, including monetarism, as advocated by Milton Friedman, supply side economics, and a return to a classical orthodoxy critical of expanding federal deficits and government spending. The amalgam of these approaches coalesced as "Reaganomics," a view made credible by the failure of Keynesian polices to cure stagflation in the 1970s.

The changing paradigm of "Reaganomics" was based on a model, advocated by economist Arthur Laffer, and accepted by conservatives in the Reagan administration, that the federal deficit could be cut if taxes were reduced. In essence, tax cuts would generate a level of economic activity that would increase tax revenues, protect programs, *and* reduce the federal deficit. The deficit reduction plans introduced to Congress in the 1980s lowered tax rates, especially for the richest segment of the population, and were rationalized as stimuli for an entrepreneurial spirit emasculated by government regulation and high rates of taxation. A crucial assumption in the Laffer analysis was that the marginal rate of taxation was already at the level, although below that of international competitors, that acted as a disincentive to investment. The enduring aspect of this assumption, however, has made the restoration of federal income taxes to levels that existed prior to 1980 impossible, even as the federal deficit quadrupled.[9] This problem is reflected in 1995 with further tax cut proposals, especially to the wealthy, but some Republicans in both the House and the Senate, leery of repeating the Reagan experience, called for deficit reduction before tax cuts. The lesson appears to have been learned, at least partially.

The Reagan tax cuts were also supported as being essential to the economy's "competitiveness": "But the description of the system as 'the economy' is part of the idiom of ideology, and obscures the real process. For what is being improved is a capitalist economy; and this ensures whoever may or may not gain, capitalist interests are least likely to lose."[10] Competitiveness is also a central rationale of deregulation and privatization, and while intuitively attractive, it belies the complexity of the process. Rather than enhance competition, they "privatize" economic decision making, concentrate economic power, and bolster the interests of the economic status quo. The ascendancy of supply side economics in the 1980s emasculated the policies of the Johnson administration, and Miliband's warning is equally applicable to the Republican "Contract with America."

Both major political parties have embraced the ideology of competitiveness. The Clinton administration accepted this precept as willingly as did the Reagan and Bush White Houses. This included the championing of "deregulation of trade" in the form of the North American Free Trade Agreement (NAFTA) in 1993, an agreement negotiated by the Bush administration, and the General Agreement on Tariffs and Trade (GATT) in 1994.11 Both NAFTA and GATT are outcomes of the process of globalization. Global trade and, more importantly, investment agreements are now codified to allow multinational corporations greater access to markets, protect profits, and limit the ability of local governments to impose restrictions that interfere with their interests. Both agreements provide enforceable rules to protect private property rights that enhance the power of multinational corporations. Trade deregulation was meant to promote export-led growth, bolster American competitiveness, and provide workers with greater job opportunities. Neither agreement, however, contained the equivalent of the European Union Social Charter, which provides minimum protections for workers. Labor standards and antitrust polices are after-thoughts in these agreements. By March 1995 there was little to promote enthusiasm of American workers, and the collapse of the Mexican peso led the administration to underwrite loans to Mexico to prevent that economy, and significant American investment, from moving into a tailspin. Ironically, this intervention, while subject to criticism by Republicans, saved many in Congress, on both sides of the aisle, from the embarrassment of voting on a support package. The "socialization" of international debt support through government intervention vividly illustrates the contradictory positions taken by promarket governments. There is one law of market intervention for the rich, another for the poor. The decline of neo-Keynesianism is more apparent than real!

As trade was being deregulated, government itself increasingly became subject to re-evaluation. The Clinton-Gore proposal to "reinvent government" is based on a premise that government should operate like the ever more deregulated private sector. Whereas inherently governmental services such as law enforcement, the judiciary, and the military may experience a limited extension of market competition, the theory accepts that many government services are potentially commercial and therefore should be subject to competitive pressures. Governments are being forced to address "competitivization."[12] The normative economic paradigm has become: If the private sector can provide the services, the private sector should provide the services. This changing paradigm has significant political ramifications, and as the Democratic party has moved to make government more market-oriented, a key question becomes less which party can make government work better, and more which can impose the greater cuts.

Downsizing and Privatization: Contemporary Currents in the Federal Government

There is a crisis in American fiscal policy concerning the demand for government to provide services and the unwillingness of the electorate to pay for them. Electorates have been promised both improved public services and lower taxes. It is a deception that has undermined both public policy and the political process; has created false expectations; and is an unworkable strategy for providing essential services, including those needed for economic viability.[13] Government has again examined downsizing in the 1990s and explored the possibilities of transferring the production and delivery of services into the private sector. The appropriate role of government in contemporary society is again problematic. The federal government contracts for more than $300 billion in goods and services a year and provides more than $200 billion to state and local governments to carry out the federal domestic agenda.[14] Contracting is therefore a significant practice even with a relatively small public sector. Efforts to "downsize" increase the pressure to contract, but it is less evident if this will reduce the deficit or increase the number of suppliers.

Privatization can take many forms, but to limit discussion to its form obscures the underlying ideology that reflects a "celebration of the private sector (which had) been manifest in peculiarly American ways. Popular distaste for government, though never wholly absent from American politics, reached a level in the 1970s and 1980s that had not been seen for over half a century."[15] This increased in virulency in the 1990s as economic, social, and political issues long considered settled, were revisited and challenged.

During the 1980s, government was portrayed as a leviathan that devoured resources and was in dire need of control.[16] Deregulation, downsizing, and privatization emerged as structural and procedural solutions designed to change the shape of government. Conservative politicians focused attention to the domestic arena with a simple yet cogent theme: Attack big government. The push for deregulation represented a refocusing of government policy by conservative elements in both parties and made the critique of liberal capitalist priorities all the easier. "Liberal" became a derogatory term in American politics.

Deregulation reformulates property rights in favor of private interests and reduces public accountability over the use of private assets.[17] It has contributed to the significant increase in economic concentration and the growth of corporate merger speculation that reduced the availability of capital for productive investment. This occurred at a time when international competition was intensifying. Deregulation ideologically fused private property, individual freedom, and democratic government, and competitive markets were posited as crucial to both political and economic democracy. Likewise privatization, government downsizing, and economic and political "freedom" were enjoined. The model was attractive to an electorate alienated from government, but it created a "grand illusion" that simply reducing government would enhance the economic well-being of the citizenry. Deregulation eroded worker freedom by enhancing employer control over the work process. Less government intervention not only changes the technique of state management, it also helps consolidate private economic power.[18] As the federal government distanced itself from an increasing proportion of the population, the privatization of poverty grew. Out of the policies of the 1980s emerged the welfare reform debates of the 1990s. It is important to note, however, that the privatization of wealth and the privatization of poverty are two sides of the same coin. The challenge of government in the 1990s is to remedy this crisis and regain a legitimacy for political solutions that were denigrated in the ideological maelstrom of the previous decade.

From Carter to Clinton: Perspectives on Downsizing Government

There have been many presidential commissions and studies concerned with the size and scope of government. A continuity exists in the recurring question of how to improve governmental performance and policy making without undermining the political structure. The Carter administration embraced deregulation as a central policy initiative. Executive Order 12,044, signed in 1978, required that federal regulations would not impose unnecessary burdens on the economy, business, individuals, and state and local government. This expanded as the regulatory reform movement grew dramatically in the 1980s.

The efforts of President Carter were extended by both the Reagan and Bush administrations.[19] President Reagan increased the centralized control of federal agencies by signing in 1981 Executive Order 12,291, which placed agency oversight with the director of the OMB, subject to the direction of the Presidential Task Force. The control of regulatory mechanisms was further consolidated in the White House with Executive Order 12,498, which directed agencies to submit to the OMB an overview of their annual regulatory policies and goals. The irony of this consolidation of control within a deregulatory environment should not be lost, and it paralleled similar controls introduced by the Thatcher government in Britain then engaged in the largest privatization program of any Western nation.[20]

In conjunction with deregulation efforts, President Reagan supported the expansion of privatization. The Grace Commission Report of 1984 claimed that its recommendations of privatization would provide substantial savings and reduce federal employment by half a million. This was followed in 1987 by the President's Commission on Privatization, whose mission was to investigate targets for privatization as "part of a fundamental political and economic rethinking that today is reassessing the roles of government and the private sector in the modern welfare state."[21]

This commission, which gave the advocates of privatization considerable legitimacy, identified and prioritized privatization opportunities; actions necessary to promote privatization; administrative policies needed to create an environment conducive to privatization; resource requirements necessary to implement the program; and recommend actions that would support privatization initiatives.[22]

Privatization was accepted by President Reagan as crucial to an "economic bill of rights" in which private solutions were portrayed as the "American way." On the other hand, social solutions based on government intervention were redefined as not only inefficient, but also, by implication, "un-American." By enveloping privatization as a key element in redefining the welfare state, Hoover and Plant note that privatization supporters view "[social] equality [as] a destructive value and should be detached from the proper role of government and the place of welfare within that role."[23]

The attack on welfare policies as a strategy to deal with the federal deficit increased the privatization of poverty, devalued labor power, cheapened the labor process, and expanded the reserve army of unemployed. Cuts in the social wage, in unemployment benefits, and in welfare programs increased the economic underclass, which contributed to the erosion of trade union bargaining power. Such policies were not merely crisis intervention at the level of the economy but were concerned with the basic relations of domination between the different classes in society.[24]

This has dramatic implications for welfare recipients. The rationale was apparently simple: Government support systems provide no incentives for those on welfare to re-enter the labor market. This leads to an entrapment in poverty that could be overcome by cutting safety nets that would force recipients back into the labor force. Government had to be cruel to be kind. Hostility and resentment toward welfare recipients allowed this convoluted logic, reminiscent of the analysis that cutting taxes would increase tax revenues, to garner considerable support and become a cogent political force. The market was the answer to the welfare question. This nascent individualism undermines the struggle for collective freedom in both political and economic arenas, and the denigration of collective political solutions exposes the class dynamic at work. "The threat to the hegemony of the class that controls capital was sufficient to evoke the response represented by the policies of Reagan and Thatcher. In the name of economic efficiency, poverty programs have been cut, regulatory systems dismantled, and entitlements reduced."[25]

Domestic political priorities were realigned to represent a new terrain of class struggle. The fiscal crisis has meant that welfare needs became increasingly circumscribed, while deregulation and privatization reflect the struggle occurring in the economic and political restructuring of contemporary America. In the Great Society era, social programs reduced income and wealth differentials but did not significantly redistribute the balance of power in society. Privatization and deregulation, on the other hand, redistribute, enhance, and consolidate economic power. Unions weakened by a decade-long onslaught were ill equipped to confront a redistribution that both enhanced the interests of capital and eroded worker and union security.

The federal policies introduced during the 1980s forced state and local governments to assume greater responsibility for the provision and funding of services. The federal fiscal crisis contributed significantly to the budgetary shortfalls in state and local government, and increased the impetus of privatization.[26] Between fiscal 1980 and fiscal 1990 federal spending on education fell by 40 percent as a share of GDP, environment and natural resources by 39 percent, and welfare and unemployment by 21 percent. General revenue sharing with the states was eliminated in 1980, and with local governments in 1986. By 1991 the U.S. Conference of Mayors noted that federal funds had declined from 17.7 percent to 6.4 percent of city budgets over the decade. Between 1978 and 1988 federal aid to state and local governments fell by more than $17 billion, and counties that had the primary responsibility for infrastructural projects experienced a 73 percent cut in funding.[27]

The Bush administration, however, expanded the policies of President Reagan by establishing the Council on Competitiveness, chaired by Vice President Quayle. This council epitomized the deregulation of government. It was established not by any formal statutory instrument, but by press release! Under the influence of the vice president, the council followed an aggressive deregulatory agenda and expanded the influence of free market ideology on government policy making. It was aided in this objective by the President's Task Force on Regulatory Relief. Executive Order 12,612, signed by President Bush, also required agencies to implement the "principles of federalism," a shorthand for limiting the scope of the federal government, and an extension of the Reagan philosophy of "new federalism."

The massive growth in the federal budget deficit was an integral element in the disastrous Reagan supply side initiatives, and its continued growth has circumscribed political choices in the 1990s. Clinton's interest in downsizing government should also come as no surprise. In response to the Reagan policies that reduced federal funding to the states, Governor Clinton of Arkansas was committed to the expansion of entrepreneurial government and its reorientation toward market goals. The irony is that a Democratic president is the champion of efforts resisted by many Democrats in Congress during the Reagan years. The Reagan and Bush administrations failed to cut both government and the deficit, and these became the mantra of the incoming Clinton administration in 1992. Early in the term, the National Performance Review was established to evaluate the role of government, and following in the tradition of the Grace Commission, it proposed cutting federal civilian employment by 252,000 jobs by 1999, and a shift to entrepreneurial government. This is an extension of the philosophy of the previous decade in advocating privatization, downsizing, and changing government administration to more closely mirror the private sector.[28] At a time when the federal deficit exceeds $4 trillion, there is enormous pressure to change the way government does business. The review argued that government structures resemble an antiquated business bureaucracy left over from an era when American companies dominated global markets. Just as American industry had to meet the challenges of the information age, so government must reassess its structure, function, and purpose, and must streamline.

The streamlining plan passed to the OMB in September 1993 proposed to cut the ratio of managerial personnel in half by 1998 and was characterized by delegation of authority, decentralization, employee empowerment, and increased accountability. It suggested that governmental micromanagement give way to simplified organizational structures with a stronger market orientation. Executive Order 12,862, signed by President Clinton on September 11, 1993, stated: "Public officials must embark on a revolution within the Federal Government to change the way it does business. . . . [the] Federal Government must become customer driven [with] customer service equal to the best in business."

Thus federal government standards were to be measured against private sector performance criteria. The National Performance Review goes beyond the policies of the ostensibly more conservative administrations that preceded Clinton in restructuring government with a market orientation. On the other hand,

Executive Order 12,866 shifted priority setting away from the OMB, with reversion to the agencies' control of policy-setting programs, and expedited review procedures.[29] This is a positive response to the criticism that the OMB under both Reagan and Bush was shrouded with secrecy.

In the 1980s federal mandates, along with reduced funding, increased the financial difficulties of lower levels of government. In 1995 Congress sought to prevent the federal government from passing on the cost of mandates to state and local government. State governors of both parties, however, know that federal downsizing will mean that lower levels of government, as the provider of many services to constituents, will be the prime target of criticism from a highly volatile electorate. While the elimination of unfunded mandates may help contain state-level financial difficulties that occurred under Reagan, fewer services will be provided. This would be exacerbated by the passage of a balanced budget amendment to the Constitution, which would necessitate the dismantling of substantial parts of the federal government over the next twenty years, with state and local governments bearing a disproportionate share of the cuts. The failure to move the amendment through the Senate early in 1995 will slow down the proposals to downsize the federal government, but the longer-term prospects of program cuts and privatization remain.

Likewise, the shift in the funding base to block grants will erode the real spending power for domestic programs. States may be left with greater "choice" of how to spend fewer dollars! Again the likely outcome is an extension of privatization, fewer services, and a significant reduction in public sector employment.

The "Contract with America" is a reaffirmation of the Reagan policies. It calls for a balancing of the federal budget while protecting defense spending and promising tax cuts. This is precisely what caused the budgetary crisis in the first place. Although the authors of the "Contract" were very careful not to provide details of where cuts would occur, the impact on means-tested programs is projected to be three times greater than the Reagan cuts in 1981 and 1982.[30] This again increases the pressure to downsize, deregulate, and privatize. Given that pressure, what was the actual experience of privatization in the 1980s?

The Promise and the Reality of Privatization

Budget reductions in the 1980s forced many state and local governments to become laboratories of privatization.[31] The urban tax base eroded as middle-income families fled to the suburbs, and companies relocated plants in search of ever greater economic development incentives. Rising unemployment reduced tax revenues while the cost of welfare escalated. Within an environment of fiscal stringency, privatization often appeared as the only option for state and local government.

Privatization is accepted by most local governments and has taken many forms. A 1984 study by the International City Management Association, investigating fifty-nine different services in about two thousand cities and counties, found some private delivery for every service offered, and for thirteen services, a majority reported private delivery.[32] A 1987 Touche Ross study indicated that more than 99 percent of local governments had engaged in some contracting out over the previous five years. In the same period 24 percent of local governments had sold off assets, but in only 15 percent of cases was service improvement the primary reason for the sale.[33] Vouchers, franchise agreements, volunteers, and joint public-private ventures have also been used in privatization programs.

Privatization in America is therefore multifaceted and packaged in various forms. One recurring element in the debate is that privatization expands "customer choice," but political choices are, at the same time, reduced. The political process allows for alternative choices not embraced by the market.[34] When government provides service there is greater potential for community access and participation, and the process is open to greater public scrutiny and accountability. Market choice, on the other hand, is patterned by the ability to pay rather than social need, and collective interest groups, including unions and environmental and civil rights organizations, are weakened as political forces when decision making is removed from the public arena. In fact, a fundamental objection to the marketing of public services arises from the fact that the public sector is part of the public realm, in which market principles are inadequate to ensure the fairness of distribution. The relationship between government and citizen cannot be solely based on property rights and exchange, and the ethics of commercialism should not be equated with that of service.

Harold J. Sullivan has taken the argument further by suggesting that privatization may lead to the evasion of constitutional responsibilities when decision-making power over who receives services is relocated in the private sector.

> When government acts directly on citizens through law or through the actions of elected or appointed officials, no question exists that it is bound by the Constitution. On the other hand, when purely private agencies act on their own without government support or participation, they are free from the restraints to which government actions are subject.[35]

Citizen rights and liberties can therefore be lost when the production and delivery of services is privatized.[36] Governments, acting in the name of economic efficiency, are unlikely to extend constitutional safeguards where the priorities are cost-cutting and deregulation.

Privatization and market liberalization are also distinct and do not always coincide. The concentration of economic power in the private sector has meant that privatization can lead to contractual monopolies with diminished information, deliberation, and accountability. Large firms dominate a significant proportion of contracting out, and studies in Massachusetts indicate that this concentration increases over time.[37]

The objectives of privatization have been summarized in terms of improved performance, lower deficits, improved "fiscal responsibility," economic growth, reduced public sector union power, and the promotion of popular capitalism.[38] As the 1980s debate continues in full force in the 1990s, it is important to examine the extent to which these objectives were achieved.

Supporters of privatization argue that the public sector is both less efficient and less effective than the private sector because federal managers confront a bureaucracy that places constraints on their ability to act. As such, they lack both the power to shape organizational development and the market discipline needed to improve their level of efficiency. Yet there is ample testimony of the inability of many private companies to compete because of their arcane organizational structures. The private sector does not have all the answers, yet the blanket belief in its superiority has been used as a justification for changing the activity of federal and lower-level governments. While public sector inefficiency must not be condoned, the market is not the only panacea of efficiency. For many publicly provided services it is not self-evident that the private sector provides better quality service at a lower price, and Starr points out that

> pervasive differences in services performed by public and private organizations often render simple comparisons misleading. Especially important are differences in clientele. Public and private schools, hospitals, and social services rarely have the same kinds of students, patients, and clients. . . . The burden of public institutions is precisely that they are often the services of the last resort; the freedom of private institutions consists in part of their ability to select the most desirable client populations. To be sure, that selectivity may make them more attractive sources of services, but it does not indicate they perform any better than do the public services when both face the same clients and the same tasks.[39]

The Presidential Commission on Privatization makes Starr's point in relation to mortgage insurance: "The Federal Housing Administration should reduce its mortgage insurance activity so that it does not compete as directly with private mortgage insurers. It should direct its efforts toward that market not served by private insurers, that is, toward buyers who have been turned down by private mortgage insurers."[40]

The competitive model appears as an emperor with no clothes. Competition is secondary to restructuring markets and profit enhancement of powerful interests in the private mortgage industry. Likewise, the sale of Conrail occurred after 1981 legislation allowed the closure of unprofitable lines. Between 1984 and 1987, when it was sold, Conrail made a total profit of $1.5 billion; it was sold for $1.6 billion. As Pack candidly suggested, "If Conrail can move from losing money to making profits by dropping unprofitable routes, the question is, why maintain unprofitable routes, not why is public production more inefficient than private production."[41] The efficiency criterion is therefore seriously open to question.

The experience of the 1980s indicates that privatization was inadequate and ineffectual in cutting the federal deficit; it rose dramatically, a problem exacerbated by steadily rising debt servicing payments. Defense expenditures epitomize federal privatized spending. Early in 1995 the president announced an unrequested increase of $25 billion in the Pentagon budget, an area also declared "protected" by the Republicans supporting the balanced budget amendment. In such an environment privatization is irrelevant to cutting the federal deficit. After two decades of budgetary retrenchment on social spending, deficits have continued to expand at all levels of government, and contractors are unlikely to lobby for reduced federal appropriations. As Starr argues, "There is much reason to question the seemingly straight forward view of privatization as a means of reducing government. Private contractors make aggressive lobbyists, as would other recipients of public funds under any proposal to retain government financing but to move production into private hands."[42]

Defense Department needs, for example, are supplied by highly privatized and monopolistically controlled contractors whose profitability depends on the expansion of federal contracts. The "peace dividend" is of limited utility to such corporations. Public funding of private delivery can therefore increase rather than reduce pressure on budgets, and the massive subsidization of market failures such as the savings and loan bailout indicates that downsizing government guarantees neither lower spending nor private drinking at the public trough. Corporate welfare, however, does not carry the same moral opprobrium as the AFDC mother and child, the prime targets of the welfare "reformers" of 1995.

The contemporary focus of downsizing has concentrated on cutting social programs and increasing contracting out, but this only deals with the expenditure side of public budgets.[43] An investigation of federal income demands a longitudinal evaluation of tax policy. Barlett and Steele argue that tax codes have become increasingly regressive since the 1950s, when the tax system was designed to encourage the growth of the middle class. By the 1990s the code had been rewritten to serve the needs of the wealthy, thus increasing downward mobility.[44] Unless there is fiscal responsibility, and a progressive taxation policy to ensure that wealthy Americans pay a fair share of the tax burden, budget cuts alone will not lead to a balanced budget. The maximum rate of the federal income tax was cut to 28 percent in 1986, having declined from 70 percent in 1980. Yet fewer than 1 percent of taxpayers were taxed at 70 percent on the last dollar earned, and 85 percent of taxpayers paid less than 40 percent at the margin. The 1986 Tax Reform Act cut taxes on average by $24,380 for those earning more than $100,000 a year, while those in the $20,000 to $50,000 income bracket received a cut averaging only $586. The 1986 legislation gave wealthy taxpayers and the middle class the same tax rate, progressivity was destroyed, and the deficit continued to expand.[45] Both parties in Congress were responsible for this development. The 1990s solution to this crisis has been the devastating attack on the poorest members of the community, the middle class already having lost substantially. While the Republican leadership in the Senate lamented in 1993 that "class warfare" was being waged against rich Americans, Barlett and Steele pointedly note:

> There has been class warfare but it didn't start with the introduction of the Omnibus Budget Reconciliation Act of 1993. Nor was it directed against the rich. In truth it began quietly in the 1960s, and continued through the 1970s and 1980s. And the target was the middle class. It was a war that middle America lost. Resoundingly.[46]

In 1995, with tax cuts again high on the Republican agenda, the argument that reducing tax rates will increase tax revenues and reduce the federal deficit is again made. The lesson from the 1980s experience of this policy is just the opposite: dramatically increased deficits.

States have argued that downsizing government will lead to economic growth and look to privatization as an economic development tool. For example, the State of Colorado Title 29 states: "[Increased] privatization will aid in the development and retention of local small businesses, industries, and construction firms, will broaden the economic base of local areas, and will contribute to the increased economic vitality throughout the state."

To accept that the shift to private ownership will simply increase economic development while ignoring market structure, market power, and competitive pressures provides a limited view of how markets operate. Public spending to private contractors can, in fact, have a negative impact on the local economy, and a Florida study indicated that community income declined by $2.40 for every $1.00 "saved" because of privatization.[47] Private contractor profits dependent on tax dollars and the employment of fewer workers at lower wages are poor indicators of economic growth or vitality.

In 1995, a fundamental premise of the "Contract with America" was that government spending has a negative impact on private sector investment and growth. David A. Aschauer, however, has cogently argued to the contrary, that government spending encourages growth, and that the slowdown in public spending in the 1970s and 1980s contributed to the decline in U.S. international competitiveness.[48] This is particularly the case for infrastructural investment where public sector capital amounts to approximately one-third of total reproducible capital in the United States. State and local government investments in capital projects such as roads and bridges, water and sewage, and mass transit and utilities amounted to 64 percent of this total. Public investment declined as international competition was intensifying, and the reduction of investment in capital-intensive infrastructural projects actually had a deleterious effect on private sector growth in the 1980s.[49] As Tobin argued:

> The Administration's view that only formation of capital by private business provides for the future of the nation is a vulgar error that sacrificed public

investment in human capital (education and health), natural resources and public infrastructure to the construction of shopping malls and luxury casino hotels.[50]

Spending cuts that harm private capital reflect the failure of Reaganomics, even on its own restrictive terms, to generate long-term economic growth. The belief that the private sector will provide the level of infrastructural investment necessary to compete in international markets, given the externalities involved in such investment, is shortsighted and conveniently chooses to ignore the recent American experience.

Another major problem facing the economy has been the trade deficit. It is difficult to make a connection between international trade and the downsizing of government. The trade deficit attained record levels of more than $150 billion in the mid-1980s and returned to this level in 1994. Both the Bush and Clinton administrations responded by deregulating trade, and international developments in privatization promote the deregulated outflow of capital from advanced economies such as the United States into developing economies, including Mexico and South American nations. This movement is lubricated by the promise of low-cost access to assets, cheap labor, governments willing to comply to the demands of international capital, and few environmental controls. In the 1980s, assets valued at $185 billion were privatized[51] as almost seven thousand state-owned enterprises in more than seventy countries were sold off. Annually many billions have been generated worldwide through privatization.[52] American capital that moves offshore in search of highly profitable privatization sales will, in the long term, only contribute to the burden of the trade deficit. Privatization is part of the new world order based on a global free-market economy, few barriers to trade, free investment flows across national borders, and access to more easily controllable workforces. This latter point has also been important on the home front, and it is to this that we now turn.

The private sector has long provided a more hostile environment for workers and unions than the public sector. Supporters of privatization portray unions as institutions that create market imperfections and promote the inefficient allocation of resources. Privatization, by consolidating power in a more private form, challenges and reduces the power of public sector unions.[53] In 1994, with fewer than 12 percent of private sector workers in unions, public sector membership stood at 38.7 percent. If the National Performance Review is implemented as planned, it would erode the membership base of organized labor in the federal sector. The proposals in the "Contract with America" promise an even greater reduction.

Unions are increasingly marginalized by privatization and deregulation, whose supporters openly advocate the mobilization of the business community to neutralize public-employee opposition to reform,[54] and coalition building to overcome union objections.[55] Contractors who employ a "social Darwinist" approach to employment relations use fewer workers, often on a part-time or contingent basis.[56] The new, leaner organization employing a smaller, more tightly controlled, and lower-paid workforce clarifies the commodity status of labor and promotes an increasingly segmented and contingent workforce in the labor market.

Women and minorities, who are subject to less employment discrimination in the public sector, also suffer disproportionately from privatization. As Suggs has documented, the growth of public employment is strongly correlated with a decline in race-based wage differentials. Cuts in public sector employment have a disparate impact on women and minorities. Workers who experience the worst effects of segmented labor markets in the private sector face greater inequality that would result from extensive government downsizing: "Strategies that eliminate or reduce the expansion (in municipal employment), such as privatization, may prevent or limit minority gains in the public sector—which is where minorities have found greater opportunity and greater earnings equity."[57]

The final argument, that privatization helps build democracy, has intuitive appeal among its supporters and is ideologically attractive as a vindication of the "American Way."[58] Yet, to the contrary, privatization can be antidemocratic when narrowly defined corporate interests are the prime beneficiaries. The channeling of public money through the contract funnel offers a fraudulent promise of "people's capitalism." Economic and political trends of the past decade show this is as spurious a solution to the problems of the public sector as "trickle down" economics was to the economy as a whole. It is no more than a blatant attempt to appropriate public resources for private profit. Superficial advantages to government carry long-term costs to the citizenry.

Conclusions

While the problems of government administration are real, privatization and downsizing are simple, quick-fix solutions rooted in political opportunism. Positive, not negative, government is required to address the issues confronting the modern nation-state. In an economic climate that emphasizes downsizing or loadshedding, smaller government and lower taxes appear attractive. But taxes are needed to finance public expenditures. Taxation policy is not neutral, and the impact of taxes on different groups in society provides a measure of core social values. Fiscal policy is a reflection of how the cost of public spending is allocated and determines the relationship between citizen and state, the boundaries of public and private activity, and the politically acceptable levels of inequality. When political parties vie for electoral victory on the basis of cutting taxes, without addressing where such cuts would be made, the outcome is a repudiation of social and political responsibility. This is central to the "Contract with America," the balanced budget amendment, and the unfunded mandates resolution. All would impose a de facto deregulated framework on the economy and prevent government from addressing the social problems that such policies would create for the cities and states of America.

Contemporary problems raise fundamental questions of the role of government in modern society. In spite of the free market rhetoric, the politics of this policy change is as important as its economic counterpart. The federal government failed to carry through its privatization programs in the 1980s. Will the Clinton administration succeed in its objectives to shift government toward entrepreneurialism and also reduce the deficit, or will it fail, as did its predecessors?

Changing ownership will not provide a cure-all for the perceived weakness or failure in government. The National Performance Review focused attention on efficiency issues in the public sector; the "Contract with America" quickly transposed this into a political attack on public services. It embraced a standard of values that led supporters to overstate the benefits of private production and understate the quality of government. Workers will not turn back this attack by defending the status quo. Unions need to develop a positive strategy to improve public services. The call for worker empowerment within the Nation Performance Review is an important step in that direction, but the proclamation must be transformed into reality. Federal sector workers threatened with job loss are rightfully dubious about worker empowerment in an environment of downsizing and increased contracting out.

Whereas workers prefer lower to higher taxes, the full impact of taxation is rarely subject to adequate debate, especially as taxes have become increasingly regressive. The poor simply pay a higher proportion of their income in taxes than do the rich, and this regressivity has worsened over the past twenty years. Proposals to reduce the capital gains tax, expand individual retirement account limits, and change the tax rules on business depreciation will primarily benefit the richest fifth of the population. Workers and their families in the other 80 percent of the population will have to pay for these cuts. As suggested earlier, the privatization of wealth coexists with the privatization of poverty and the cheapening of labor. This is not a neutral agenda and it must be challenged politically. To return to the arguments of the 1980s that tax cuts will pay for themselves will further expand the deficit even with draconian cuts in social programs. To fine-tune the differences between the parties is to abnegate the social responsibility of government for the well-being of the population. Such an approach will serve only to heighten political alienation and further erode public confidence in the democratic process.

Economic policy has always been affected by the demands of indigenous and international capital. The international system of trade, production, and finance all place considerable strains on economic policy making. The dilemmas of social democratic regimes within capitalism are manifest in deregulation, downsizing, privatization, fiscal restraint, and the changing international division of labor. Proposals to reconfigure government must be appraised in view of a conservative agenda that seeks to restructure state agencies to better serve the needs of the wealthy. The real losers are those most in need in our society. The illusion of the 1980s was that prosperity would result from hard work, but the mink coats did not trickle down, and the federal deficit exploded. An intensification of the 1980s solutions in the 1990s will consolidate ever greater economic inequality, social and urban devastation, and political alienation. Progressives must continue to challenge the ideology of privilege and the concentration of economic power that has dominated the political debate for the past twenty years and demystify the conservative political agenda for what it is: a not-so-grand illusion.

Notes

1. Donald L. Barlett and James B. Steele, *America: What Went Wrong* (Kansas City: Andrews and McMeel, 1992), 105–23.
2. S. Breyer and R. Stewart, *Administrative Law and Regulatory Policy* (Boston, 1985), 655.
3. Kevin Phillips, *The Politics of Rich and Poor: Wealth and the American Electorate in the Reagan Aftermath* (New York: Random House, 1990), 91–101.
4. Jeanne Kirk Laux and Maureen Appel Molot, *State Capitalism: Public Enterprise in Canada* (Ithaca, NY: Cornell University Press, 1988), 1.
5. See Cosmo Graham and Tony Prosser, *Privatizing Public Enterprises: Constitutions, the State, and Regulation in Comparative Perspective* (Oxford: Clarendon Press, 1991), 1. Also Ronald Moe, "Exploring the Limits of Privatization," *Public Administration Review* 453 (1987), who suggests that administrative historians will conclude that privatization was the single most important concept of the 1980s.
6. James Laxer, *The Decline of the Super-Powers: Winners and Losers in Today's Global Economy* (New York: James Lorimer, 1989), 22–23.
7. See Ben Fine, "Scaling the Commanding Heights of Public Enterprise Economics," *Cambridge Journal of Economics* 14 (1990): 127–42. This argument was powerfully made in "Tory Paradox: In Thatcher's Britain Freer Enterprise Leads to More State Control," *Wall Street Journal* (October 6, 1988): 1, 10. The article highlights the centralization of state control in Britain after nine years of privatization by the Thatcher government.
8. Seymour M. Lipset, *Political Man* (New York: Heinmann, Mercury Books, 1963), 406.
9. See James Tobin in P.M. Jackson, ed., *Policies for Prosperity: Essays in the Keynesian Mode* (Cambridge, MA: MIT Press, 1987), 72.
10. Ralph Miliband, *The State in Capitalist Society: The Analysis of the Western System of Power* (London: Weidenfeld & Nicholson, 1969), 73.
11. The Clinton administration negotiated "side agreements" to NAFTA on labor and environmental issues, but these agreements are emasculated of any sanctioning power, and leave corporations with a relatively free hand to ignore these concerns at will.
12. John C. Hilke, *Competition in Government-Financed Services* (New York: Quorum Books, 1992), 7.
13. Stewart Lansley and Doug Gowan, *Fair Dues: Defusing the Tax Time Bomb* (London: Campaign for Fair Taxation, 1994), 3.
14. National Performance Review, *From Red Tape to Results: Creating a Government That Works Better and Costs Less* (September 1993), 48.
15. John D. Donahue, *The Privatization Decision: Public Ends, Private Means* (New York: Basic Books, 1989), 3.
16. The image is taken from Thomas Hobbes, an English philosopher writing in the seventeenth century who compared the modern state to a mythical sea monster. He contended that government had become too large, powerful, and dominating in the lives of the citizenry, advocated a reduction in the size and scope of the modern state, and predated the contemporary debate by three centuries. See Thomas Hobbes, *The Leviathan* (Oxford: Michael Oakshot, n.d.).

17. Barry Price and Roslyn Simowitz, "In Defense of Government Regulation," in Marc R. Tool and Warren J. Samuels, eds., *State, Society and Corporate Power,* 2d ed. (New Brunswick, NJ: Transaction Books, 1989), provide a succinct analysis of the ideological edge the deregulation movement honed in the late 1970s and early 1980s. They also develop a concise review of the process by which government regulation redefines property relations and property rights.

18. See Paul Starr, "The Case for Skepticism," in William T. Gormley, Jr., ed., *Privatization and Its Alternatives* (Madison, WI: University of Wisconsin Press, 1991), 25.

19. Paul R. Verkuil, "Is Efficient Government an Oxymoron?" *Duke Law Journal* 43 (1994): 1223–24.

20. See *Wall Street Journal,* "Tory Paradox," and Vladek, "Proceedings of the Fifth Annual Robert C. Byrd Conference on the Administrative Process: The First Year of Clinton/Gore: Reinventing Government or Refining Reagan/Bush Initiatives?" *Administrative Law Journal of the American University* 8 (1994): 30. For an excellent discussion of the history of government attempts to resolve problems of organization and regulation see Angel M. Moreno, "Presidential Coordination of the Independent Regulatory Process," *Administrative Law Journal of the American University* 8 (1994): 461.

21. David Linowes, "Privatization: Toward More Effective Government," *Report of the President's Commission on Privatization* (1988), xii.

22. Ibid., p. 258.

23. Kenneth Hoover and Raymond Plant, *Conservative Capitalism in Britain and the United States* (London: Routledge, 1989), 51.

24. Sam Rosenberg, "Restructuring the Labor Force: The Role of Government Policies," in *The Imperiled Economy Book II: Through the Safety Net* (New York: Union for Radical Political Economics, 1988), 27–38.

25. Hoover and Plant, *Conservative Capitalism,* 12.

26. Max B. Sawicky, *The Roots of the Public Sector Fiscal Crisis* (Washington, DC: Economic Policy Institute, 1991), 3. Sawicky argues that such policies create "collateral damage" for states and localities. The Gulf War terminology is particularly apposite for masking the damage created by such policies.

27. GAO Federal-State-Local Relations, *Trends of the Past Decade and Emerging Issues,* Report to Congressional Committees (Washington, DC: GAO/HRD–90–34, 1990).

28. This includes the call to privatize the air traffic control system, increasing private sector partnerships with government, and outsourcing noncore Department of Defense functions. See Al Gore, *Creating Government That Works Better and Costs Less: The Report of the National Performance Review* (New York: Plume Books, 1993).

29. See Vladek, "Proceedings," 30.

30. Center on Budget and Policy Priorities, *The New Fiscal Agenda: What Will It Mean and How Will It Be Accomplished?* (Washington, DC, 1994), 2–3.

31. Poole has argued that between 1973 and 1983, state and local contracting increased between 200 percent and 300 percent, a trend that continued throughout the decade. See Robert W. Poole, "The Limits of Privatization," in Michael A. Walker, ed., *Privatization: Tactics and Techniques* (Vancouver, BC: Fraser Institute, 1988), 79–91.

32. Carl F. Valente and Lydia D. Manchester, "Rethinking Local Services: Examining Alternative Delivery Approaches," *Management Information Services Special Report* 12 (March 12, 1984).

33. Touche Ross & Co., *Privatization in America: An Opinion Survey of City and County Governments on Their Use of Privatization and Their Infrastructure Needs* (Washington, DC, 1987), 20.

34. See Paul Starr, "The Case for Skepticism," in Gormley, ed., *Privatization and Its Alternatives,* 9.

35. Harold J. Sullivan, "Privatization of Public Services: A Growing Threat to Constitutional Rights," *Public Administration Review* 6, no. 47 (November–December 1987): 461–67.

36. Ibid. Also Mark H. Flener, "Legal Considerations in Privatization and the Role of Legal Counsel," in Lawrence K. Finley, ed., *Public Sector Privatization: Alternative Approaches to Service Delivery* (New York: Quorum Books, 1989), 141–52.

37. Mark Schlesinger, Robert A. Dortward, and Richard T. Pulice, "Competitive Bidding and States' Purchase of Services: The Case of Mental Health Care in Massachusetts," *Journal of Policy Analysis and Management* (October 1987): 262.

38. Steve H. Hanke, "Privatization versus Nationalization," in Steve H. Hanke, ed., *Prospects for Privatization: Proceedings of the Academy of Political Science* 36, no. 3 (1987): 2.

39. Paul Starr, *The Limits of Privatization* (Washington, DC: Economic Policy Institute, 1987), 6.

40. Linowes, "Privatization," 32.

41. Janet R. Pack, "The Opportunities and Constraints of Privatization," in Gormley, ed., *Privatization and Its Alternatives*, 292.

42. Starr, *The Limits of Privatization*, 8.

43. Janet R. Pack, "The Opportunities and Constraints," 285.

44. Donald L. Barlett and James B. Steele, *America: Who Really Pays the Taxes?* (New York: Touchstone, 1994), 22.

45. Ibid., 88–94.

46. Ibid., 94.

47. D. Marshall Barry, *The Negative Local Economic Impact of Privatization* (Center for Labor Research and Studies, Florida International University, 1989).

48. David A. Aschauer, *Public Investment and Private Sector Growth: The Economic Benefits of Reducing America's "Third Deficit"* (Washington, DC: Economic Policy Institute, 1990), 5–11. This also gives rise to a major distortion when discussing the federal deficit in that the assets that result from much of the spending, such as the broad infrastructure of the nation, does not appear as an offset to the spending required to produce such assets. This results in a lopsided view by concentrating attention on the flow of funds, not the accumulation of social assets.

49. Ibid., 11.

50. See James Tobin, *Policies for Prosperity*, 86.

51. John B. Goodman and Gary W. Loveman, "Does Privatization Serve the Public Interest?" *Harvard Business Review* (November–December 1991): 7–8.

52. Rodney Lord, "Privatisation: The Boom Goes On," *Multinational Business* 3 (1991): 1–7.

53. Hanke, "Privatization versus Nationalization."

54. Stephen Moore, "Contracting Out: A Painless Alternative to the Budget Cutter's Knife," in Hanke, ed., *Prospects for Privatization.*

55. Lance Marston, "Preparing for Privatization: A Decision-Maker's Checklist," in Steve H. Hanke, ed., *Privatization and Development* (San Francisco: Institute of Contemporary Studies, 1987), 68.

56. F. Valente and Manchester, "Rethinking Local Services," 12.

57. Robert E. Suggs, *Minorities and Privatization: Economic Mobility at Risk* (Washington, DC: Joint Center for Political Studies, 1989), 28. Suggs noted that minorities made up 30 percent of the workforce in Phoenix but suffered 88 percent of job loss during an agency privatization. Marilyn Dantico and Nancy Jurik, "The Effect of Privatization on Women and Minority Workers," in *The Privatization/Contracting Out Debate* (AFSCME, 1988), 29–33, found similar levels of discrimination in contracting-out situations.

58. Steve H. Hanke, "Toward a People's Capitalism," in Hanke, ed., *Privatization and Development.*

4

The Swedish Model:
From the Cradle to the Grave?

Norman Eiger

Defining the Swedish Model

The term "Swedish model" was already coined in the 1930s[1] in Marquis Childs's sense of Sweden as the land of the middle way between the Soviet command economy and the unregulated market capitalism of the United States. Since then the expression has been used almost like a mantra when discussing modern Sweden. There are many definitions of what constitutes the Swedish model and much depends on whether one takes a narrow or a broad view of Swedish society, or on one's ideology and values. Some focus on its mixed economy, others on its unique labor relations system and active labor market economy, while still others focus on its corporatist compromises, its advanced welfare programs, or its social democratic goals of solidarity and equality.[2] Using the broadest possible view, Rojas[3] settles for nothing less than defining it as synonymous with the entire social fabric of contemporary Sweden.

Our examination uses a broad definition of the Swedish model, though not quite as far ranging as Rojas's. It covers many characteristics to aid our understanding of the far-reaching changes that have taken place and the direction of the current transition. Drawing on many perceptions of the model, the following elements that have existed in varying states of harmony and tension with each other and that together give Swedish society its distinctiveness will be examined:

1. *Labor relations component.* The great social-class compromise between powerful universally organized employee and employer organizations that has led to stability in labor relations. Collective bargaining that is highly centralized, with settlement patterns led by the Swedish Trade Union Confederation (LO), the central confederation of wage workers.

2. *The economic-labor market component.* Economic goals of full employment, efficiency, and equality achieved through the application of the Rehn-Meidner strategy: a solidarity wage policy; fiscal policies that recapture excess profits; wage restraint coupled with low interest rates; low inflation; and an active labor market policy. The corporatist model is reflected by the strategy of labor market parties to negotiate solutions on economic issues and be represented on policy and administrative government boards.

3. *The political component.* Relative stability in the politics of the society coinciding with the long-term political rule of the Social Democratic Workers Party (SAP), often through coalitions it has dominated.

4. *The welfare component.* A welfare state that unites the working class and the new middle class behind its cradle-to-the-grave programs because it provides universal social entitlements. It is not minimalist in its benefits, and it extends to all classes equal qualitative benefits.[4]

The Swedish model has been considered the most successful evolution of the social democratic project in the world. The model largely reflects the values and institutions of the Social Democratic labor movement, which has held government office for fifty-two out of the past sixty years—the longest tenure in power of any labor movement. Yet support of the model extends beyond the labor movement to include broad sections of the population that vote for at least two of the three major non-socialist parties. Even the moderates within the Conservative Party, which is hostile to social democratic goals, have on occasion supported aspects of the model. Nevertheless, the major contours that shape the model came from the political and economic institutions of the labor movement. It represents the most significant effort to create a social democratic model in one country. Fundamental challenges linked to far-reaching international economic and technological change raise the question of whether the model can any longer be developed in one country.

The Demise of the Swedish Economic and Labor Relations Model

There is a widespread perception that Sweden discovered a successful third way between laissez-faire capitalism and the East European command economies. Sweden's economic and labor market policies, from 1945 to the early 1970s, did achieve complex policy balances that led to relatively full employment, even during global recessions; economic growth without inflation; and one of the highest living standards in the world. Sweden also pursued the goal of greater wage equality without undermining efficiency and motivation. This was achieved in the context of political democracy, an economy based on private property relations, social harmony, an almost universally unionized workforce, and an interventionist economic policy that corrected for market failures.

Antiunion conservatives in other countries find Sweden's success, with the highest rate of unionization in the Western world, difficult to understand. While union membership in many countries declined between the 1960s and the 1980s, Sweden's unions experienced a steady growth rate, rising to 80 to 85 percent of the workforce in the late 1980s. The 2.3-million-member LO, comprising twenty-seven national unions with largely blue-collar memberships, is the major union federation. With its close ties to the SAP, the LO is considered the economic backbone of the social democratic project in Sweden. As the public sector and service industries grew since the 1960s, 75 percent of white-collar workers (1.3 million employees) organized into the twenty union affiliates of the Salaried Workers' Federation (DC). A third union confederation, SACO/SR, with 280,000 members, succeeded in organizing the majority of professional workers in the public sector.

In the private sector, until the 1980s, the unions led by the LO at the central level negotiated with the powerful Swedish Employers' Confederation (SAF), and its thirty-five industry federations representing forty-five thousand member companies. Some idea of the resources available to the SAF and its associated federations can be gauged from the well over one thousand staff members in its secretariat.[5]

According to neoclassical economists and conservative ideologues, a regulated mixed economy with a powerful labor movement was not supposed to succeed. They were proven wrong; but since the 1970s a number of internal structural changes, the abandonment of parts of the economic model, and external pressures arising from changes in global markets and capital mobility have made the economic dimension of the Swedish model problematic and subject to heated debate and radical change.

Sweden's economic model began in the 1930s with the great class compromise between labor and capital symbolized by the historic Saltsjobaden agreement. Swedish labor-management relations evolved from a period of bitter strikes and lockouts at the turn of the century toward agreements and cooperative strategies after the 1932 election of the first Social Democratic government. The long-term hegemony of a strong labor government encouraged business to reach cooperative understandings rather than pursue sharp adversarial relations. Saltsjobaden laid out the rules and procedures for collective bargaining that paved the way to centralized national bargaining in the late 1950s between the powerful unions affiliated with the LO and the strong and disciplined employers' organization, the SAF. The national agreement established a series of framework guidelines that were generally adhered to by each LO and SAF industry affiliate. Supplementary agreements at the industry and company levels fine-tuned the details, including local-level equity adjustments. Therefore, centralized collective bargaining and positive sum agreements formed the base of the labor relations pillar of the model. As a result the Swedish labor movement, despite wage restraint and without major conflict, achieved wage levels in the post–World War II period that were among the highest in the advanced industrialized countries.

Centralized bargaining was essentially instrumental as a means to achieve broader social ends. The two goals at the heart of the Swedish Social Democratic model are full employment and equality.[6] The challenge was to achieve these goals without sacrificing price stability, efficiency, and economic growth.

Although social democratic economists had anticipated Keynesian demand-management to fight the Great Depression of the 1930s, they recognized that other strategies were needed in periods of expansion and inflationary pressure. Consequently, two LO economists, Gosta Rehn and Rudolph Meidner, developed a set of economic and labor market strategies to achieve full employment and an egalitarian income distribution that have become known as the Rehn model. It was adopted by the LO Congress in 1950 and by 1960 was implemented by the Social Democratic government without serious opposition from the business community. In summary, labor unions utilized centralized bargaining to achieve a solidarity wage policy of greater income equality; it was the government's role to achieve redistribution through taxation, transfer payments, and the universal social net of the welfare state. The normally conflicting goals of full employment and price stability were to be achieved through moderately restrictive fiscal and monetary policies that placed restraints on profits as well as wages. Business cycles were to be sharply reduced through a set of contracyclical strategies designed to promote the appropriate level of investment.

The solidarity wage policy meant that "work of a similar nature should, to the greatest possible extent, cost the same for all employers."[7] Simply put, it involved a policy of equal pay for equivalent work. Unlike bargaining in the United States, the nature of the work, not the profitability of firms, is the standard for pay settlements. This necessitated centralized bargaining with the SAF and close coordination between the blue-collar and white-collar unions in both the private and public sectors.

The outcome of the policy focused labor's resources on raising wages of the lower-paid groups and narrowing industry and occupational differentials arising from market forces and power positions. It also favored the more productive companies and encouraged greater productivity in the less efficient. Inefficient companies, unable to pay the industry average wage, were forced to lay off workers or were indirectly encouraged to close. However, since downsizing and closing of marginal, inefficient firms would create unemployment and conflict with the other key goal of labor, an active labor market policy had to be central to the model.

This involved an array of strategies to ease the transfer of workers to the stronger firms: worker mobility through relocation allowances; labor flexibility through retraining programs; sophisticated employment services; subsidies to the private sector to hire the hard to employ; and the use of public works as the employer of last resort. Active labor market policy combined with contracyclical investment strategies, and fiscal and monetary policies, maintained the lowest level of unemployment among the Western industrialized countries (with the possible exception of Switzerland). Aggregate demand was controlled by corporatist agreements on wage restraint and high rates of progressive taxation; excess profits were taxed and channeled to investment in human resources and research.

Achieving full employment without inflation required union cooperation on wage restraint in tight labor markets. The problem was complicated because the solidarity wage policy generated very high levels of profits among the most efficient firms. Extremely low unemployment coupled with high profits was an inducement for wage drift at the local plant level.

The LO Congresses in the 1960s grappled with the problem and in 1971 commissioned Rudolph Meidner to head a study group to develop a proposal to recapture excess profits for an investment fund controlled by workers. In addition, the study group's charge was to propose a plan to counteract capital concentration stemming from self-financing and to enlarge employee influence on company decision making. The 1976 LO Congress accepted the Meidner Plan for the creation of employee investment funds.[8] These funds would be created by taking 20 percent of excess corporate profits in the form of new equity share issues. Capital would remain in the enterprise, but as a result of the gradual transfer of shares, it was estimated that within twenty years, majority ownership in major Swedish enterprises would be shifted to the employee-controlled funds. The funds and the local unions at the enterprise would share in the voting rights of the shares. The Swedish labor movement's program had moved from influence over decision making through collective bargaining and codetermination to changing the structure of ownership and decision making.

The proposal unleashed the most bitter debate since the late 1950s, when similar principles were involved in the pension funds conflict. With property rights being challenged, the SAF militantly led the opposition, accusing labor of intending to socialize Sweden's industry and end the market economy.[9] Heated discussions within the LO and the SAP increased, and differences sharpened between the LO and the salaried workers of the DC. The majority of the public were confused over the complex issue, and polls consistently showed a majority against the proposal. This radical step toward the democratization of ownership and control of capital failed when the LO was unable to unify a blue-collar–white-collar coalition, while the right was mobilized and unified effectively.

When a Social Democratic–led coalition received a parliamentary majority in 1981, a diluted version of the collective capital funds proposal was passed. Two additional goals were added to the original concept: to increase capital formation, and to strengthen the pension system. But various provisions were introduced into the proposal that severely limited the size, coordinating ability, and duration of revenues from the profits tax and that prevented the funds from obtaining majority control in any single firm.[10] Claiming this was the "nose under the camel's tent of collectivism," the business community launched an all-out political offensive climaxing on October 4, 1983, when one of the largest demonstrations in Swedish history marched through Stockholm's commercial district. Some eighty thousand to one hundred thousand chief executives from small firms to the largest enterprises marched with managers and salaried employees to the parliament to protest against the wage earner funds.[11]

An LO evaluation of the funds after three years of implementation claimed that the predictions of catastrophe were proven groundless; although indications that the funds contributed to the economy could not be definitely proved. But Meidner's and the LO's predictions were fulfilled when profits that were not recaptured by this skeletal investment fund fueled wage drift, which promoted inflationary public sector settlements, or were invested abroad. Wage drift accelerated the breakdown of the solidarity wage policy. The employers' victory was compounded when the nonsocialist government elected in 1991 announced that the employee funds would be dissolved and the accumulated capital, which the unions wanted for the weakened pension funds, were allocated to entrepreneurial research and development. One of the central instruments the workers' movement had devised to further economic democracy was largely stillborn.

Other events occurred that indicated a decline in the corporatist spirit of Saltsjobaden. Sweden's employers had taken an extremely hard line in the 1977 bargaining round with the LO. The SAF demanded basic changes in the legislated system of illness benefits and vacation and working time. In 1980 the breakdown in central contract negotiations led to a massive employee lockout that paralyzed Sweden for two weeks. Though subsequent bargaining rounds were settled without such crises, changes within the unions, the economy, and employer strategies fundamentally altered the Swedish bargaining model.

Centralization and wage solidarity have also been affected by structural shifts involving the growth of the service and public sectors. The powerful salaried worker and civil servant unions arising from these changes became increasingly dissatisfied with a policy of wage setting based on the LO and SAF patterns set in the competitive export industries.[12] Wage agreements tied to formulas based on the export industries began to break down in the second half of the 1970s.[13]

In an economy that is not growing and with relative stagnation in real wages, the tradition of cooperation between blue- and white-collar unions and private and public sector unions gave way to tensions that sometimes erupted into direct conflict. This erosion of interunion unity undermines the wage solidarity model and contributes to the forces promoting wage drift and a cycle of inflationary pressures.

After the nonsocialist coalitions were unable to resolve inflationary pressures and increasing budget deficits, the Social Democrats turned the economy around when they were returned to power in 1982. The budget deficit was eliminated without cutting social policy entitlements, the economy grew at an annual rate of 2.7 percent, unemployment was brought down for several years below 2 percent, and trade deficits turned into surpluses.[14] Yet the underlying forces shaping the

Swedish economy had not changed. The profit boom and speculation that followed the government's devaluation strategy were not controlled by fiscal restraint, and the wage drift that followed profit expansion fueled further inflationary rises. In response, the government tried to introduce an incomes policy to moderate wage settlements through informal agreements on tax rates, dividends, and price restraints. However, these corporatist-type interventions were not able to withstand the increasing inflationary pressures at the end of the decade.

The temporary abandonment of centralized collective bargaining by the SAF in 1984 in favor of separate industry negotiations became fixed when the SAF stated that from 1991 onward, all collective negotiations would be conducted by the industrial federations.[15] Employers fundamentally challenged the system of centralized bargaining and wage solidarity, claiming they prevented the wage differentials and labor flexibility needed to adapt to global market pressures. Meyerson[16] summed up the employer view by charging that "The Swedish labor market had come down with sclerosis," which required fundamental changes.

Moreover, in the 1980s the ideology of free market conservatism and neoclassical economics that swept Western economies infiltrated the Finance Ministry of the Social Democratic government.[17] The Rehn-Meidner strategies were abandoned in favor of fighting inflation with rising unemployment in 1990—the worldwide neoliberal nostrum. With the election of a nonsocialist government, deflation was caused by sharply rising interest rates. Sweden plunged into a prolonged deep recession, a budget deficit of Skr 100 billion, declining investment, stagnant productivity rates, and continued steep increases in unemployment.

The demise of Sweden's commitment to full employment and reliance on unemployment as a trade-off against inflation were vividly illustrated in projections of 5.2 percent unemployment in 1993 by Sweden's Business Research Institute (KI),[18] and the even worse scenario of the Labor Market Board (AMS) of 7 percent unemployment.[19] Either projection represents crisis levels of unemployment compared to what is acceptable in Sweden. During 1993 the unemployment rate reached an unprecedented 13 percent. However, a painfully slow recovery reduced the rate to 10 percent in 1994, with projections of further reductions. No longer is the Swedish response a Keynesian expansionist strategy and active labor market program but rather reduced public sector expenditures and fewer employment and training services.[20] Today the priority is to protect the currency, slow the export of capital and distribute wealth toward the owners of capital. In economic downturn the policy responses of the nonsocialist government, and to a lesser extent the SAP, dramatize what has been clear for some time: The Swedish economic and labor market model now appears unrecognizable.

What are the underlying causes of this breakdown in the class compromise in labor relations and the economic model? For one explanation we must turn to the global restructuring of capitalism. Social democracy failed to reduce the concentration of capital ownership and wealth and win a measure of control of capital investments in Sweden. The giant companies that dominate Sweden's private sector have grown larger under policies that pursued a profit-led private sector expansion. Twenty companies employ 30 percent of the workforce and account for 40 percent of export sales and 70 percent of research and development. Until the 1980s these corporations, for several reasons, largely invested their profits in Sweden. First, there were restrictive policies on capital export as well as on competitive foreign investments in Sweden. Second, a highly skilled, well-trained labor force, ample raw materials, access to venture capital, and attachment to the nation encouraged domestic investment. The turnabout came in the mid-1980s, when the European Community (EC) announced it was going to pursue a single market by 1992. This increased the motivation to have direct access to the new market through local production and EC-based subsidiary headquarters. Swollen with cash reserves resulting from the Social Democratic government's devaluation and other economic strategies in 1981, Swedish firms increased their acquisition of foreign firms and investments in global markets. The phasing out of controls on capital exports and imports contributed to a 77 percent increase in direct foreign investments from 1985 to 1986 alone. Foreign investment doubled by 1988,[21] and nearly 33 percent of the employees of Swedish companies were outside of Sweden by 1990.[22]

With more assets held abroad, companies are less influenced by the policies and controls of nation-states, particularly those of small countries. Similarly, they are less influenced by the policies of national labor movements. In this new and unequal international playing field, the rules of Saltsjobaden, if not less relevant, are certainly less motivating for management. There is a lessening of interest by Swedish firms in domestic demand stimulation.[23] Hence Keynesian programs are opposed by business even in recession, in favor of shrinking transfer payments and social programs.[24] When rates of capital investment abroad continued in 1990, neoconservative stopgap measures were introduced by the Social Democrats, including the abandonment of the commitment to full employment. Further, the government abandoned its ambivalent position on the EC and proposed Sweden's membership by 1995. Aside from capital mobility, there are the related constraints on an export-dependent nation operating in an increasingly competitive world economy. Reliance on exports makes Sweden highly vulnerable to loss in market share if it pursues policies that are significantly at variance with the production and social costs of its competitors.

The greatly expanded role and volatility of international monetary policy, currency speculation, and capital flows reduce the autonomy of social democratic macroeconomic policies. The deregulation of the foreign exchange and domestic money markets in the 1980s left the country without tools to defend itself against currency speculators. In the absence of foreign exchange controls, marginal interest rates in 1992 soared to 500 percent before the krona was left to float. The high interest rates wiped out several hundred thousand jobs, threw the country into its deepest depression, and enlarged the budget deficit to crisis levels.

The struggle for the social democratic project, which can no longer be realized in one country, must now be raised to the European level with the effort to create a social Europe that goes beyond the current stalled, minimalist social program; other options include international workers' councils to represent workers at multinational companies and coordinate bargaining strategies. Sweden's labor movement, despite the new hostile political and economic environment, has not suffered declines in membership and still remains the best organized in the world. It will have to play a major role in furthering the goals of social democracy on the larger landscape of the new European economy.

The Changed Political Dimension of the Swedish Model

At least four major characteristics describe the political model: (1) a Social Democratic–led government for fifty-four out of the past sixty years; (2) a highly stable voting pattern;[25] (3) a strong identification with party by voters; and (4) extremely close ties among the LO; its affiliated blue-collar unions, which have organized one-fourth of Swedish society; and the SAP. Dramatic changes in each of these areas since the 1970s were particularly glaring in the 1991 elections.

In September 1991 political shifts shook all four of the traditional parties and led to the election of its most conservative government since 1982. The election left the Social Democrats with 37.6 percent of the vote, its lowest performance since 1928, and a loss of twenty-three seats. The Green party lost all of its seats, because it fell short of the 4 percent threshold under the proportional representation rule; the Liberal and Center parties lost about 3 percent of their previous vote, capturing only 8.5 percent and 9.1 percent, respectively.[26] However, the Moderates, the most conservative of the traditional parties, increased their vote by 3.6 percent, winning 21.9 percent, which gave them the right to form the governing coalition for the first time in sixty-one years.[27]

These results had been predicted, but particularly stunning was the arrival on the scene of Sweden's first right-wing protest party—the New Democracy, which gained 6.7 percent of the vote and twenty-six parliamentary seats, and held the balance of power in the new parliament with the sectarian Christian Democratic party, which similarly gained twenty-six seats, with 7.1 percent of the vote. The ability of these parties to pass the 4 percent threshold was a sign of a political revolt that is generally alien to Sweden's cultural norms. The volatility of the new political scene was further reflected in the demise of the New Democracy party and the drop in support for the Christian Democrats in the swing to the left in September 1994.

Although there are immediate explanations for what happened in 1991 and 1994, a longer-term view is needed to understand labor's defeat in 1991 and its victory three years later. First, the stable voting traditions of the electorate have turned highly volatile. In the elections of the 1950s and 1960s only 5 percent of the voters switched their party support, in contrast to 20 percent and 25 percent switching in 1988 and 1990, respectively.[28] The erosion of Social Democratic support over the past fifteen years occurred when an increasing proportion of its voters split their votes in local and municipal elections.[29] The weakening of the commitment to the SAP is also evidenced by the decline of those strongly identifying with the party.[30] This decline of party loyalty was also found among the other three traditional parties.[31] Among the major factors explaining the decline in party attachment is the reduction in class voting and disenchantment with political leaders in a slow or no-growth economy.

A conventional view suggests that the successes of the SAP in increasing security and raising living standards actually contributed to the decline in class voting. As the problems of traditional capitalism were ameliorated, increasing numbers of working-class voters, particularly highly skilled artisans, as well as service and younger workers, identified their interests with nonsocialist parties. The impact of affluence and the growth of the service and public sectors influenced the demographics of Swedish voting patterns. In the less affluent northern Sweden, the SAP received close to 50 percent of the vote, whereas in the more affluent Stockholm metropolitan area, with its much larger proportion of salaried workers, it received but 27 percent.[32]

Perhaps a more salient explanation is the changing class composition of the society resulting from the shift from mass production to service and information industries. Technological change and deindustrialization reduced the number of traditional blue-collar production workers, the core of the Social Democratic movement's base. The growth of the welfare state has led to an expansion of the public-sector (largely female) workforce; the mobility of workers has led to the growth of suburbs and the breakup of the old working-class communities. These changes have transformed the Social Democratic movement. Internally, the shift to the service, information, knowledge, and public sectors has restructured the class composition of Sweden. The numerical decline of the traditional working class has led academics to argue that left parties face secular decline as the proportion of workers in the labor force, and thus in the electorate, is falling at a precipitous rate.[33] Despite the strong case for this scenario made by Przeworski, this extreme pessimism is not warranted in the Swedish case. Sweden's Social Democrats have understood that their base in the blue-collar working class would always be an electoral minority and that creatively fashioned alliances were needed with other classes to achieve a Social Democratic–led government. The weakness in Przeworski's view is its failure to recognize the potential for appealing to both the proletariat and the salariat on the basis of commonly shared interests. In challenging Przeworski, Esping-Anderson[34] suggests the potential of an alliance of blue- and white-collar workforces on the basis of a Social Democratic program that extends economic democracy and speaks to their shared "desire for full employment, improvements in work life, and employee participation."

Appealing to the needs and interests of the greatly enlarged female workforce is a challenge for social democracy. With some justification, women credit social democracy for the economic gains they have made since the 1960s: the vast expansion of jobs, mainly in the public sector, that were opened to them, and the social services that support the family and permit women to work with less anxiety. The SAP receives 5 percent more votes from women than from men,[35] but complacency about this support continuing would be very shortsighted. Serious problems exist with occupational segregation and with patriarchal structures and values within the labor movement. As unemployment rises, women see their aspiration to successfully combine working life and home life threatened. Social Democrats must therefore once again champion their commitment to full employment, a perception that was eroded by the neoliberal economic program the government pursued prior to being voted out of office.

The SAP has developed programs designed to appeal to the interests of the new middle classes and the multinational corporations. This led to tensions in the relationship between the LO and the party. Although cross-class appeals and compromises have always been part of their pragmatic political strategies since the 1930s, Social Democratic policies leading up to the 1991 election debacle were perceived as betrayals of basic principles of the workers' movement. A major problem was the government's tax reform, regarded by the LO as being regressive and favoring higher-income groups. The 1994 Social Democratic tax program contains progressive aspects in reducing the budget deficit and may be a step toward reversing labor's perceptions. Other policies that contributed to the alienation of trade unionists and activists and a lower level of voter mobilization were the government crisis proposals in February 1990 for a temporary ban on strikes; a wage, price, and dividend freeze; and changes in sick benefits. Finally, these wounds were salted by labor's perception that its government was abandoning the commitment to full employment. For many, the party appeared to be losing its soul.

Bodies as well as soul have been lost—membership in the SAP dropped from a record high of 1.2 million during the first half of the 1980s to just 260,000 in 1992, largely as a result of the termination of union locals collectively affiliating their memberships. Budgets of the SAP have been depleted by about Skr 4 million. Additionally, tens of millions of krona have been lost to party treasuries because of declining government subsidies.[36]

One constant in the life of the party had been the overwhelming support of the blue-collar unions for formal, close ties with the Social Democrats. This sentiment changed dramatically toward the latter half of the 1980s. In 1988 fewer than 24 percent of the members of Metall, the metalworkers' union, felt that cooperation with the Social Democrats should be reduced or eliminated altogether. This increased to 44 percent in 1992.[37] The president of Metall, Leif Blomberg, even called for LO unions to draw a clear dividing line between the unions and the SAP.[38]

Finally, the party received much criticism for its lack of openness in debating divisive issues. Besides the government's retreat to neoliberalism in 1990, there was a lack of full discussion in the labor movement on the proposals to join the European Community, tax reform, the Øresund bridge issue, and environmental-energy concerns.[39] What does the future hold politically for the labor movement and the SAP? It is difficult to envision an optimistic scenario, either in the short or the long run. Periods like the continuous forty-four-year unbroken rule of the Social Democrats are phenomena of the past. On the other hand, those analysts who said the conservative victory in 1991 ushered in a long-term shift to the right were proven wrong only three years later.

Between 1991 and 1994 the nonsocialist government once again failed to cope with a growing economic crisis. The electorate turned toward the Social Democrats, as it did in 1981 after the economic mess created by the previous divided nonsocialist ruling coalition. The Social Democrats were returned to office in September 1994. With 45.6 percent of the vote and 162 seats in the parliament, Ingvar Carlsson, the new prime minister, decided to form a minority government and to rely on the Left party and Green votes or their passive support to maintain office.[40] They spurned overtures from the Liberal party to form a coalition government, and are depending on being able to gather majorities on an ad hoc basis to pass specific parts of its program.

In the future the trade unions will be more independent of the SAP, but leaders in both wings of the workers' movement discount any serious rupture. The trend is toward a "more explicit recognition of their respective role and autonomy," according to Knut Rexed,[41] the deputy secretary of the DC.

The institutions of Sweden's workers' movement have historically exhibited an ability to change under criticism and to use crisis as an opportunity for change.[42] In response to the criticism on internal democracy and technocratic decision making, internal dialogue is being broadened to include broadly scoped educational forums and study circles, as in the 1970s,[43] on such potentially divisive issues as the proposal to join the EC; the 1990 Social Democratic Congress has recognized the need for programmatic and structural reform in its program for the 1990s; and a task force made up of the nongovernmental younger members of the SAP and its youth organization was recently formed to study the "undercurrents of modern society and ways to handle them."[44]

Swedish social democracy can draw on the high density of union organization in both the blue- and white-collar workforce. The organization of the salaried occupations was greatly assisted by the LO in the post–World War II period, and a long tradition of cooperation and goodwill exists that provides a foundation for a revitalized political as well as economic alliance. On the other hand, there is resistance to such collaboration. The emerging workforce is multifissured by a range of diverse and sometimes opposing interests. Growing challenges arising from technological change are jurisdictional disputes between blue- and white-collar workers. Solidarity among these employee interests depends on restoring coordinated bargaining strategies. The tasks are formidable, for they must be undertaken against a background of stagnant growth rates, a budget deficit running at 11 percent of the GNP, the different interest claims of public-sector and private-sector workers and workers in "sunset" and "sunrise" industries.[45]

The forces weakening the Swedish social democratic model are formidable. Will the new Social Democratic government rise to the challenge? Now that they are once again the government, will the Social Democrats find an alternative to the neoliberalism of the 1980s? In opposition, the Social Democrats restored their support and raised expectations by attacking the conservative government's policy of intentionally allowing unemployment to rise and proposing to curtail sickness benefits and other social programs. The central question is whether the Social Democrats will be able to pursue, in an environment of unbalanced corporate power, a program that again points the way toward reconciling economic efficiency and competitiveness with solidarity, equality, and economic democracy. In view of our analysis, optimism is not warranted, and to date the preliminaries are not promising.

The once self-confident SAP that built the Swedish model and even proposed changing the basis of capitalist property relations in the 1970s, basically feels powerless and frustrated to make major changes. Ingvar Carlsson voiced this frustration in an interview shortly after moving into the prime minister's office: "National political leaders have only a formal right to make decisions over a situation in which they feel increasingly powerless. This brings politics into ill repute. . . . Democracy could be damaged [by this]." Swimming against the tide of globalized market forces and the threat of financial speculators, Carlsson clearly states the dilemma, but strategies to resolve it are not offered. Instead Carlsson seeks to balance the demands of the multinational corporations for what they consider a favorable business climate, and the needs and expectations of workers and their organizations.

One of the first initiatives of the new Social Democratic government was the formation of two councils of business leaders, one consisting of the CEOs of Sweden's largest multinationals and the other comprising representatives of small business. Both will meet regularly and advise the government on policy. Allen Larson, who was designated as the government's representative on the big business advisory council, promised that the government would "listen" to business and "seriously try their suggestions."[46]

Also in a post-election interview, the future Social Democratic finance minister, Goran Persson, went on record that there would be no change in the conservative government's monetary policy. He also suggested that the LO was simply an interest group that will have limited influence on economic policy. Asked to respond to the current "profit explosion" in Sweden, which is 2 to 3 percent higher than even during the record-breaking years of the early 1980s, Persson did not see any need for a policy on excess profits similar to that of previous Social Democratic governments. Instead, he believed "business needs several years of very big profits before we will get sufficient investment."[47] How such an approach can be fitted into an anti-inflationary policy was not addressed. Labor's response to this policy by its own government remains to be heard.

Whither the Welfare Model?

The economic and labor market models advanced by Rehn and Meidner with the support of the labor movement have been significantly dismantled and the political model transformed. Is this the fate of the welfare model? Since all advanced capitalist societies have various forms of welfare systems, where does Sweden fit? In what ways is it different? According to Richard Titmus,[48] as modified by Gosta Esping-Anderson,[49] social welfare models could be grouped as either weak welfare states of the marginal, residual type or strong welfare states of the institutional type. In the "residual" model the state intervenes as a helper of last resort to assist individuals who have been marginalized by social and market forces. In quantitative and qualitative terms it provides a minimal level of support for temporary periods. The United States is an example of the residual type.

Sweden is an advanced example of the institutional type of welfare system in which government provides cradle-to-the-grave security based on the following principles: (1) It is comprehensive in the range of services provided; (2) it is universal, not means-tested, and the services are a right of citizenship; (3) its transfer payments approximate the average standard of living;[50] (4) it aims at a fairer redistribution of basic resources among income groups; and (5) it unites the working class and the middle class behind its system of universal social rights.

By taking services such as health care, child care, sickness compensation, employment security, job training, continuing education, and general income maintenance into the welfare state, when combined with its labor market policy, Sweden has attempted to decommodify labor. Along with progressive taxation, this advanced welfare state represents the government's contribution to the social democratic goal of equality. In the United States, the trend has been toward greater inequality among classes, greater commodification of labor power, and minimalist social insurance and services that weaken labor's bargaining power. This encourages social atomism, family breakdown, and hopelessness and conflict among the powerless and among ethnic and racial groups. Such estrangement is reflected when desperate workers in the United States assume the role of strikebreakers, a phenomenon unheard of in states with strong institutional types of welfare (as well as legal prohibitions against striker replacements). In contrast to the rampant individualism of the American welfare system and the resentments it fosters among people from all strata, the Swedish system encourages a greater sense of social obligation among classes.

Sweden's Social Democratic party recognized that welfare transfer payments and the decommodification of basic social services would not change the basic structure of wealth distribution in the vertical sense. To win over the emerging new middle-class stratum, and to build a majority coalition, welfare expenditures had to be financed out of economic growth. This was a view shared by European socialist leaders, as Michael Harrington observed their "euphoric and utopian" assumption in the post–World War II era that the socialist perspective was based on a "limitless process of growth—financed social decency in a capitalist economy under socialist political control."[51]

Thus the Swedish welfare state program expanded qualitatively as well as quantitatively during several decades of economic growth and relatively low levels of international competitive pressures. However, growth under capitalism could not be continuous and, with economic downturn, painful allocative choices would be required. Consequently, the rightist movement among neoconservatives in the Moderate party and among young conservatives called for significant rollbacks in welfare programs.

Prime Minister Carl Bildt, leader of the first "actually existing" conservative-led government in sixty years, told Parliament, "The age of collectivism is at an end now.[52]

American mass media proclaimed that the defeat of the Social Democrats was a vote against the welfare state and one more national conquest for laissez-faire market economics. But it cannot be seen as a mandate to roll back the welfare state. The parties in the conservative-led coalition ran on a platform of improving the welfare state through greater choice among services and responsiveness to individual needs.[53] When the government began to cut employee rights and social programs, its support dwindled.

While people complain about inadequate child care openings or grumbling occurs about paternalistic service agencies, and young conservatives rail against egalitarian social policies, very few Swedes would do away with the services. Indeed, the values of a strong, institutional-type welfare system pervade most sections of the society. Most political observers agree that it would be suicidal politically for any party to run against this consensus.[54]

On the other hand, the major pressure to curtail social programs is the disintegrating economy. According to the AMS, 436,000 or 9.7 percent of Sweden's workforce were jobless in August 1994. An additional 3.4 percent of the unemployed are covered by active labor market programs.[55] Sweden's vaunted training programs were swamped to the point that Gota Berhardsson, director-general of the AMS, said "they cannot cope with much bigger numbers if they are to do their job properly."[56] The rest of the jobless will be forced to rely on unemployment benefits or on other forms of public assistance, which will greatly increase the already ballooning budget deficit.[57]

In contrast to the conservative government's program of reducing expenditures by Skr 30 billion over three years, which focused mainly on reductions in sickness benefits, housing interest rate subsidies, and grants to local authorities for public services,[58] the Social Democrats proposed an increase of more than Skr 80 billion to deal with the unemployment crisis. At a time when social insurance costs at the county and local levels are rising, additional cuts in national aid threaten to break many community budgets.[59]

There are at least four major factors restraining a significant rollback of the welfare state that appear more salient than those that tend toward its dismantling. First is the continued power and density of the trade unions. Militant collective actions would confront any fundamental changes.[60] Second, as suggested, the new middle class does not oppose the social services and benefits of the welfare model. However, it does want qualitative changes, such as greater choice and less bureaucracy and paternalism. A broad cross-class coalition exists that prevents a backlash that would savage social services. Third, contrary to the conservative myth that welfare state support that enhances worker security destroys motivation, the Swedes long ago understood that the welfare state has played a key role in permitting Swedish industry to restructure more easily. Workers assured of little income loss from structural and technological changes are more likely to accept necessary change. Consequently, unions are better able to negotiate rationalization agreements that further productivity even if they result in job losses, and workers are more motivated to participate in problem solving and new forms of work organization. Finally, the Social Democrats are mandated to prevent further erosion of the welfare state. Although further expansion is unlikely, only careful pruning of programs or readjustment of priorities may take place. As far back as the 1986 LO Congress, the labor movement recognized that with one-third of the workforce in the public sector, the issue was not further expansion but how best to use existing resources. Toward this end the LO called for reforms that could be carried out by shifting priorities and allocations—for example, to deal with child-care and old-age-care demand, to expand higher education opportunities for working-class youth, to extend paid paternal leave from twelve to eighteen months, and to provide more subsidized housing.[61] These reforms will probably wait until the new Social Democratic government manages to reduce unemployment.

If the conservatives cannot directly attack the basic principles of the institutional welfare state, they effectively mined a vein of discontent toward its bureaucratic character. Conservatives in Sweden, as in other countries, have tapped into certain widespread populist concerns. Their solution is to expand the choice given to individuals, including the right to purchase social services such as day care in the marketplace. All sides of the political spectrum recognize that many welfare state services have become too centralized (despite the fact that most programs were decentralized to the county and municipal levels in the 1970s); some programs have become rigid and dominated by a professional elite that discourages individual and community participation. Conservatives have taken advantage of this dissatisfaction by calling for privatized, market-based programs. This lends urgency to the efforts of the architects of Sweden's welfare state to reform social services in accordance with their vision and principles. There are many indications that the SAP has "smelled the coffee," as Joanne Barkan put it, and is awakening to the shortcomings of the welfare state, policy proposals project reform based on greater choice and citizen participation.[62]

With the end of a serious commitment to full employment and other foundations of the economic model, the maintenance of the strong welfare model in Sweden assumes even greater social importance. The social values it embodies of security, solidarity, and equality as buffers to the harshness of market forces are central to the vision the SAP must again articulate, but in ways that reflect the changed social structure. However, not only does Sweden's strong universalistic welfare model receive broad-based commitment across social strata and not only are its solidaristic values deep-rooted, but also the need for social stability leads to the recognition that the long-term budgetary and social costs of failing to provide essential human services as citizenship rights are politically prohibitive. Therefore, it was not surprising to find that the most conservative government in Sweden's modern history became increasingly frustrated as its "major ideological and fundamental nonsocialist bills were turned into mincemeat before decisions are reached."[63]

Conclusions

Social Democracy in One Country from the Cradle to the Grave

Sweden has gone farther down the long evolutionary road toward the goals of social democracy than any other society. Has it reached the end of the road and taken a sharp U-turn? Some concluding observations can be made based on current trends in each of the components of the Swedish system we have discussed.

First, what looked like a linear progressive development from political to social and finally economic democracy has become, in the past two decades, an erratic evolution to a retreat from the latter goal. If a Polaroid snapshot were taken today of Sweden and compared to one taken even a few years ago, it would be unrecognizable. A fundamental transformation has occurred in the economic and labor market dimensions of the model. We have seen that the Swedish labor movement's struggle to go beyond social reform of the economy toward social ownership and democratic control of capital was soundly defeated. The shift of power away from labor, despite the Social Democratic election victory, leaves internationalized capital driving economic and social policy. Until recently it would have been inconceivable to witness economic policy, in a deep recession, based on budget cuts and social belt-tightening. The Rehn-Meidner economic strategy, to reconcile the values of full employment, price stability, equality, and efficiency, is a memory. Active labor-market strategies are being severely strained by the highest levels of unemployment in decades. Solidarity between the unions and occupational interests is being weakened. The withdrawal of employer representatives from government labor market and welfare policy boards is emblematic of the breakdown of corporatist arrangements. Adamant employer opposition to centralized bargaining and the solidarity wage policy epitomizes the breakdown of class compromise.

Similar profound changes have occurred in the political dimension of the model. Long envied for its stability, Swedish political life can no longer be considered an exception as its uniqueness gives way to the volatile patterns long familiar in other advanced industrial countries. Social democratic hegemony has been replaced by shifting alliances between fragile nonsocialist and Social Democratic coalitions.

The Swedish model is under intense economic and political pressures, and its further growth is unlikely to occur, but simultaneously the model cannot be easily reduced by its opponents. Indeed, the institutional welfare state appears to be the lasting legacy of social democracy in one country. Underlying these seismic shifts is the harsh reality of a profoundly changed international and domestic economic landscape. If any single conclusion can be reached, it is that a small economy, highly dependent on exports and subject to uncontrolled capital investment decisions of transnational corporations, cannot fully realize the social democratic project in one country. This naturally raises the question of the prospects for an international realization of the model. Although discussing such prospects would take us far beyond this chapter, a few observations are in order. Developing international labor strategies in the past has been caught between the shoals of narrow nationalism and the currents of market forces. In the post-Fordist era national capitalist economies and corporations have become globalized. Breaking down economic and even political borders in Europe, which seemed utopian as recently as 1985, now appears as an almost inexorable, although a slow and rough, process. While internationalization opens opportunities for the hegemony of capital, it also offers labor movements and their allies new possibilities for developing at least a European-level countervailing force toward further international labor solidarity. To achieve the aim of participation by people in the decisions that shape their environment requires that labor share in the control of the institutions of international finance, codetermine with capital the organization and strategic decisions from the workplace level to the transnational enterprise level, and have broad influence over European regional and international macroeconomic policy. In short, it means the fulfillment of the social democratic vision of extending the realms of freedom and rights from the national to the international economy.[64]

Notes

1. A.Rojas, "The Swedish Model in Historic Perspective," *Scandinavian History Revue* 39, no. 2 (1991).

2. Rudolph Meidner, "The Swedish Model Goals, Methods and Experiences," in W.J. Dercksen, ed., *The Future of Industrial Relations in Europe: Preliminary and Background Studies* (The Hague: Netherlands Scientific Council for Government Policy, 1990).

3. See Rojas, "Swedish Model."

4. Caveat: All models are grossly simplified frameworks for analyzing complex phenomena. "Models," according to Henry Theil in *Econometrics* (New York: John Wiley & Sons, 1976), "should be used, not believed." One example among many of the problems

of simplification is that these components are not autonomous. Though we examine each one separately, they are linked to each other, and while not completely dependent on each other, change in any one seriously affects the others. Their greater dependency, however, is on the forces in the largely changed international economic environment.

5. Hans-Goran Myrdal, *Employers' Associations in Europe: Policy and Organization* (Baden-Baden: Momos Verlag, 1991).

6. Meidner, "The Swedish Model Goals."

7. Gosta Rehn and Birger Viklund, "Labor Development in the 1980s," in *Recent Development and Future Prospects for Trade/Union Policies and Industrial Relations in Europe, 1988.*

8. Rudolph Meidner, *Employee Investment Funds* (Boston: George Allen & Unwin, 1978).

9. "Viewpoint," *The Federation of Swedish Industries* 6, no. 4 (1983).

10. Jonas Pontusson, *Public Pension Funds and the Politics of Capital Formation in Sweden* (Stockholm: Arbetslivcentrum, 1984).

11. "Viewpoint," *The Federation of Swedish Industries* 6, no. 4 (1983).

12. Kristina Ahlen, "Recent Trends in Swedish Collective Bargaining," *Current Sweden* 358 (1988).

13. Fritz W. Scharpf, *Crisis and Choice in European Social Democracy* (Ithaca, NY: Cornell University Press, 1987).

14. Jonas Pontusson, "At the End of the Third Road: Swedish Social Democracy in Crisis," paper presented at Swedish Information Service Seminar, Graduate Faculty of New York School for Social Research, New York City (November 16, 1991).

15. Myrdal, *Employers' Associations in Europe.*

16. Per-Martin Meyerson, *The Welfare State in Crisis: The Case of Sweden* (Stockholm: Federation of Swedish Industries, 1982).

17. Pontusson, "At the End of the Third Road."

18. See *Svenska Dagbladet* (February 28, 1992).

19. Sven Svensson, "A Dead-End Budget," *Sweden Report* 1 (April 1992).

20. Hans Bergstrom, *Dagens Nyheter* (October 15, 1991).

21. Paulette Kurzer, "The Internationalization of Business and Domestic Class Compromises: A Four-Country Study," *Western European Politics* 4, no. 4 (October 1991); Dan Magenerot, *Dagens Nyheter* (November 5, 1991).

22. Myrdal, *Employers' Associations in Europe.*

23. Pontusson, "At the End of the Third Road."

24. The SAF lobbied the new government to cut back sickness benefits from almost 100 percent of income to 67 percent in the first two weeks of sick leave. See *Dagens Nyheter* (May 25, 1992).

25. Axel Hadenius, *A Crisis of the Welfare State? Opinions about Taxes and Public Expenditures in Sweden* (Stockholm: Almquist and Wiksell, 1986).

26. See *Swedish News* (September 19, 1991).

27. See *Dagens Nyheter* (September 17, 1991).

28. From Peter Esaisson's presentation at Swedish Information Service Seminar, New School for Social Research, New York (November 16, 1991).

29. See Bergstrom, *Dagens Nyheter* (October 15, 1991).

30. Fifty percent of SAP voters strongly identified with the party in 1976, in contrast to 41 percent in 1988. See Hans Bergstrom, *Dagens Nyheter* (October 15, 1991).

31. From Peter Esaisson's presentation at Swedish Information Service Seminar.

32. Ingemar Worland, "The Electoral Decline of Social Democracy: Is There a Geographical Factor?" in L. Karvonen and J. Sundberg, eds., *Social Democracy in Transition* (Brookfield, VT: Dartmouth Publishing Co., 1991).

33. Adam Przeworski, *Paper Stones: The History of Electoral Socialism* (Chicago: University of Chicago Press, 1986).

34. Gosta Esping-Anderson, *Politics Against Markets: The Social Democratic Road to Power* (Princeton, NJ: Princeton University Press, 1985).

35. Ulf Lindstrom, "From Cadres to Citizens to Clients," in Karvonen and Sundberg, eds., *Social Democracy in Transition.*

36. See Stenberg, *Dagens Nyheter* (April 30, 1992).

37. Data reported in a poll of Metall's membership by SIFO (Swedish Institute for Public Opinion). The extent of support of formal Metall-SAP ties varies with level of pay, skill, and education of union members. The higher the level in each of the categories the more likely the member is to criticize formalities or cooperation between the union and the party.

38. See Anna Danielsson and Tommy Oberg, *Svenska Dagbladet* (April 7, 1992).

39. See Stenberg, *Dagens Nyheter* (April 30, 1992).

40. See *Swedish Notes* (September 19, 1994).

41. Knut Rexed, "Swedish Labor During the 1990s," paper presented at Swedish Information Service Seminar at Graduate Faculty of the New School for Social Research, New York City (November 16, 1991).

42. In response to wildcat strikes of the late 1960s, Sweden's unions and the SAP developed a wide-ranging workplace and economic democracy program.

43. Norman Eiger, "Education for Workplace Democracy in Sweden and West Germany," in R.N. Stern, ed., *The Organizational Practice of Democracy* (New York: John Wiley & Sons, 1986).

44. Rexed, "Swedish Labor During the 1990s."

45. During the 1980s the SAP again demonstrated its ability to appeal to significant sections of the middle class. In the 1982 elections support for the SAP among white-collar groups ranged from 43 percent of the clerical and service workers to 25 percent of upper-level white-collar employees. See Eric S. Einhorn and John Logue, *Modern Welfare States* (New York: Praeger, 1989). The cross-class appeal also appeared successful in 1994, with real unemployment at double-digit levels.

46. See *Dagens Nyheter* (October 8, 1994); *Sveska Dagbladet* (October 3, 1994).

47. See *Sveska Dagbladet* (October 3, 1994).

48. See Richard Titmuss, *Essays on Social Policy* (London: George Allen & Unwin, 1958); Richard Titmuss, *Social Policy* (London: George Allen & Unwin, 1974); "Viewpoint," *The Federation of Swedish Industries.*

49. Esping-Anderson, *Politics Against Markets.*

50. Sven E. Olsson, *Social Policy and Welfare State in Sweden* (Lund: Lund University, 1990).

51. Michael Harrington, *Socialism: Past and Future* (New York: Arcade, 1989).

52. Craig R. Whitney, "Swedish Coalition Plans Overhaul of Policies," *New York Times* (October 6, 1991).

53. A bitter struggle occurred within the nonsocialist coalition over the Christian Democrats' proposal for subsidizing parents who cared for their own children through a universal allowance that also allows the parents to replace existing day care services with market choices.

54. See *Dagens Nyheter* (January 21, 1992).

55. See *European Industrial Relations Review* 249 (October 1994): 11.

56. See *The Economist* (February 22, 1992).

57. See *Swedish Report* (April 1992).

58. See *Financial Times* (April 27, 1992).

59. Hans Bergstrom, *Dagens Nyheter* (October 15, 1991).

60. The proposal that the first two days of sick leave would not qualify for benefits met with widespread protests, and more than half a million wage earners signed petitions denouncing the proposal. See *Dagens Nyheter* (May 5, 1992).

61. See LO Congress Report, "The Trade Union Movement and the Welfare State" (1986).

62. Joanne Barkan, "End of the Swedish Model?" *Dissent* 39, no. 2 (1992).

63. See *Dagens Nyheter* (May 7, 1992).

64. The leaders of the Scandinavian Social Democratic parties met in May 1992 to discuss a common strategy toward influencing the direction of the European Community, with the highest priority being full employment. In the campaign to achieve a "yes" vote on joining the Community in 1995, Ingvar Carlsson stressed this priority. Sweden will join with Finland and Austria; Norway's voters rejected the proposal to join the European Union.

5

Labor Relations and the Social Structure of Accumulation: The Case of U.S. Coal Mining

Michele I. Naples

Introduction

The U.S. coal-mining industry has had strong unions and disruptive industrial conflict since the 1920s. Moreover, miners have often been forerunners for the U.S. labor movement as a whole. In a recent dispute, the UMWA campaign of civil disobedience and widespread grassroots organizing succeeded in preventing Pittston from running away from the union and its retirement fund. These methods and results point a hopeful beacon for labor in the 1990s. Is such optimism regarding a change in the climate of labor relations warranted? This chapter will place labor relations in coal in an analytical framework known as the Social Structure of Accumulation (SSA). The SSA refers to the overarching institutional structure that shapes and channels class conflicts.[1] The history of this paradigm is linked to macroeconomic long waves of prosperity and crisis. This macro-institutional perspective can help throw light on changes in economic and labor conditions in one sector, U.S. coal mining.

This chapter applies the SSA framework to the U.S. mining industry and attempts to compare the results to other theoretical alternatives. The focus of this study is on the history of labor relations in U.S. coal mining since World War II, which includes the events surrounding the Pittston strike and their implication for current labor relations in U.S. coal.

The Social Structure of Accumulation

Theoretical Framework

The Social Structure of Accumulation comprises the set of institutions that constitute class relations. Components of the SSA shape relations between, for example, financial and industrial interests, national and foreign firms, and labor and corporations (e.g., the structure of union-management relations). The SSA manages and channels class conflicts, treating only specific forms and objects of conflict as legitimate. Thus the postwar labor-relations paradigm attenuated such disruptive forms of conflict as strikes and especially wildcats, substituting grievance procedures and contract negotiations. This truce focused attention on a subset of issues least threatening for accumulation (e.g., income equivalents rather than working conditions). This in turn benefited productivity and motivated investment. A successful SSA provided the context for accelerated accumulation, reducing unemployment nationwide.

Class conflicts are neither eliminated nor necessarily reduced by the SSA; they are managed. Consequently, the SSA embodies contradictions. The SSA framework is essentially a nation-state framework for dealing with socioeconomic conflict. As the logic of the system of rules is applied to more aspects of relations in more areas, the inability of the SSA to resolve fundamental conflicts becomes manifest—that is, the SSA contains some of the seeds of its own destruction. Moreover, the very success of an SSA in facilitating accumulation can create economic conditions that bring to light the faults in the SSA. For instance, in coal the combination of lower unemployment and the contradictions of the labor-relations system generated actions by miners that brought to the fore the contradictions of the SSA, raising labor costs.[2] As a result, the historical paradigm for social behavior faces a crisis before any new system evolves. Conflicts within and between classes can become wide-ranging and disruptive as a crisis unfolds. The "natural" or "unregulated" state of capitalism is stagnation, not the harmonious equilibrium of neoclassical economists.[3]

Times of economic crisis such as the present are also intertwined with social and political crises and thus are moments for epistemological breaks. As many institutionalists observe, there need not be a complete collapse in the social and economic fabric. However, it is recognized that the old rules or ways of being do not work anymore. Some actors seek to undo the old system (to "deregulate"), while others defend aspects of it, perhaps fearing that an institutional void would be worse.

The process whereby a new SSA is hammered out is conflict-ridden. Paradigm shifts are potential revolutions; they are transformations that require political realignments and are the outcome of class struggles. The new SSA will be reached by consensus among some sectors or class factions but will be imposed on others. After the fact, social scientists see the prevailing SSA as "obvious" and functional; consider, for instance, the characterization of postwar unions as "mature."[4] But in the crisis phase, the requirements for a successful SSA are unclear, in part because success is measured by the system's ability to manage ongoing class conflicts.

Before a new worldview takes shape, many novel practices are experimented with. Once an SSA achieves ideological hegemony, early in the long-wave upturn, difference and challenges to the meta-rules in any single sector are no longer tolerated. Concrete institutional developments become more straightforward, and the parameters have already been set; it is simply a question of applying the meta-regulatory approach to particular problems.[5] Experimentation is least viable once a new worldview has achieved political dominance.

Alternative Frameworks

The SSA framework can be contrasted with other views of labor relations and strike activity. Neoclassical theory treats strikes as wasteful mistakes, and labor-management accommodation as the rational way to increase the size of the pie to be parceled out. Institutionalists recognize that strikes are labor's weapon, and unions are labor's voice in a conflict-ridden labor-management relationship.[6] Institutional analyses tend to be static, so a crisis in labor relations must arise from such exogenous factors as pressures from international competition. Of course, it all depends on whether competition is viewed as an internal factor in a larger framework of globalization.[7] Traditional Marxian theory recognizes unemployment as the key constraint on strikes,[8] yet Marx also saw the massive unemployment generated by depressions as motivating greater labor militancy. This approach pays less attention to institutional factors.

The regulation approach is closest to SSA analysis,[9] although its emphasis is on technological rather than social relations in production. From its perspective the technology of mass production and the assembly line served as a basis for the postwar expansion by introducing a social consumption norm. Real wages were tied to productivity, and social welfare programs were introduced, stabilizing demand. Thus Fordism resolved the underconsumption problem that had contributed to the Great Depression. The postwar pattern of collective bargaining would face a crisis once the productivity advantages of capital-intensive production had been fully realized.

But technological exhaustion and a productivity slowdown did not cause the upsurge in labor unrest in coal in the 1960s. Productivity growth did not slow appreciably until 1967 (see Figure 5.1);[10] strike activity rose after 1964 (see Figure 5.2). Furthermore, disruptive forms of conflict, especially regarding safety and health issues, appear to have contributed to the productivity decline of the early 1970s.[11]

The regulation analysis also suffers from functionalism: It focuses on why particular institutional developments were functional for accumulation, but not how they came to predominate. This invokes a historical determinacy that ignores the conscious intervention of labor, capital, and their representatives as subjects shaping their own environment. There was no disinterested engineer running the state who chose institutional structures based on macroeconomic considerations. Rather, individual class segments acted in their own self-interest to discover, promote, and/or impose what became the prevailing vision for labor-management relations.

Figure 5.1 **Labor Productivity in Coal Mining, 1949–92**

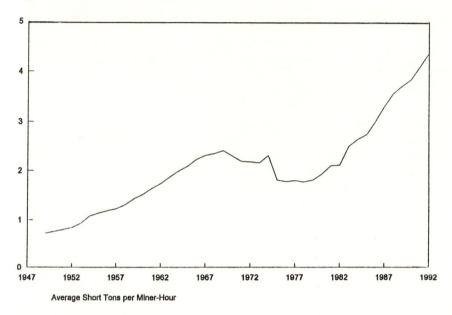

Average Short Tons per Miner-Hour

Source: U.S. Department of Energy, Energy Information Administration (Washington, DC: U.S. Government Printing Office).

Generalizations

The SSA approach thus provides ten generalizations regarding the history and future of U.S. coal-mining labor relations:

G1.   Institutional innovation, change, and challenges to the meta-rules will be most widespread during the late expansion and into the long-wave crisis.

G2.   The advent of collective bargaining under the SSA manages class conflict, attenuates its disruptive forms, and focuses attention on a subset of issues less threatening for accumulation.

G3.   Difference and challenges to the worldview are not tolerated under the newly hegemonic SSA in the early expansion.

G4.   The structure of U.S. labor relations tends to be consistent with the meta-social bases of the general SSA.

G5.   The structure of labor relations in U.S. coal comes to resemble the national SSA pattern.

G6.   Once in place, the SSA in U.S. coal benefits unit labor costs, accumulation, and profitability, and ultimately leads to reduced unemployment.

G7.   Labor relations in one sector are not static. The logic of the new rules is applied on an extended scale so that the full system of national union/rank-

Figure 5.2 All Strikes and Strikes over Working Conditions in Coal Mining[a]

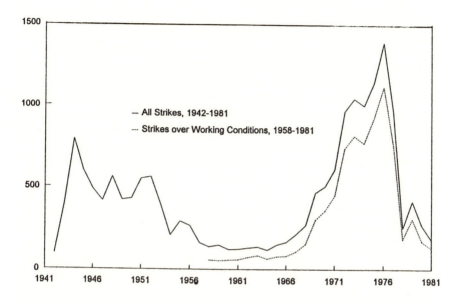

Source: U.S. Department of Labor, Bureau of Labor Stataistics (Washington, DC: U.S. Government Printing Office); not available after 1981.
[a]Years 1940–52, bituminous coal only; in 1953 these were 94 percent of all coal strikes.

and-file/management relations only becomes fleshed out over time.

G8.   Sustained low unemployment and the contradictions of the labor-relations system in U.S. coal generate actions by miners that bring to the fore the contradictions of that paradigm.

G9.   The emergence of these fault lines in the labor-relations SSA hurts productivity and profits.[12]

G10. Consequently, firms seek to undo the old system, to deregulate themselves, or to run away from commitments under the old SSA.

The ensuing history will seek to explore these generalizations, demonstrating the analytical capabilities of the long-wave SSA analysis, and developing implications for labor relations in U.S. coal into the next century. Unlike strictly institutional analyses, this materialist approach incorporates economic forces into the study of institutional development. Economic self-interest motivates actors; availability and control of resources affect the reproduction of the SSA. The inertia of the regulatory framework gives it only relative autonomy, not absolute autonomy, from economic elements.

The Pattern in Coal Before Dominance by the Postwar SSA

The 1930s organizing drives along industrial lines in the United States owed much to the efforts of John L. Lewis, the Mineworkers' president who helped found the CIO. The United Mineworkers of America (UMWA) originated the practice of deducting union dues from paychecks, which permitted union leaders to focus more on other activities and less on chasing down their salaries (G1). During World War II, most new industrial unions learned to work with management under an emerging paradigm of negotiation and compromise. Most unions signed a no-strike pledge for the duration of the war. Lewis and the mineworkers considered such a promise a sellout to management and refused to sign.

The intense pace of production under wartime conditions and rising industrial accidents put U.S. mineworkers at the forefront of the wildcat strikes that accelerated in 1943 and 1944 (G1). Miners' continued militancy may have been related to coal's longer history of unionization along industrial lines than most sectors, dating from the 1920s. Furthermore, 90 percent of all coal came from UMWA mines in the 1940s, and coal provided half of U.S. energy needs.

The emerging postwar SSA recognized unions as long as they accepted certain rules of the game: a separation between politics and the economic, such that government policy would be addressed through the two major political parties, especially the Democratic party, rather than by political strikes; an acceptance of economic issues as the relevant province of collective bargaining negotiations; a definition of the economic that presumed pecuniary equivalents for every qualitative workplace demand (e.g., unsafe working conditions could be compensated for by higher wages); and a willingness to negotiate in good faith to avoid strikes and so benefit both management and labor (G2). An administrative union hierarchy developed to negotiate and implement contracts, replacing the more activist, democratic structure that the CIO organizing drives had fostered.

Most unions consented to require members to sign an anticommunist oath under the 1947 Taft-Hartley Act. Lewis challenged the law and refused to enforce it, aware that leftists were effective organizers for the miners; this meant that the UMWA could not use the National Labor Relations Board (NLRB) election mechanism. At the time there was very little support outside coal for Lewis's instrumentalism vis-à-vis the left (G3). The new paradigm was hostile to communism in the international arena, and to Communist organizers' unwillingness to abandon ongoing workplace struggle (G4).

The UMWA continued to fight to retain miners' right to walk out of any unsafe mine, as other unions focused on productivity increases and technical change. The miners' ongoing strike activity continually prompted President Truman to call in the National Guard to assure coal production. Despite the UMWA's hostile relations with the government and lack of adherence to the emerging model for labor relations, the union won a precedent-setting medical and pension fund in 1947. Lewis insisted that company contributions to the pension fund be tied to output rather than employment, anticipating that company pressures to replace labor with equipment would ultimately succeed. From 1948 to 1952, miners' hourly pay outstripped that of other unions; however, short hours meant that their annual earnings were just above the manufacturing average.

The mineworkers broke with both the CIO and the AFL before the 1949 CIO purges of dissident unions. Nor did the inter-union raids of 1949–52 directly affect coal. But the unbending political climate of McCarthyism and the hegemony of the new labor-relations paradigm meant that the miners would be isolated from the labor movement and the government if they tried to maintain a militant front against company pressures to automate. Partly because industrial conflict made coal an unstable energy source, many consumers were attracted to the new, affordable postwar alternatives of Mideast petroleum and domestic natural gas. While the changeover required capital investment and took time, retail deliveries of bituminous coal fell by 58 percent between 1944 and 1954, and railroad consumption fell by 87 percent. Faced with a precipitous decline in coal consumption, and low profit rates except for the inflationary years of 1947 and 1948, coal operators cut back production—worker employment fell by one-fourth between 1948 and 1952.

To summarize this period in coal, there was a clear regularity to labor-management relations, where labor appeared to have tremendous influence. However, this pattern did not fit the emerging SSA and was continually challenged by its advocates. Nor could the UMWA's strategy be maintained when faced with the transformation in coal's economic context. The rules for labor relations would change quickly, in a direction that was not "natural" but that was directed by the national understanding of appropriate collective bargaining behavior (G5).

The UMWA Signs the Truce

In 1952 the UMWA signed a watershed contract with the newly organized Bituminous Coal Operators' Association (BCOA). The union agreed to permit automation in exchange for higher wages and increased benefits (G2). Although the UMWA had always supported efforts to legislate minimum safety standards, including the 1952 federal Coal Mine Safety Act, Lewis now contended that getting miners out of the mines was the best way to deal with accidents and fatalities. This new concern with saving the industry, at a cost of 58 percent of production-worker jobs by 1961,[13] meant that the UMWA leadership took no initiative toward seeing the 1952 legislation enforced. This helps explain the finding of Lewis-Beck and Alford[14] of no trend impact of the law on fatalities, despite its novel enforcement provisions.

The new technology created worse health problems for miners. The continuous miner increased noise and coal dust levels significantly (the dust produced was too dense to see through). Mechanization had mixed effects on safety: The rate of lost workday accidents fell by one-third from 1947 to 1959, and was flat through the 1960s, but the fatality rate showed no such reduction (see Figures 5.3 and 5.4).[15] Mechanical crushing and cleaning of coal above ground also spread: The amount of coal mechanically cleaned rose from 30 percent in 1948 to 66 percent in 1959. This reduced contact between such workers and those at the face, requiring greater efforts to renew the informal ties that sustain a strong union.

Increasing demand in the West made Western sub-bituminous mines more attractive despite their lower-quality coal. Because coal is so heavy to transport (more than one-third of the price of delivered coal is transportation cost), the railroads had burned top-grade lump coal; the new electric utilities generally were less concerned about weight. The share of industry output from surface mines rose from 9 percent to 29 percent between 1940 and 1959. The new surface mines proved difficult for the UMWA to organize. Surface mines were safer in this period, as overhead cave-ins and ventilation of gases and coal dust were less of a problem. Production workers operated huge pieces of earth-moving equipment, and work groups had less autonomy than underground workers. Because strip-mined seams in the western United States are quite thick, averaging thirty-five feet (as against fewer than ten feet in underground mines),[16] strip miners faced less rapid changes in natural conditions than miners underground, and workers had to make fewer judgments. These factors and surface workers' lack of a mining heritage contributed to the difficulty of unionizing strip mines.

After the 1952 contract, the number of strikes fell off (G2). Continued wildcat strikes focused heavily on job-security issues—one-third of all strikes in the 1950s concerned job security, while only 13 percent of strikes from 1960 to 1981 did.[17] The UMWA even financed the introduction of continuous mining equipment through a union-controlled bank in Washington. The heavy capital investment was explicitly encouraged by the new SSA in coal (G2, G6); it in turn confirmed management's commitment to industrial harmony, since idle capital made strikes more costly.

In the period 1952–62 there were no new coal contracts, and the existing contract was amended by agreements not subject to member ratification.[18] To maintain industrial peace, UMWA officials disciplined wildcat strike leaders with fines and threats of expulsion.[19] In this period of the new SSA's consolidation, there was not the tolerance of difference Lewis had shown militants in the 1940s (G3). Like the national SSA, coal's labor-relations paradigm reduced the disruptiveness of class struggles and shifted the objects of conflict from safety and health and working conditions to wages and fringes (G5). Institutionalization of labor relations meant increasing autocracy in many unions. Lewis's rule of the mineworkers was autocratic even before the truce. For instance, by World War II he had placed most union districts under administrators he appointed. And a clause in the union constitution punished those convicted of circulating a

Figure 5.3 **The Accident Rate in Coal Mining, 1931–93**

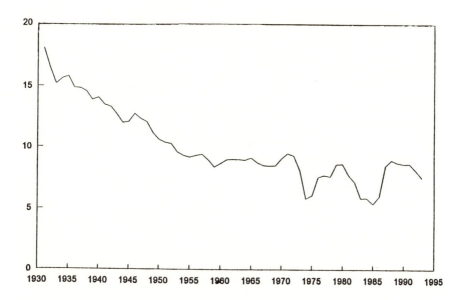

Source: U.S. Department of Labor, Mine Safety and Health Administration (Washington, DC: U.S. Government Printing Office).
Rate per 200,000 hours worked.

"wrongful" condemnation of any decision by a union officer by six months' suspension from the union and exclusion from holding office for two years.[20] That undemocratic structure served Lewis well as he steered the union toward an accommodation with coal operators.

After Lewis's retirement in 1960, the new regime under Tony Boyle (Thomas Kennedy was nominal head until 1963) further reduced member influence over union policy, in keeping with the logic of the new paradigm's increasing centralization of union power: The number of local-union endorsements needed to nominate a candidate for office was increased from five to fifty, the Executive Board was given the right to postpone union conventions, the president was empowered to fill international-officer vacancies, and the term of union office increased from four years to five years.[21] This illustrates how the rules of the game, in this case increasing autocracy, are applied on an expanded scale over time (G7).

The benefits of the new truce, including mechanization, and the rise in surface mines contributed to rapid productivity growth and declining unit labor costs in the 1950s (see Figures 5.1 and 5.5). By 1958, when the number of wildcat strikes

Figure 5.4 **The Fatality Rate in Coal Mining, 1930–93**

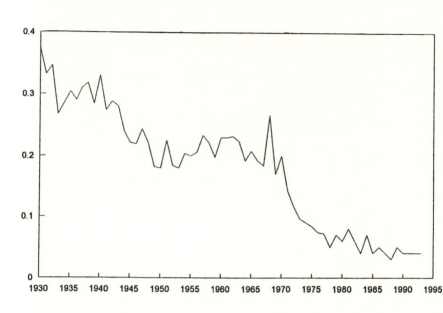

Source: U.S. Department of Labor, Mine Safety and Health Administration (Washington, DC: U.S. Government Printing Office).
Rate per 200,000 hours worked.

finally dropped off (see Figure 5.2), the decline in coal's share of the energy market abated.[22] This suggests that as well as low costs, stable labor relations and therefore stable output were key to stopping the flight from coal and restoring profitability (G6).

After-tax returns on net worth in coal averaged only 2.9 percent in the 1950s (as against 8.9 percent in manufacturing), seeming to belie the advantages of the truce. However, 3 percent of all bituminous coal corporations accounted for 92 percent of all net profits after taxes, while 78 percent had more than $6 million in net losses (data are for 1957); many marginal operators reported losses for years, and remained in business only because continued operation enabled them to cover some of their fixed costs. Low average profitability therefore had two causes: excess industry capacity, and the disincentive to exit (coal-mining equipment and structures have virtually no alternative use). In the years of industrial harmony, miners' relative wage position slipped behind steelworkers', and they failed to negotiate such new benefits as paid holidays, supplemental unemployment benefits, and cost-of-living adjustment (COLA) clauses. While the theory of regula-

Figure 5.5 **Real Unit Labor Costs in Coal Mining, 1958–91**

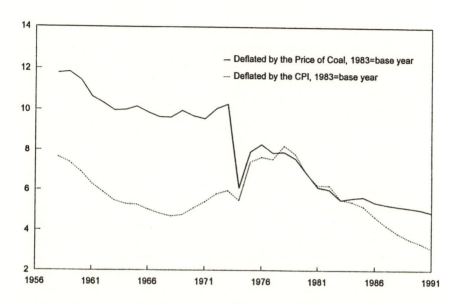

Sources: U.S. Department of Energy, Energy Information Administration; U.S. Department of Labor, Bureau of Labor Statistics (Washington, DC: U.S. Government Printing Office).

tion implies that institutionalized collective bargaining would increase real wages, and stabilize their growth by tying them to productivity, real wages fell in every year except one from 1958 to 1963.[23]

In the early 1960s the Welfare and Retirement Fund recorded a higher incidence of respiratory complaints, later attributed to the generation of high coal-dust levels by continuous mining. Yet the trustees, including Tony Boyle, decided against demanding dust controls for fear of overburdening loss-ridden operators.[24] Although at the time the UMWA was probably the richest union in the country, when coal companies ran away from their obligations and when revenues fell in the early 1960s, the fund cut back on benefit levels and eligibility. In coal, industrial harmony corresponded to a relative decline in material benefits for workers.

The Unraveling of the Truce

As suggested above, any accommodation between capital and labor is tenuous, given the conflict built into class relations. The more the union acquiesced to

management concerns about productivity, industrial peace, and flexibility in fir-
ings and layoffs, the more the rank and file doubted they had a voice through
their union. The more undemocratic the union's structure became, the more
difficult it became for members to work within that structure to make change.
While dissatisfaction with the new paradigm for labor relations might fester
among coal miners, it was not until the secular drop in unemployment in the
long-wave expansion of the 1960s gave them greater economic security that they
acted on that dissatisfaction (G8).

After years of declining demand and high unemployment in coal, the long
economic boom of the 1960s brought some relief. Layoffs in coal mining became negligible, and the quit rate rose after 1960, doubling by 1965 and tripling
by 1969, to almost 1 percent per month.[25] Unauthorized strikes began to increase
after 1964, accelerating after 1968, and represented more than 90 percent of all
coal strikes; strikes over working conditions also increased (see Figure 5.2). This
was clearly a change from the 1950s pattern, when top-level negotiations extended the 1952 contract. In the 1960s the rank and file participated by walking
out. Strikes during the term of contracts were particularly disruptive, and the
willingness to raise "noneconomic" issues (i.e., those outside the understood
scope of collective bargaining), increased coal's strike-proneness.

In 1964–68 a number of large wildcat strikes over noneconomic issues racked
coal. In 1964 wildcat strikes shut down most mines in West Virginia and eastern
Kentucky when the union announced plans to close five union hospitals.[26] In
1965 seventeen thousand miners refused to cross picket lines, in protest of the
unfair discharge of six miners.[27] Fifty-nine thousand struck in 1968 in sympathy
with members at a newly certified Pennsylvania mine where conflicts had bro-
ken out with police.[28] The growing importance of wildcat strikes is indicated by
a 1968 contract that granted a $120 Christmas bonus, to be reduced if wildcat
activity continued (see Table 5.1).[29]

This greater willingness of miners to walk out, particularly over nonwage issues,
was the context for "Jock" Yablonski's announced candidacy for union president in
1968. Yablonski criticized Boyle's cooperation with management, lack of attention
to occupational safety and health, and corrupt bureaucracy (G8). Miners' attention to
nonwage issues continued to build. In March 1969, the state of West Virginia
considered a bill providing compensation for victims of coal's black lung disease.
Rather than work through the union, the Black Lung Association was formed, and
successfully called out forty-five thousand West Virginia miners in wildcat strikes.
Many visited the state capital, and stayed out until the bill was signed into law,
suggesting their lack of confidence that the governor would sign.[30] In August eleven
thousand miners in Pennsylvania and West Virginia struck for two weeks in sympathy with five local union officials who had been fired.[31]

A 1968 fire that killed seventy-eight miners had drawn national attention to
mine safety.[32] Boyle absolved Consolidated Coal of responsibility for the fire.
But under pressure of Yablonski's candidacy, continued wildcat strikes, and

Table 5.1

Percent of Coal Strikes During the Term of the Contract

Year	Number of all strikes	Number of strikes during contract term	% of strikes during contract term
1960	126	50	39.7
1961	122	108	88.5
1962	129	119	92.2
1963	135	122	90.4
1964	116	100	86.2
1965	148	141	95.3
1966	164	141	86.0
1967	210	195	92.9
1968	268	252	94.0
1969	464	446	96.1
1970	504	496	98.4
1971	608	599	98.5
1972	963	953	99.0
1973	1,039	1,038	99.9
1974	996	983	98.7
1975	1,139	1,131	99.3
1976	1,386	1,382	99.7
1977	958	952	99.4
1978	250	236	94.4
1979	414	404	97.6
1980	267	256	95.9
1981	178	162	91.0

Source: U.S. Department of Labor, Bureau of Labor Statistics (Washington, DC: U.S. Government Printing Office, 1985).

concern about mass demonstrations in Washington (like those in West Virginia) he could not control, Boyle was active in getting a strong version of the federal Coal Mine Health and Safety Act (MHSA) of 1969 passed in November. Although coal accidents did not immediately decline, the fatality rate did. By 1973 the fatality rate was 55 percent below its average for the 1960s, and after 1977 it averaged one-third of its former level (see Figure 5.4).[33]

Boyle claimed victory in the union election, but Yablonski challenged the results, citing numerous voting irregularities; he was subsequently murdered. Here was union autocracy in the extreme, and its overthrow would be equally vigorous (G8). A meeting after Yablonski's funeral led to the formation of Miners for Democracy (MFD)[34] to unseat the entrenched leadership. Most held Boyle responsible for Yablonski's death; he was convicted in 1971. But his regime remained ensconced—for example, fifty-four thousand miners struck for a week in 1971 when a federal court ordered Boyle to step down as trustee of the UMWA Welfare and Retirement Fund.[35]

Arnold Miller was elected by the MFD to oppose Boyle.[36] Miller's successful election led to a major restructuring of the union constitution to ensure greater democracy: district officials and executive board members would be elected; the rank and file would ratify contracts; contracts would be uniformly enforced across different regions; and the salaries of top officials were reduced by 30 percent.[37] This culmination of the efforts begun with Yablonski probably spurred rank-and-file activism—certainly wildcat strike activity stayed high (see Table 5.1).

Unionized miners' struggles also constrained productivity growth (G9).[38] Strikes over working conditions had started accelerating even before the 1969 MHSA (see Figure 5.2). Miners continued to take health and safety matters into their own hands rather than entrusting matters to the government bureaucracy. Connerton, Freeman, and Medoff[39] discovered that the productivity advantage of union over nonunion underground mines in the eastern United States in 1965 became a disadvantage in 1975, which they attributed to more contentious labor relations. The union presence also helped the MHSA be implemented.[40] This, too, constrained management and therefore productivity (G9). Union safety stewards could provide inspectors with information that management might "overlook" and could call in inspectors when conditions were judged especially unsafe without fear of losing their jobs. In the late 1970s union mines were found to have a significantly lower fatality rate than nonunion mines,[41] and there have been a scant number of major disasters at union mines since 1972 (MSHA). At the same time, real unit labor costs continued to rise in the 1970s in coal relative to the consumer price index (see Figure 5.5). However, the oil price increase of 1973 permitted coal price increases as well, which were facilitated by oil company ownership of coal subsidiaries.[42] Consequently coal sustained windfall profits and suffered little in the recession of 1973–75.

Miller's first opportunity to negotiate a contract, in 1974, proved to be a tremendous success. The combination of an energy crisis, low coal unemployment, and miners' subversion of the postwar SSA combined to give the UMWA great leverage in negotiations (G8, G9). After a four-week strike, the UMWA obtained parity with the United Autoworkers and United Steelworkers of America, including a COLA clause and all layoffs on a seniority basis. The union also regained its role as innovator, obtaining five paid personal days, increased staffing requirements at the coal face for safety, company-paid safety training, and quarterly inspections by UMWA safety stewards of all mines.

The Stalemate in U.S. Coal

The breakdown of the SSA for labor relations in U.S. coal, as in other sectors, created problems for unionized operators. Because of the oil shortage, this did not immediately translate into a contraction of employment industrywide. But coal operators did run away from union mines, to nonunion strip mining in eastern Kentucky even more than to the West.[43] The UMWA's share of coal tonnage fell from 74 percent in 1968 to 44 percent in 1980 to 33 percent by the late 1980s (G10).[44]

The threat from nonunion coal, however, did not immediately make itself felt, as UMWA militancy was sustained through the mid-1970s. Even in 1977, one-third of all strikes nationwide involving more than ten thousand workers were in coal.[45] The neglect of mine-level negotiations under Lewis and Boyle and the focus on national contracts meant that there was little institutional history of effectively handling local grievances. Coal operators may have expected little from the grievance mechanism, since unlike Lewis, Miller seemed unable to control his discontents.[46] This may help explain the documented ineffectiveness of 1974 contract initiatives to improve grievance processing.[47]

The 1977 amendments to the MHSA mandated the involvement of mineworkers' representatives in the inspection and enforcement process. Miners could now accompany inspectors and respond to operators' challenges to inspectors' findings. Health and safety training was also extended to nonunion miners, and minimum requirements for such programs were mandated.[48] By codifying some union practices and extending them to nonunion workers, these amendments reduced both the costs of unions for operators and the incentive for miners to become union members. In the 1977–78 strike, the longest in the UMWA's history (110 days), miners ignored the Taft-Hartley injunction imposed by President Carter. Because most major coal suppliers had been taken over by conglomerates, there were ample resources to subsidize struck mines, which probably extended the strike. The new contract did provide substantial wage increases, but in exchange for eliminating the recently won COLA, permitting employers to fire the leaders of wildcat strikes, introducing productivity incentives (absent since 1945), and transferring the health and welfare funds to individual company private insurers.[49] The contract revamped the grievance mechanism, granting authority to grievants and supervisors to handle problems at the work site, and providing for training of union and management grievance handlers.[50]

While several aspects of the agreement are reminiscent of the earlier SSA, and productivity subsequently rose again, industrial conflict did not end. Strikes over working conditions returned to the relatively high levels of the late 1960s, and wildcat strikes were not back to the levels of the early 1960s even by 1981 (see Figure 5.2 and Table 5.1). This reduction came in the context of a rapid decline in the number of mines, dropping by 28 percent from 1978 to 1983, and a corresponding drop in employment as the oil crises of the 1970s[51] became the oil glut of the steep world recession of the early 1980s.

Miller was widely criticized after the 1978 contract did not live up to the expectations generated by his earlier successes. Miller's vice president, Sam Church, succeeded him when he stepped down for health reasons. An advocate of labor-management cooperation to save the industry, Church proved unable to sell what he considered a favorable settlement to a membership dissatisfied with his regime in 1981.[52] After eleven weeks on strike, mineworkers ratified a contract that prevented probationary periods for new miners and restrained employers' right to subcontract or sublease mines to nonunion firms, and also included a new dental plan.[53] In 1982 Church was unseated by the MFD candidate, Richard Trumka.

Trumka's first contract negotiations took place in a new national climate. In 1981 President Reagan fired air traffic controllers and replaced them with strikebreakers, setting a pattern for other employers to follow. Conservative appointees to the NLRB, OSHA, and Mine Enforcement and Safety Administration (MESA) further "unraveled" the postwar structure of labor relations (G10).[54] While other unions were besieged by demands for givebacks, the mineworkers were able to negotiate companywide re-employment rights for laid-off employees despite continuing declines in the number of mines and in employment. In a shrinking market Trumka sought to assure industrial consumers that coal could be a reliable resource, by settling without a national strike for the first time in twenty years.

Trumka did call a selective strike against A.T. Massey Company, which would not sign the national agreement. The fifteen-month, often violent strike (e.g., miners' homes were shot up) challenged Massey's double-breasting, the practice of opening nonunion subsidiaries and transferring to them coal lands from union mines. The strike reportedly forced Massey to sell three subsidiaries, to close three others, and to post an 80 percent decline in profits in the first six months of 1985.[55] The settlement did not reverse the unemployment and antiunion consequences of double-breasting, but awarded 250 laid-off miners compensation; 400 laid-off miners who received no compensation later sued the UMWA.[56]

Innovation: Pittston and Its Implications

The UMWA did have some success in protecting past gains despite a contracting industry. But the fear that Massey's union evasion would be widely imitated prompted the UMWA to explore new avenues for promoting miners' interests. As G1 indicates, experiments with possibilities for the next SSA are most widespread during the crisis phase of the long swing. In 1986 the mineworkers approved a merger with the Oil, Chemical, and Atomic Workers' Union (OCAW) to form a national energy union, but the OCAW backed out at the last minute.[57]

Early in 1988 the UMWA joined the AFL-CIO for the first time, hoping to expand its war chest for the confrontation expected during the 1988 negotiations.

A major coal company, Pittston Coal, had started double-breasting in 1986. A year later it left the BCOA, which now included only thirteen coal companies and represented only 35 percent of industry tonnage.[58] The 1988 contract was successfully concluded without a national strike, and furthered laid-off miners' rights to other coal jobs. Pittston rejected such re-employment rights, and seeking to divest itself of responsibility for its retired miners, refused to sign. To provoke a walkout, Pittston cut off the health insurance and death benefits of retirees and their families and stopped arbitrating grievances. But, as I have argued elsewhere,[59] management does not control the strike decision. Two thousand mineworkers stayed on the job for fourteen months while the union pursued other creative means of pressuring Pittston to come to terms (G1): corporate campaigns against Pittston subsidiaries such as Security (which involved depositors withdrawing from banks that did business with Brinks); pressure on members of the Board of Directors (one quit his bank position); and demonstrations in Virginia, Connecticut, New York, at Pittston's headquarters, and at the homes of its CEO, Paul Douglas, often in concert with other groups. Trumka called two weeks of memorials in May and June 1988. Some ten thousand unionists used the time to testify at MSHA hearings against reduced safety regulations.

A new force in this conscious grassroots organizing was Jobs with Justice, an organization the UMWA founded with several unions, civil rights, community, and women's organizations in 1987 to promote job security, a decent standard of living, and union rights. Members committed themselves to engage in five actions during the course of a year, supporting strikes, union recognition, anti-apartheid efforts (the UMWA competes with South African coal), etc. Jobs with Justice helped organize a support rally of twelve thousand at the Wise County, Virginia, fairgrounds where Jesse Jackson spoke.

By December 1988 the UMWA Executive Board called on all union locals to get involved in the Pittston campaign. On April 5, 1989, the union called a selective strike against Pittston, advocating discipline and solidarity in the face of likely provocation. Pittston hired the same security company Massey had, and the governor of Virginia sent 350 state troopers to "maintain order," or to ensure the flow of coal. Strikers practiced civil disobedience, sitting down in front of company gates and getting arrested. A walkout by 300 area high school students protesting the arrests appeared on national television. Two weeks into the strike, thirty-nine women who only identified themselves as Daughters of Mother Jones occupied Pittston headquarters in Lebanon, Virginia, for thirty hours.[60] Subsequently miners and supporters blocked trucks and set up rolling mile-long roadblocks (fallen trees, etc.). One local in southwestern Virginia set up Camp Solidarity on a ten-acre site. It became a springboard for outside supporters to participate in civil disobedience.

In May the union mounted a proxy fight at Pittston's stockholders' meeting to show how mismanaged the company was. While union initiatives lost, they succeeded in getting strong support from institutional investors and embarrassing Pittston's directors.[61] Shortly thereafter both sides agreed to arbitration, but a month later CEO Douglas refused to meet further with Trumka.[62] At the same time three UMWA officials were jailed for continuing to promote civil disobedience.[63] In response, some forty thousand miners walked off the job for a two-week period in eleven states.

In September ninety-eight miners and a minister staged the first sit-down strike since the 1930s, occupying a Pittston preparation plant, Moss 3, for days (G1);[64] sit-downs had been outlawed by the Taft-Hartley Act. Thousands of supporters quickly massed at the gates to prevent state police from removing the strikers. A federal injunction ended the occupation, but the miners successfully melded into the five thousand who rallied at the gates. UMWA vice president Cecil Roberts promised that plant occupations would continue if the conflict were not resolved.[65]

In mid-November the new secretary of labor, Elizabeth Dole, appointed William Usery to help mediate and return Trumka and Douglas to the bargaining table.[66] In January a successful settlement was finally passed, and "strikers won big."[67] While the company had forgone some $60 million in profits, it lost in its effort to abandon the trust funds, force miners to pick up 20 percent of health care costs, and prevent miners' access to nonunion jobs. It did win mandatory overtime and Sunday work which the union had fought. In the course of the strike, more complaints were filed by both sides with the NLRB than during any preceding strike. The NLRB mechanism's bias toward management was cited by a House labor subcommittee staff report, given prompt injunctions against UMWA picketing and delayed hearings on Pittston's unfair labor practices.

Conclusions

The Pittston experience may have far-reaching consequences for mineworkers and the labor movement as a whole. Miners practiced civil disobedience, mobilized a grassroots movement, used tactics that attracted media coverage, and directly challenged the state by ignoring injunctions and biased labor laws. The campaign required a high degree of organization by the union to coordinate so many disparate participants; it also required discipline and adherence to a nonviolent philosophy to reinforce the sympathies of a U.S. population far from the coalfields.

Several lessons emerge from the Pittston strike. The success in getting re-employment rights for union workers in nonunion shops may prove to be a viable basis for extended organizing. Laws lose their legitimacy when large numbers of citizens practice civil disobedience to violate them. But the large numbers are key, and the effectiveness of Jobs with Justice in mobilizing supporters suggests this as a promising new institutional mechanism for multiplying labor's clout. This is especially true since mainstream U.S. weeklies and newspapers tended to write off the strike as a certain loss for the union until the final settlement was reached. Theatrical tactics that attract television coverage (such as the high school student strike and the clergy pickets in Connecticut) become effective means of getting labor's message out.

The union has been involved in other conflicts since Pittston, but none that involved such broad-based coalitions. The federal black lung program under President Reagan had tightened eligibility requirements for receipt of benefits: On average, 6 percent of applicants qualified in 1983–90, as opposed to 30 percent in 1979–82.[68] While the MSHA claimed that better mine ventilation accounted for the decline, the Clinton Labor Department discovered that five hundred mining companies had probably colluded to tamper with coal dust samples used to test for the risk of black lung disease.[69] Criminal charges were filed, and dozens of companies and individuals ultimately pled guilty.[70] Such running away from institutionalized obligations characterizes both the deregulatory (G10) and the experimental (G1) periods.

Another recurring problem had been companies bowing out of the joint industry-union fund that covered retirees' health care benefits, claiming for a variety of reasons that they were no longer responsible (e.g., Pittston). In the early 1990s, Congress finally passed a bill requiring every company that had employed UMWA miners since 1950 to pay for such benefits.[71] This relieved both unionists and those companies that had been shouldering the full responsibility.

In its ongoing fight against double-breasting, the UMWA had decided that the only way to end the "corporate shell game" was by dealing with the holding companies that could move around subsidiaries' coal resources.[72] Otherwise, within seven years existing union mines would be exhausted and union jobs would be gone. In early 1993 the UMWA struck several coal companies for refusing to provide information on their corporate structure. The selective strike was steadily expanded until 17,700 miners were out in six coal companies covering seven states.[73] The strike lasted seven months, and William Usery was again appointed as mediator. The union finally won a commitment for 60 percent of all new jobs, even in new or newly acquired mines of parent companies and related subsidiaries.[74] In exchange, a new industrywide, labor-management cooperation committee was established to try to troubleshoot before contract expiration. And operators were allowed to change work rules radically, subject to local-union ratification and increased union employment.

The ongoing economic pressures in coal partly reflect the *national* economic crisis. The malaise of the past few years will be ongoing, given sustained high levels of bank and business failures and continuing high debt levels economy-wide. There is a political vacuum, given the demonstrated inability of traditional political forces to take constructive initiative, rather than simply undo old systems that no longer work. This opens the way for new visions, strategies, and tactics if they can be shown to benefit working people, as the Pittston effort clearly did. These are fertile years for labor to demonstrate the bankruptcy of the *old* SSA and to experiment with tactics and programs that have widespread appeal. Given current economic "downsizing," labor's message will resonate with groups that traditionally thought themselves insulated from economic downturns. During the crisis of the 1930s, the slide from 1929 to 1933 was a period of great leverage for large corporations vis-à-vis both labor and smaller firms; the same was true in Reagan's 1980s. After the trough in 1933, political coalitions succeeded in constraining large firms, to the benefit of small businesses as well as labor.

There is no definite structure that the next SSA must adopt. By working in coalition with other groups, through vehicles such as Jobs with Justice, labor can open up the whole question of what the economy of the future will look like. As recent Russian history illustrates, what is unimaginable today may become reality tomorrow. Workers can control their work, lives, and economic well-being only if they will be able to make economic decisions regarding employment and investment that would enliven their communities, as the 1993 strike averred. The Pittston experience teaches us that preparedness, coordination, and creative protest are powerful means for changing the course of economic history.

Notes

1. See S. Bowles, D.M. Gordon, and T.E. Weisskopf, *After the Waste Land: A Democratic Economics for the Year 2000* (Armonk, NY: M.E. Sharpe, 1990); D.M. Gordon, "Up and Down the Long Roller Coaster," in Union for Radical Political Economics, ed., *U.S. Capitalism in Crisis* (New York: Union for Radical Political Economics, 1978), 22–35; D.M. Gordon, R.C. Edwards, and M. Reich, *Segmented Work, Divided Workers* (New York: Basic Books, 1982); D.M. Kotz, T. McDonough, and M. Reich, *Social Structures of Accumulation: The Political Economy of Growth and Crisis* (New York: Cambridge University Press, 1994); and M.I. Naples, "The Unraveling of the Union-Capital Truce and the U.S. Industrial Productivity Crisis," *Review of Radical Political Economics* 18, nos. 1–2 (Spring–Summer 1986): 110–31.

2. See Naples, "Unraveling of the Union-Capital Truce."

3. See David M. Kotz on natural states in Kotz, McDonough, and Reich, *Social Structures of Accumulation.*

4. For example, see R.A. Lester, *As Unions Mature: An Analysis of the Evolution of American Unionism* (Princeton, NJ: Princeton University Press, 1958).

5. See Michael Reich's essay in Kotz, McDonough, and Reich, *Social Structures of Accumulation.*

6. R.B. Freeman and J.L. Medoff, *What Do Unions Do?* (New York: Basic Books, 1984).

7. See C. Bina and B. Yaghmaian, "Postwar Global Accumulation and the Transnationalization of Capital," *Capital & Class* 43 (Spring 1991): 107–30; and C. Bina and C. Davis, "Labor and the World of Coercive Competition," a paper presented at the Allied Social Science Associations (ASSA) meetings, Anaheim, CA (January 1993).

8. R. Boddy and J.R. Crotty, "Class Conflict and Macro-Policy: The Political Business Cycle," *Review of Radical Political Economics* 7, no. 1 (Spring 1975): 1–19.

9. See M. Aglietta, *The Regulatory Crisis of Capitalism* (London: New Left Books, 1979); R. Boyer, "Wage Formation in Historical Perspective: The French Experience," *Cambridge Journal of Economics* 3, no. 2 (June 1979): 99–118; and M. Piore and C. Sabel, *The Second Industrial Divide* (Chicago: University of Chicago Press, 1984).

10. M.I. Naples, "Social vs. Technical Determinants of Bituminous Coal Mining Productivity Growth" (Trenton, NJ: Working Paper, Trenton State College, 1995).

11. Ibid.

12. See Naples, "Unraveling of the Union-Capital Truce."

13. U.S. Department of Labor (U.S. DOL), Mine Safety and Health Administration (MSHA), *Summary of Selected Injury Experience and Worktime for the Mining Industry in the United States, 1931–77*, Information Report 1132 (Washington, DC: U.S. Government Printing Office [US GPO], 1984).

14. M.S. Lewis-Beck and J.R. Alford, "Can Government Regulate Safety? The Coal Mine Example," *American Political Science Review* 74, no. 30 (September 1980).

15. U.S. DOL, MSHA, *Summary of Selected Injury Experience.*

16. U.S. Library of Congress (U.S. LOC), Congressional Research Service (CRS), Environment and Natural Resources Policy Division, *The Coal Industry: Problems and Prospects, a Background Study* (Washington, DC: U.S. GPO, 1978), 28

17. U.S. DOL, Bureau of Labor Statistics (BLS), "Historical Work Stoppages, United States, 1953–81," magnetic tape (1985).

18. P. Navarro, "Union Bargaining Power in the Coal Industry, 1945–81," *Industrial and Labor Relations Review* 36, no. 2 (January 1983).

19. Lester, *As Unions Mature*, 102.

20. Ibid., 101.

21. G. Green, *What's Happening with Labor?* (New York: International Publishers, 1976), 131.

22. Navarro, "Union Bargaining Power."

23. U.S. DOL, BLS, *Employment and Earnings, United States, 1909–78*, Bulletin 1312–11 (Washington, DC: U.S. GPO, 1979).

24. U.S. Congress, Office of Technology Assessment (OTA), *The Direct Use of Coal* (Washington, DC: U.S. GPO, 1979), 13.

25. U.S. DOL BLS, *Employment and Earnings, United States, 1909–78.*

26. S. Aronowitz, *False Promises: The Shaping of American Working Class Consciousness* (New York: McGraw-Hill, 1973), 28.

27. U.S. DOL, BLS, *Work Stoppages Involving More than 10,000 Workers* (Washington, DC: U.S. GPO, 1965–77), 22.

28. Ibid., 21.

29. Ibid., 23.

30. Green, *What's Happening with Labor?*

31. U.S. DOL, BLS, *Work Stoppages*, 16.

32. Lewis-Beck and Alford, "Can Government Regulate Safety?"

33. U.S. DOL, MSHA, *Summary of Selected Injury Experience.*

34. Green, *What's Happening with Labor?* 200.

35. U.S. DOL BLS, *Work Stoppages*, 19.

36. Green, *What's Happening with Labor?* 200.

37. Ibid., 200–201.

38. Naples, "Social vs. Technical Determinants."

39. Freeman and Medoff, *What Do Unions Do?*

40. See a related analysis of the Occupational Safety and Health Administration (OSHA) in D. Weil, "Enforcing OSHA: The Role of Labor Unions," *Industrial Relations* 30, no. 1 (Winter 1991): 20–36.

41. J. Braithwaite, *To Punish or Persuade: Enforcement of Coal Mine Safety* (Albany, NY: State University of New York Press, 1985), 9.

42. See C. Bina, *The Economics of the Oil Crisis* (New York: St. Martin's Press, 1985); and C. Bina, "Competition, Control, and Price Formation in the International Energy Industry," *Energy Economics* 11, no. 3 (July 1989): 162–68.

43. R.M. Simon, "Hard Times for Organized Labor in Appalachia," *Review of Radical Political Economics* 15, no. 3 (Fall 1983).

44. See Navarro, "Union Bargaining Power," 228; and *Business Week* (July 3, 1989).

45. U.S. DOL, BLS, *Work Stoppages,* 8–10.

46. Freeman and Medoff, *What Do Unions Do?*

47. US LOC, CRS, Environment and Natural Resources Policy Division, *The Coal Industry,* 37–38.

48. National Research Council, Commission on Engineering and Technical Systems, Committee on Underground Mine Safety, *Toward Safer Underground Mines* (Washington, DC: National Academy Press, 1982), 57–58.

49. Navarro, "Union Bargaining Power"; Simon, "Hard Times for Organized Labor;" and M. Yarrow, "The Labor Process in Coal Mining: Struggle for Control," in A. Zimbalist, ed., *Case Studies in the Labor Process* (New York: Monthly Review Press, 1979).

50. US LOC, CRS, Environment and Natural Resources Policy Division, *The Coal Industry.*

51. See C. Bina, "Limits of OPEC Pricing: OPEC Profits and the Nature of Global Oil Accumulation," *OPEC Review* 14, no. 1 (Spring 1990): 55–73.

52. T. Ghilarducci, "The Impact of Internal Union Politics on the 1981 UMWA Strike," *Industrial Relations* 27, no. 3 (Fall 1988): 371–84; and Simon, "Hard Times for Organized Labor."

53. Navarro, "Union Bargaining Power"; and C. Seltzer, *Fire in the Hole: Miners and Managers in the American Coal Industry* (Lexington: The University Press of Kentucky, 1985).

54. For instance, see *UMW Journal* (November 1982).

55. M. Wolford, "Mine Workers End Massey Strike—Dispute Unsettled, Will Go to Court," *Labor Notes* 84 (February 1986): 5.

56. *New York Times* (August 23, 1988): A18.

57. Unless otherwise specified, the *UMW Journal* is the source for the ensuing history.

58. *Business Week* (October 9, 1989).

59. M. I. Naples, "An Analysis of Defensive Strikes," *Industrial Relations* 26, no. 1 (Winter 1986–87): 96–105.

60. *Mother Jones* (1989).

61. *Forbes* (June 12, 1989): 41–42.

62. *MacLean's* (November 20, 1989): 72.

63. *The Nation* (October 1989): 410.

64. *Mother Jones* (January 1990): 37.

65. *The Nation* (October 16, 1989): 409.

66. *MacLean's.*

67. *U.S. News & World Report* (January 15, 1990): 45.

68. *New York Times* (March 17, 1991): IV5.

69. *New York Times* (April 5, 1991): A12; and *New York Times* (April 2, 1992): A15.

70. *New York Times* (October 26, 1991): A20.

71. *New York Times* (December 9, 1993): B16.

72. *New York Times* (February 6, 1993): I6.

73. *New York Times* (November 20, 1993): I10; and *New York Times* (December 15, 1993): A25.

74. *New York Times* (December 9, 1993): B16.

6

Shop Floor Relations: The Past, Present, and Future of Mass Production

David Fairris

Introduction

A crisis emerged on the shop floor of many mass-production manufacturing firms in the United States during the 1960s. The crisis reflected the unfolding of a contradiction in the postwar industrial relations system, a central foundation of which was the mistaken belief that a clear distinction could be established between "managerial prerogative" and labor's right to influence its "conditions of employment." The crisis emerged after management attempts, beginning in the late 1950s, to bolster its control over shop floor production following a decade of gains by shop floor workers. The rising injury rates and increased pace of production resulting from management's more aggressive stance led to reduced worker cooperation in production, and in turn to slower productivity growth and to profit rate decline in the later 1960s.

Employers have been experimenting for more than two decades with new institutional arrangements regulating labor-management relations in production. These experiments have been spurred in part by the shop floor crisis of the 1960s and in part by increased global competition. Employee involvement through quality of work life programs and team production methods are examples of recent attempts by employers to address the problems associated with the shop floor crisis of the 1960s. Most of these experiments ultimately grant workers greater responsibility for production and shop floor dispute resolution, but without a substantive enhancement in worker shop floor power.

Are these changes likely to elicit greater cooperation, and thereby increased productivity, from workers? Those who answer in the affirmative often point to the similarity between recent U.S. experiments and Japanese-style shop floor management, which can claim superiority on a number of important measures of productive performance, due in part to greater labor-management cooperation. Workers cooperate with management when managerial authority is seen as legitimate and when shop floor outcomes are viewed as fair. Similar forms of managerial authority may be deemed legitimate by workers in one country, but illegitimate by workers in another. Similar distributions of shop floor rewards (between productivity and, e.g., health and safety) may seem fair to workers in one country, but unfair to workers in another. The history of shop floor relations in the United States suggests that enhanced worker cooperation is more likely to emerge from a system of shop floor governance in which workers are granted significantly greater decision-making power than is found in recent employer experiments.

Past

The labor movement that emerged in the mass-production manufacturing industries of the 1930s rested on the active participation of rank-and-file workers and unpaid staff members from shop stewards on up.[1] One consequence of this decentralization of power in union structures is that a significant amount of control over union goals was in the hands of the rank-and-file. This was especially true for shop floor decisions, whereas in the days before World War II, labor-management disputes were often settled through collective shop floor power-brokering, sometimes with workers simply "knocking off" until the dispute was favorably resolved.[2] Although workers were significantly empowered during the early development of industrial unions, the way in which this power was to be wielded and the issues it would be allowed to influence remained very much unclear.

By the end of the 1940s an informal and rather vague understanding or "accord" had emerged among significant segments of employers, the state, and the labor leadership. Employers would willingly enter into negotiations with labor over wages, hours, fringe benefits, and their distribution to workers in the plant (through the definition of job titles, job evaluation schemes, and seniority agreements). The government would support, through legislation and various government-financed agencies, the process of responsible collective bargaining. And if labor would not dictate to employers how they should market their products or where they could invest their profits, employers would not refuse to discuss a wide range of shop floor conditions such as safety, speedup, and technology. Applied to the shop floor, the understanding envisioned a system in which contract language and the grievance procedure would serve as adequate mechanisms for the joint regulation of shop floor conditions and the orderly resolution of shop floor disputes. I refer to this system as "shop floor contractualism."

Shop floor governance in the mass-production industries of the late 1940s bore little resemblance to this vision of shop floor contractualism. Compared with the situation a decade earlier, shop floor relations had indeed become less openly conflictual. The "quickie strike" was less common, and although the slowdown was still employed in those industries and departments whose production processes left some control over pace in the hands of workers, these older expressions of shop floor power had become integrated with a new form of dispute resolution referred to as "fractional bargaining."[3] Fractional bargaining was a decentralized and strategic form of workplace dispute resolution involving foremen, shop stewards, and informal work groups. It often operated as a strategic process of grievance filing, shop floor slowdowns, and occasional shutdowns, through which the rank-and-file was able to bring its power to bear on the conditions of production in the labor process. Its existence rested on the power, though not necessarily the right, of foremen and shop stewards to strike extra-contractual deals governing shop floor conditions. Fractional bargaining served as an adequate mechanism for policing contractual agreements on workplace issues as well as an important source of rank-and-file empowerment in influencing those work standards that were largely determined noncontractually.

The "accord" or understanding forged in the late 1940s had an important impact on the direction of future developments in shop floor relations. The state was constantly refashioning bits and pieces of labor law in the hope of realizing the industrial peace and enhanced productivity the accord seemed to promise. Unions shifted their focus to bureaucratic, centralized bargaining structures to ensure the monetary gains the accord made possible. And employers were freed, subject to the rank-and-file's shop floor power, to enlarge their control over the labor process, allowing them the possibility of offsetting the monetary gains that the accord effectively conceded to labor, and of reappropriating those shop floor gains that workers had won in past struggles. The result of these developments was a gradual bureaucratization of shop floor relations, leading to the erosion of rank-and-file power at the point of production and increased appropriation of working conditions by employers in the labor process.

Much of management's energy in eliminating the system of fractional bargaining was devoted to making shop floor governance structures more legalistic, a by-product of which was increased bureaucratization. Company policy on production and strict procedures for grievance handling were formalized. This entailed an increase in the size of industrial relations departments; the hiring of young, recently educated industrial relations experts with an exceedingly legalistic approach to the resolution of workplace disputes; and the schooling of foremen and supervisors in the strict contract/grievance approach to shop floor governance.[4]

The government's role in this process was to clarify the rather vague line separating managerial prerogative from bargainable workplace issues, to do so in a way that left sufficient scope for the former, and to shore up the system of grievance arbitration. In its 1958 *Borg-Warner* decision, the U.S. Supreme Court attempted a clarification of the issues that were proper subjects for collective bargaining by stipulating some things as "mandatory subjects" of bargaining and others as only "permissible subjects."[5] And in a series of important decisions in the late 1950s, the National Labor Relations Board (NLRB) and the Court threw their weight behind the private arbitration of industrial disputes.[6]

Unions became more bureaucratic as well. Given the nature of the U.S. industrial relations system and the centralization of union power, multiplant and multiemployer bargaining agreements, as well as contract negotiations conducted by well-trained experts, were crucial for winning wage and fringe benefits demands from firms within an industry. However, the bureaucratization of union structures served one set of workers' interests at the expense of another. As the power to affect wages and fringes grew, the ability to control shop floor conditions diminished.[7]

Fractional bargaining thus slowly gave way in the late 1950s and early 1960s to increased reliance on contract language and use of the grievance procedure—that is, to the system of shop floor contractualism. This amounted to the containment of the rank-and-file's freedom to act by granting workers certain limited shop floor rights in contract language. The decisions of rationally minded industrial relations experts, union leaders, and arbitrators were clearly preferable, in the minds of managers and government leaders, to those of foremen and the rank-and-file. And in committing a large number of disputes to the grievance procedure, management gained the right to act unilaterally until some resolution was reached.

Workers' first inclination on their loss of shop floor power was to seek working conditions protection through contract language.[8] As a result of these rank-and-file initiatives, more working conditions issues began to appear in contracts, but as Livernash[9] makes clear, the issues of deep concern to workers were largely noncontractual in nature; their resolution required decentralized forms of power and decision making on the shop floor, and neither the company nor union bureaucracy was willing to grant this. When contract language failed them, workers turned to the grievance procedure wherever possible to address their workplace concerns. The number of grievances rose, but to the extent that they got resolved at all, such resolution was protracted, far too biased in result, or the process could only address a narrow range of issues.

What emerged in the late 1960s as a result of this diminution in shop floor power were widespread expressions of workplace discontent by rank-and-file workers.[10] Workers viewed the enhanced managerial authority as illegitimate and the altered distribution of shop floor rewards, as reflected in lower levels of safety and the increased pace of production, as unfair.[11] The discontent appeared in a variety of forms: There was an increase, for example, in both the percentage of strikes over working conditions and the percentage of wildcat strikes. There was also a growing separation and tension between the rank-and-file and the labor leadership, resulting in increasing contract rejections by the rank-and-file and in movements to depose union leaders.

While the bureaucratization of shop floor dispute resolution beginning in the late 1950s was successful in eliminating the source of workers' shop floor power, and produced a short-lived spurt in productivity and profits in the early 1960s, the long-run consequences for employers were negative. Rank-and-file discontent with shop floor conditions in the second half of the 1960s produced significant losses for employers in the form of declining productivity growth and reduced profits rates.[12]

The 1973–74 recession greatly reduced rank-and-file shop floor revolts, but not the underlying worker discontent, nor the bureaucratic structures of shop floor governance that partially fueled this discontent. Both of these aspects of the system of shop floor contractualism plagued employers' efforts to revive productivity and profits. The elimination of fractional bargaining meant that workers were less successful in protecting contractual rights, and much less successful in winning rights surreptitiously. Workers responded to this alienation with an uncooperative shop floor posture and a "work to rule" mentality with respect to work. The negative impact on labor productivity, even in periods of greater unemployment, has been significant.

Present

Employers' recent shop floor experiments are an attempt in part to address these labor-related aspects of the productivity slowdown.[13] Quality of work life (QWL) programs can be directly traced to efforts by management to solve problems associated with the failed mechanisms of worker shop floor voice and bureaucratic methods of dispute resolution of 1960s shop floor contractualism. Team production and pay-for-knowledge schemes were often introduced in these settings as ways of joining QWL-style labor-management communication with a formal institutional structure for decentralized shop floor decision making.

QWL programs, or roughly similar entities with different names, expanded throughout the 1970s. An integral part of these programs is joint committees of production workers and lower-level managers meeting regularly on company time to solve problems encountered by both labor and management in production. Discussions include such topics as how to improve productivity and product quality as well as workers' concerns about noncontractually regulated shop floor conditions. These early experiments were generally credited with reducing grievance rates and absenteeism and with improving some shop floor conditions, even though committees were severely constrained in their scope and received little support from industrial relations departments and local union officials.

Interest in participation schemes witnessed a tremendous surge in the late 1970s and early 1980s, this time with a slightly different focus, owing in large part to increased international competition. There was still some devotion to resolving workers' noncontractual shop floor concerns, but increasingly cost-cutting measures in production became the major focus of QWL committees. Indeed, many of the new participation programs were explicitly designed as joint labor-management "cost study teams."[14] One of the stated goals of management in these new efforts was to decentralize shop floor decision making in the hopes of increasing worker participation and making better use of the knowledge of production possessed by the rank-and-file worker.

In situations where the progress of participation schemes was neither stalled nor blocked entirely by entrenched bureaucracies, cracks began to appear in the structure of shop floor contractualism. The efforts of union leaders to maintain a separation between those issues discussed in QWL committees and those covered by contract language faced serious challenges. Local agreements—which are independent of the national contract, but procedurally determined by collective bargaining—witnessed a proliferation of work-rule practice changes in many industries. In many cases these changes constituted concessionary moves by unions to enhance productivity without a concomitant increase in shop floor power. The unmistakable trajectory of these changes, however, was toward the further devolution of shop floor decision making to workers and supervisors directly concerned with production in a setting absent of formal contract language. What remained to be worked out was the specific institutional form for combining these participation schemes with actual shop floor decision making. This is where team production entered the scene.

A number of alternative developmental paths toward team production emerged in U.S. manufacturing during this period, making it difficult to describe team production in general terms. Most team production systems, however, contain the following attributes: a dramatic reduction in job classifications, occasionally to a single classification for all production workers; workers becoming skilled in a much fuller range of production activities; work teams composed of ten to fifteen workers who meet weekly to discuss such issues as the efficiency and ergonomic features of job design and the job assignments of team members; a team leader (typically a union member in union plants) from the ranks of workers and a group leader (a salaried, nonunion employee) from the ranks of management as coordinators of team activity; and a pay-for-knowledge system that encourages workers to acquire different skills in the plant by awarding increased wages for skill acquisition. Detailed contract language governing shop floor conditions is generally eschewed. Workers and supervisors are encouraged (indeed, forced) by this structure to resolve shop floor disputes speedily, with a minimum of bureaucracy.

Team production builds on workers' natural desire to produce a quality product in surroundings that are safe and pleasant and under conditions of relative autonomy. While the team concept acknowledges these desires, it never truly fulfills them. In most cases, teams are given the freedom to design and assign jobs subject to tightly prescribed production standards. The new employer experiments are most properly viewed as a system of management control in which the responsibility for producing is squarely placed on workers' shoulders while the production goals and job standards are dictated by management. Experience to date suggests that in exchange for an increase in the intensity of labor effort, decreased safety, the attenuation of seniority as a criterion for labor allocation, and an ideological structure that promotes competition among workers (across teams, plants, and firms), workers receive the promise of limited job security, wage increases for newly acquired skills, a quicker turnaround time for the resolution of workplace disputes, and a very limited say in the nature of work.[15]

The downside of team production for workers stems from the fact that an institutional void has been both created and then filled by management's initiative. That work teams primarily focus on, and allow for the realization of, management's concerns with production costs and productivity, should therefore be no great surprise. Management has essentially replaced shop floor contractualism, which contained minimal contractual rights for workers, little rank-and-file responsibility, and few shop floor freedoms, with a system that contains significantly fewer contractual rights, greater rank-and-file responsibility, and a marginal change in shop floor freedom. In essence, team production restores the decentralized atmosphere of shop floor relations during the days of fractional bargaining but severely constrains workers' ability to act.

The Future

The historical analysis of this chapter suggests that a change in shop floor governance is necessary because of the contradictory nature of postwar institutional arrangements rather than exogenous shocks such as technological change. The system of shop floor contractualism is inefficient; it serves neither labor's nor management's interests. Struggling to maintain and protect such a system seems senseless. Many sorts of new institutional arrangements would lead to superior economic performance and enhanced rewards from production. In comparison to existing arrangements, some would produce gains for both labor and management mutually, with varying degrees of inequality in the sharing of enhanced rewards; others would yield advantages for one party only, with losses for the other. Some institutional arrangements of shop floor governance contain greater rewards in the aggregate, and thus are more socially efficient, than others.

The analysis of this chapter suggests that new institutions of shop floor governance emerge because of their inherent technical and organizational efficiency as well as their impact on control over production and related distributional consequences. A comparison of measures of economic performance (e.g., productivity growth and improvements in shop floor conditions) under fractional bargaining and shop floor contractualism suggests two tentative conclusions: (1) Management opts for shop floor institutional arrangements that enhance managerial authority even at the risk of potential productive inefficiencies; and (2) economic performance, including productivity growth, can be enhanced by institutional arrangements that offer workers greater control in production. Greater worker participation in shop floor production renders managerial authority legitimate and ensures fairness in the distribution of rewards from shop floor production. Legitimacy and fairness foster cooperation and enhanced productivity.

Are the recent employer experiments with Japanese-style shop floor institutions—QWL programs and team production—likely to be seen by labor as yielding legitimate managerial authority and fair shop floor outcomes, and thereby leading to enhanced cooperation and increased productive efficiency? Or, rather, do these arrangements conserve managerial authority at the possible expense of superior productive performance that could be attained by alternative arrangements, such as the works council system in Germany, that concede greater power to labor? Based on its record of continued productivity growth and relatively smooth adjustment to changing technologies and international competition, Germany certainly stands out as a possible alternative model for reform of U.S. shop floor institutions. Comparing the German and Japanese models of shop floor governance suggests that the latter may prove to be the relatively inferior shop floor regime for adoption in the United States.

Before considering their differences, it is instructive to point out the striking similarities in German and Japanese shop floor institutional arrangements. In both countries, production managers typically have extended experience as production workers; there is significant employment security; investment in worker training is high; bureaucratic structures that inhibit the immediate resolution of shop floor disputes are held to a minimum; the earnings of management relative to labor are low; production workers have more responsibility and are expected to display greater versatility in job tasks; and there exist plant-level mechanisms for worker representation. Perhaps there are strategic features that contribute positively to labor-management cooperation in a variety of normative settings, and would do so in the United States as well.

As a model for U.S. shop floor governance, the Japanese system has a number of advantages. It would significantly reduce the costs of contracting and contract enforcement, and would eliminate many of the structural rigidities associated with the formal constraints of shop floor contractualism. It would also enhance shop floor labor-management communication. However, the vacuum created by the absence of formal constraints on the behavior of labor and management in Japan is filled by informal norms of cooperation. Workers in Japan participate in shop floor decisions but possess few substantive rights of shop floor decision making.[16] The legitimacy of managerial authority and the fairness of shop floor outcomes are assured by the normative commitment to "harmony" through "mutual understanding."[17]

This takes the specific form of a relationship in which workers are obligated to their superiors "for favors received and [are] duty bound to repay in hard work and loyalty."[18] The immediate superior is expected, in return, to advise and protect the worker, looking out for his or her interest in relations with superiors. The superior is expected to act with benevolence toward his subordinates, to exhibit, in the words of Dore,[19] "concern for the interests and dignity of subjects, a concern for justice, tempered with the optimistic faith which puts more reliance on the judicious use of rewards than on punishments."

Are legitimate structures of authority and fair shop floor outcomes likely to emerge in the United States under formal institutional arrangements of shop floor governance similar to those in Japan? If history serves as a guide, the answer would seem to be in the negative. The industrial organizing drives of the 1930s were attempts by workers to establish formal and informal measures to protect them from the abuses of managerial prerogative in production, even though in many cases management was well informed of workers' shop floor concerns through in-house company unions. Some thirty years later it became apparent that even contractual rules and regulations could not serve as adequate mechanisms for ensuring workers' shop floor interests. Replacing the protections against speedups and unsafe working conditions currently embedded in the "job control" language of U.S. collective-bargaining agreements with mechanisms of joint consultation and an enlarged realm of shop floor managerial prerogatives is not likely to yield fair shop floor outcomes or to be seen by workers as a legitimate set of institutional arrangements for managerial authority.

German institutions of shop floor governance offer many of the same advantages as the Japanese system, yet contain fewer drawbacks as a shop floor model for the United States. German workers possess formal rights of shop floor participation that grant them significant decision-making power. Because these are statutory rights, and therefore less subject to private manipulation, fewer resources would be devoted to establishing and protecting shop floor rights under this system than under the system of "shop floor contractualism." Because shop floor rights are broadly defined, in contrast to the "job control" approach in the United States, flexibility in shop floor organization would also be enhanced.

The statutory rights of works councils—plant-level bodies that represent workers' interests in workplace decisions—are the most important of these formal arrangements for our purposes. In exchange for the legal obligation to "cooperate" with management "for the good of the plant and its workers,"[20] works councils are granted rights of codetermination with management for some workplace conditions (e.g., discipline procedures and safety) and the right to be consulted by management on decisions concerning other conditions (e.g., job design and technology).[21] Works councils are able to sign agreements with management that have legal force; they are the focal point for workers' shop floor grievances; and they serve as equal participants with management on boards of arbitration.

The fairness of shop floor outcomes and the legitimacy of authority in German industry rest, in part, on the shop floor decision-making power that works councils grant workers. But normative features of shop floor labor-management relations play a prominent role as well. It is often claimed, for example, that there is a collective commitment to work and to the creation of high-quality products in Germany. Arguably more important is the claim that managerial authority in Germany is based on the superior knowledge of the manager,[22] and that management relates to labor on the basis of "professional cooperation" rather than "pure surveillance."[23] Shop floor management in Germany is ostensibly authoritative, not authoritarian.

The degree to which the formal arrangements of shop floor governance in Germany mesh with the history and informal norms of behavior in the United States should not be exaggerated. In comparison to the most privileged workers under the U.S. system, German workers possess less control over the allocation of labor in the plant and are unable to legally withdraw their labor from production over shop floor issues. (Works councils are legally barred from striking.) The collective commitment to quality products and the grounding of managerial authority in superior knowledge are features of the German system that contribute to labor-management norms of cooperation, and yet may be difficult to develop in other cultural settings.

The German system does, however, provide for the existence of a plant-level organization that represents workers' shop floor interests and possesses significant decision-making power over shop floor outcomes. This system would make possible such things as continuous negotiations between labor and management over changing shop floor conditions, the more immediate resolution of shop floor disputes, and the elimination of the "obey now, grieve later" aspect of shop floor contractualism that offends even traditional notions of due process. Formal arrangements of shop floor governance similar to those in Germany would appear to offer solutions to the illegitimacy of managerial authority and the unfairness of shop floor outcomes that plague U.S. shop floor relations and foster uncooperative norms of shop floor behavior.

How might we get from here to there? Although enhanced worker participation in production can increase productive efficiency—by decreasing the costs of bureaucracy and promoting worker cooperation with management—it also enhances labor's power to lay claim to a larger share of the rewards from production, which makes the system problematic for employers. Thus participation is not likely to be achieved without significant worker struggle to force the issue. The irony is that workers must organize collectively in opposition to employers' recent initiatives in order to influence the shape of the new institutional arrangements of shop floor governance in a direction that fosters greater cooperation and productive efficiency in the future. This organizing activity should take place on the shop floor, in the local community, and at the level of national policy.

Several unions have approached management's rhetoric of participation in team production with proposed contract language that would grant workers limited rights of participation in shop floor decision making. Some of the kinds of things that have been proposed are the following: that a team's request for a new supervisor be honored by the company, that decisions at team meetings not be unilaterally overturned by management, and that any changes in job content or design be approved by teams.[24] The International Association of Machinists'

Local 1125 at General Dynamics in San Diego proposed contract language that, in addition to some of the above, included a modification of the "rights of management" clause in the contract and language governing the monitoring capabilities and health and safety impact of new technology.[25]

Actions that offer workers insights into a different way of organizing production, with greater decision-making power for shop floor work groups, must also be fostered. Several local unions in the auto, cement, and aerospace industries who were facing significant concessions demands by employers during contract negotiations in the mid-1980s adopted a form of in-plant struggle in lieu of striking that serves as an example.[26] Working without a contract, and therefore without the constraining aspects of the contract and grievance system of shop floor contractualism, workers were free to formulate their own institutional arrangements for shop floor governance. Increased attention was given to matters of health and safety, and workers brought shop floor disputes to the immediate attention of management, often by entire departments' "knocking off" work until disputes were resolved.

At the level of the local community, a variety of methods for empowering workers in their dealings with employers over health and safety issues have recently come from coalitions of workers and community activists. Workers' links with environmental activists have been an important part of this effort, under the theory that many toxic substance emissions that threaten the environment begin inside the plant and thus adversely affect the health of workers as well. These movements have offered workers a sense of the right to a healthy and safe workplace far more tangible than the rhetoric and loosely enforced standards of existing government regulations.

The Occupational Safety and Health Act of 1970 granted workers the right to a safe and healthy workplace. However, federal standards fail to reflect the important health and safety concerns of workers, and local enforcement of existing standards is lax. Grassroots pressure from worker/community coalitions resulted in the passage of federal standards granting workers the "right to know" about the health hazards they face on the job. A recent New Jersey initiative proposed to extend this to the "right to act."[27] Such legislation would give workers equal rights of participation with management in on-site hazard prevention committees. These committees would be assigned the task of workplace inspection and the investigation of accidents, and given the power to stop hazardous work if problems are not corrected.

The Oil, Chemical, and Atomic Workers' Union (OCAW) has been at the forefront of coalition building with environmental activists to empower workers in their efforts to combat health hazards. OCAW locals in the chemical plants concentrated along the Mississippi River from Baton Rouge to New Orleans have teamed with various local and national environmental groups to explore the connection between worker control and environmental impact. Coalition activity has led to research relating the lack of rank-and-file shop floor power to fires, explosions, and chemical releases which endanger workers as well as communities and the environment, and to efforts to inform and empower workers so as to prevent chemical catastrophes both large and small.[28]

The struggle for greater worker participation in production must also be waged nationally (and, ultimately, internationally). Employers are likely to resist any move to genuinely empower workers in production, and to shift production to sites with little or no worker participation if these exist. Thus participation must be "removed from competition" through national standards. There is much debate currently about the ability of the Democratic party to serve as the representative of labor's concerns in national policy making. Skeptics have recently begun efforts to organize a national party to better serve labor's interests. Labor Party Advocates, as the organization is known, has as its immediate goal educating the public on the need for a labor party and agitating for a new economic, social, and political agenda for labor.

The national goal should be to institute centralized bargaining arrangements to replace the seriously deteriorated multiemployer bargaining structures of the postwar period, and to combine centralized bargaining over wages and fringe benefits with plant-level works councils to regulate shop floor conditions in cooperation with management. A legislative effort should set out the specific rights of works councils, stipulating rights of strict codetermination with management over such crucial issues as worker health and safety, and consultative and information rights with respect to areas of less concern to workers.

A first step in this regard could be achieved by the passage of legislation requiring joint labor-management safety committees in all workplaces of a certain minimal size. If labor's equal representation on such committees was guaranteed and, contrary to the current language, full rights to information, inspection, and shutdown were granted to committees, this bill might serve as the basis for a set of collective worker rights in shop floor determination. Labor representatives on governing committees could be elected through a government-mandated works council system of worker representation, and similar legislative rights with respect to the choice of production technologies and other aspects of shop floor organization could be extended to works councils themselves (in the case of consultative or information rights) or plant-level labor-management committees (in the case of codetermination rights) in the immediate future.

Notes

1. The historical material in this section of this chapter draws heavily on David Fairris, "Appearance and Reality in Postwar Shop Floor Relations," *Review of Radical Political Economics* 22, no. 4 (1990): 17–43.

2. Nelson Lichtenstein, *Labor's War at Home: The CIO in World War II* (Cambridge, Eng.: Cambridge University Press, 1982).

3. See Neil W. Chamberlain, *The Union Challenge to Management Control* (New

York: Harper & Brothers Publishers, 1948); and James Kuhn, *Bargaining in the Grievance Settlement* (New York: Columbia University Press, 1961).

4. George Strauss, "The Shifting Power Balance in the Plant," *Industrial Relations* 3 (1962): 81.

5. NLRB v. *Wooster Division of Borg-Warner Corp.*, 356 U.S. (1958): 342, 348.

6. Katherine Stone, "The Postwar Paradigm in American Labor Law," *Yale Law Journal* 90, no. 7 (1981): 1509–80.

7. Arnold Weber, "Stability and Change in the Structure of Collective Bargaining," in Lloyd Ulman, ed., *Challenges to Collective Bargaining* (Englewood Cliffs, NJ: Prentice-Hall, 1967).

8. David Brody, "The Uses of Power I: Industrial Battleground," in *Workers in Industrial America: Essays on the Twentieth-Century Struggle* (New York: Oxford University Press, 1980), 173–214.

9. Robert E. Livernash, "Special and Local Negotiations," in John T. Dunlop and Neil W. Chamberlain, eds., *Frontiers of Collective Bargaining* (New York: Harper & Row, 1967).

10. Richard Herding, *Job Control and Union Structure* (Rotterdam: Rotterdam University Press, 1972).

11. Injury rates in manufacturing declined significantly with the emergence in the 1930s and 1940s of the industrial labor movement. See U.S. Bureau of the Census, *Historical Statistics of the United States, Colonial Times to 1970*, Series D–1029 (Washington, DC: U.S. Government Printing Office, 1975). Injuries continued their decline in the postwar years, reaching a low of 11.4 work injuries per 1 million employee-hours in 1958. Injury rates turned upward thereafter, however, increasing with much rapidity in the years between 1963 and 1967, from roughly 12.0 to 14.0 injuries per 1 million employee-hours. See U.S. Department of Labor, Bureau of Labor Statistics. *Injury Rates*, Reports 295 and 360 (Washington, DC: U.S. Government Printing Office, 1963, 1967).

12. See Michele I. Naples, "Industrial Conflict, the Quality of Work Life, and the Productivity Slowdown in U.S. Manufacturing," *Eastern Economic Journal* 14, no. 2 (1988): 157–66; Samuel Bowles, David M. Gordon, and Thomas E. Weisskopf, "Power and Profits: The Social Structure of Accumulation and the Profitability of the Postwar U.S. Economy," *Review of Radical Political Economics* 18, nos. 1 and 2 (1986): 132–67; and J.R. Norsworthy and Craig Zabala, "Worker Attitudes, Worker Behavior, and Productivity in the U.S. Automobile Industry," *Industrial and Labor Relations Review* 38, no. 4 (1985): 544–57.

13. Further elaboration on the material in this section can be found in David Fairris, "The Crisis in U.S. Shop Floor Relations," *International Contributions to Labour Studies* 1, no. 1 (1991): 133–56.

14. Sally Klingel and Ann Martin, *A Fighting Chance: New Strategies to Save Jobs and Reduce Costs* (Ithaca, NY: ILR Press, 1988).

15. Mike Parker and Jane Slaughter, *Choosing Sides: Unions and the Team Concept* (Boston: South End Press, 1988); and Clair Brown and Michael Reich, "When Does Union-Management Cooperation Work? A Look at NUMMI and GM–Van Nuys," *California Management Review* 31, no. 4 (1989): 26–44.

16. Robert M. Marsh, "The Difference Between Participation and Power in Japanese Factories," *Industrial and Labor Relations Review* 45, no. 2 (1992): 250–57.

17. Tadashi Hanami, *Labor Relations in Japan Today* (Tokyo: Kodansha International Ltd., 1979).

18. Robert E. Cole, *Japanese Blue Collar* (Berkeley: University of California Press, 1971), 184.

19. Ronald Dore, *Taking Japan Seriously* (London: The Athlone Press, 1987), 94.

20. Andrei S. Markovits, *The Politics of the West German Trade Unions* (Cambridge: Cambridge University Press, 1986), 49.

21. Alfred L. Thimm, *The False Promise of Codetermination* (Lexington, MA: Lexington Books, 1980).

22. Peter Lawrence, *Managers and Management in West Germany* (London: Croom Helm, 1980).

23. Marc Maurice, Francois Sellier, and Jean-Jacques Silvestre, *The Social Foundations of Industrial Power* (Cambridge, MA: MIT Press, 1986), 125.

24. Parker and Slaughter, *Choosing Sides,* 46–51.

25. Dan La Botz, *A Troublemaker's Handbook* (Detroit: Labor Notes, 1991), 47.

26. See Tom Balanoff, "The Cement Workers' Experience," *Labor Research Review* 7 (Fall 1985): 5–33; Jack Metzgar, "Running the Plant Backwards," *Labor Research Review* 7 (Fall 1985): 35–43; and La Botz, *A Troublemaker's Handbook.*

27. David Moberg, "Knowing Is Not Enough; Labor Wants Power to Act," *In These Times* (May 1989): 3, 9.

28. Richard Leonard and Zack Nauth, "Beating BASF: OCAW Busts Union-Buster," *Labor Research Review* 9, no. 2 (1990): 35–49.

7

An Alternative Strategy: Lessons from the UAW Local 6 and the FE, 1946–52

Victor G. Devinatz

Introduction

Throughout the 1980s, the American trade union movement sustained major losses both at the bargaining table and on the picket lines. With the United Autoworkers (UAW) agreeing to wage concessions at Chrysler, the 1980s ushered in an era of concession bargaining that hit virtually every major industrial union in the United States. In addition, the government's breaking of both the air traffic controllers' strike and the controllers' union (PATCO) in 1981 gave the green light to private sector companies to take on their unions in all-out struggles. As a result of this strategy, bitter and violent (as well as losing) strikes often ensued such as when the United Steelworkers Union battled Phelps-Dodge Corporation in the Arizona copper mines in 1982–84 and when the United Food and Commercial Workers' Union Local P-9 took on Hormel in Austin, Minnesota, over drastic wage cuts in 1985–86.

Although it was not until the 1980s that the crisis of the American labor movement became apparent even to the most casual observers, the roots of the crisis date back to the immediate post–World War II period when the strategy of major sections of the labor movement focused on conceding control of the shop floor in exchange for an increasing array of wages and benefits. Along with this strategy, the majority of trade unions viewed the collective bargaining agreement as "the workplace rule of law,"[1] encompassing and limiting the workers' rights to what is explicitly contained in the contract.

Through a historical comparison of the UAW Local 6 and the Farm Equipment Workers Union (FE) from 1946 to 1952, I will argue that the crisis of American labor in the 1980s resulted from the post–World War II strategy pursued by the majority of industrial unions, such as UAW Local 6, in institutionalizing collective bargaining and honoring "the workplace rule of law." Additionally, this institutionalization increased control over shop floor militancy, and reduced the ability of trade unions to develop an alternative strategy when the "social contract" between labor and capital broke down in the 1980s.

Contrary to the dominant trend in American labor relations in the late 1940s, one industrial union did not institutionalize collective bargaining in the postwar era, the FE. As opposed to constructing a trade unionism based on institutionalized collective bargaining, the FE built a shop floor unionism independent of formal collective-bargaining structures. This form of trade unionism concentrated power in the hands of the rank-and-file workers, not the leadership, resulting in a vastly different trade unionism from that practiced by the FE's rival in the agricultural implement industry, the UAW.

This chapter will examine the views of C. Wright Mills and Victor L. Allen in relation to the proposition that the majority of American trade unions regarded the collective bargaining agreement as the "workplace rule of law" and its practice involved the institutional suppression of workplace conflict. The impact of such institutionalization on the formation of trade union structure and function will then be examined in relation to Antonio Gramsci's theory of trade union bureaucratization. Based on this theoretical perspective, the relationship of shop floor unionism to the institutionalization of collective bargaining will be considered. Empirical evidence will be presented using data from the two unions that organized workers in plants owned by International Harvester Corporation. A comparison will be made between UAW Local 6, which was the most militant of the UAW Harvester locals, and FE locals from 1946 to 1952. Finally, we must consider the implications of the strategies of both UAW Local 6 and the FE for labor in the 1990s and beyond.

Collective Bargaining and Capitalism: Mills and Allen

Based on his study of the initial growth and stabilization of the Congress of Industrial Organizations (CIO), C. Wright Mills developed the thesis that to engage in a mature collective-bargaining relationship with corporations, unions were forced to bureaucratize and parallel the organizational structure of business. He stated:

> Stabilization requires further bureaucratization of business enterprise and labor union. Given present industrial arrangements, it also involves amalgamating the union bureaucracy with the corporation's. This may occur either in the technical place of work, in the economic enterprises making up a given industry, or among the industries forming the political economy as a whole.[2]

Mills saw this incorporation taking place to the greatest extent on the shop floor. As unions bureaucratized, they began to adopt functions similar to those of the companies with which they were dealing. This led to a "partial integration of company and union bureaucracies," resulting in the union becoming involved in the discipline of the rank-and-file through collective bargaining, a function that in the past had been left to the company.[3] Thus bargaining became a mechanism not only for the trade union to obtain economic gains from the employer, but also a vehicle for both the union and the firm to cooperate in controlling a potentially dissident workforce. Mills stated: "They [the company and the union] are disciplining agents for each other, and both discipline the malcontented elements among the unionized employees."[4]

Mills's analysis leads to reasoning that is more fully elaborated in the work of Victor L. Allen. Since unions were initially established as a reaction to capitalism, initial goals and objectives were in direct opposition to the interests of capital. However, once the unions were established and were "accepted" by management, they were forced to modify their behavior. The continued survival of unions depended on the establishment of a "successful" collective bargaining relationship with the corporations. The goals of management and unions converged in most areas of industrial relations, especially control over rank-and-file workers.[5]

Both Mills and Allen realized that a major function of collective bargaining under capitalism was the institutional suppression of workplace conflict. However, neither theorist emphasized the importance of the ideology of union leaders in this process. Antonio Gramsci discussed the importance of this ideology and provided a methodology for a different approach to collective bargaining under capitalism.

Gramsci's Theory of Trade Union Bureaucratization

Gramsci's theory of trade union bureaucratization,[6] which analyzes the removal and transfer of power from the rank-and-file to the union leaders, can be constructed from his writings on trade unions between 1919 and 1921. In this period, Antonio Gramsci explored the role of trade unions in a capitalist society and the transformational potential of unions within capitalism. Within Gramsci's theory his analysis of the institutionalization of collective bargaining is crucial for understanding the issues at hand.

Gramsci argued that the union goal of ensuring that workers received the highest price for their labor power would lead to the institutionalization of collective bargaining. Institutionalization focused leadership's attention on the purely administrative aspects of trade unionism rather than on specific knowledge of their industries. He stated that trade union leaders are never chosen "on the basis of industrial competence, but rather simply on the basis of juridical, bureaucratic and demagogic competence."[7] Gramsci argued that this led to the separation between the rank-and-file and the leadership concerning what really occurs on the shop floor. He stated:

> The trade-union movement, as it has expanded, has created a body of officials who are completely detached from the individual industries, and who obey purely commercial laws. A metal-workers' official can pass on indifferently to the bricklayers, the bootmakers or the joiners. He is not obliged to know the real technical conditions of the industry, just the private legislation which regulates the relations between entrepreneurs and labor force.[8]

Institutionalized bargaining also led trade union officials to accept "industrial legality as a permanent state of affairs" and was defended by trade union leaders "from the same perspective as the proprietor."[9] Gramsci defined "industrial legality" as the establishment and honoring of the contractual relationship between the trade union and the employer within the confines of the capitalist economy. Thus Gramsci viewed union leaders as only being concerned with the negotiation and administration of collective bargaining agreements and as not seeing any way that this relationship, embedded in a specific historical period, could be transcended.

However, Gramsci did not believe that the institutionalization and acceptance of industrial legality by union leaders were inevitable outcomes. He pointed out that the organizational structure of a union also depends on the ability of members to guide and shape the union. He stated:

> The trade union is not a predetermined phenomenon. It becomes a determinate institution, i.e., it takes on a definite historical form to the extent that the strength and will of the workers who are its members impress a policy and propose an aim that define it.[10]

Thus, for Gramsci, the role of collective bargaining would be different in a union where it was institutionalized and where "industrial legality as a permanent state of affairs" was accepted than in one that refused either to institutionalize bargaining and rejected permanent industrial legality. The significance of this argument will be illustrated when we consider the empirical evidence concerning the UAW Local 6 and the FE.

Institutionalizing Collective Bargaining: The Shop Floor Effects

Gramsci argues that institutionalized bargaining focuses union attention on contract negotiation and administration. Industrial disputes or problems, such as changes in working conditions, that may have been resolved through a variety of procedures at the point of production, are increasingly handled within the grievance procedure of the contract.

In addition, after institutionalization, the union becomes increasingly concerned with its organizational security and is less likely to adopt policies that may jeopardize its established relationship with the employer. Even though the collective bargaining relationship between the union and the employer is "at root conflictual," the stability of the relationship leads "to the development of shared understandings" as well as an awareness that the two parties possess "a growing area of common interest."[11]

Institutionalization of collective bargaining impacts on shop floor unionism by controlling rank-and-file militancy. Industrial militancy has been defined as "any method of making solutions by means other than negotiation."[12] As Mills has argued, once collective bargaining becomes institutionalized, trade unions adopt functions similar to the companies with which they are dealing, including becoming involved in the discipline of the rank-and-file, including the control of shop floor militancy.[13] This leads to the "incorporation of workplace trade unionism," in which shop stewards are no longer able to initiate "collective actions" but are responsible for ending them whenever they occur.[14] Union leaders attempt to stifle rank-and-file militancy ("wildcat strikes," slowdowns, etc.) because they believe that such behavior will interfere with the attainment of collective bargaining objectives. However, at specific times, leaders find it necessary to encourage shop floor militancy as a pressure tactic in support of such objectives. Gouldner, for example, argued that union leaders may actively encourage wildcat strikes (albeit clandestinely) while officially declaring that they are opposed to the action.[15]

The UAW, FE, and Harvester: Historical Backgrounds

Both the UAW and the FE were organizing agricultural implement workers by the late 1930s. Beginning as the Farm Equipment Division of the Steelworkers' Organizing Committee in July 1938, the CIO chartered the FE as the international union whose jurisdiction was the farm equipment industry. The UAW gained a foothold in the agricultural implement industry in 1937 when it obtained a collective bargaining agreement with J.I. Case's Racine, Wisconsin, plant. In the same year, the UAW modified its constitution to include agricultural implement workers in its jurisdiction.[16]

Before World War II, the UAW's main strength in the agricultural implement industry was at John Deere. The union had also obtained representation rights at the West Allis, Wisconsin, tractor plant, several J.I. Case plants, and a number of smaller agricultural implement companies. Until 1945, the rivalry between the UAW and the FE was handled by dividing the jurisdiction over the truck plants. However, this arrangement came to an abrupt end after World War II, with both unions competing to organize new plants. In addition, the UAW attempted to raid the FE plants for the first time.[17]

This rivalry between the unions became increasingly important throughout the late 1940s and 1950s, in both organizing drives and ideology. Walter Reuther, elected UAW International president in 1947, and other leaders in the Reuther Caucus anticipated that unions would become accepted and essential elements of the corporate structure, while the leaders of the Communist party (CP) led the FE and viewed the union's role as defending workers, both on and off the shop floor, and challenging the prerogatives of capital on a daily basis.[18]

A proposed merger of the FE and the UAW in 1947 was rejected by the UAW membership when the Reuther Caucus actively opposed the merger because the addition of the FE to the UAW would greatly strengthen the CP-supported Thomas-Addes forces. When the FE was expelled from the CIO in 1949, along with ten other Communist-dominated unions, the CIO sanctioned raids by the UAW against the FE. In an attempt to protect itself from such attacks, the FE merged with the United Electrical Workers (UE), another CIO union expelled for ties with the CP, and formed the FE-UE.[19] This battle between the two unions only ended after the FE's merger into the UAW in 1955, after six years of UAW raids on FE plants.

Beginning in 1946, Harvester was a major battleground for the UAW and the FE. Both unions attempted to organize workers at new Harvester facilities, including the Melrose Park plant (thirteen miles west of downtown Chicago), where UAW Local 6 defeated FE Local 103 in a November 1946 NLRB certification election. In addition, the UAW began a series of raids at the FE Harvester plants in 1949, which continued almost unabated until the 1955 UAW-FE merger. This provides a backdrop for a historical summary of union activities in the Harvester corporation that demonstrate the company's importance in agricultural implement and related industries in the 1940s and 1950s.

Formed through a merger between the McCormick Company and a number of manufacturers of harvesting and haying machines in 1902, International Harvester Corporation emerged as one of America's largest corporations, with twenty-eight manufacturing plants (as well as steel mills and iron mines) located predominantly in Chicago and elsewhere in the Midwest. The company produced a full line of agricultural implements, plus trucks and earthmoving equipment; refrigeration equipment was also manufactured until 1956.[20]

From 1902 until 1957, Harvester was the major producer of agricultural equipment in the United States. However, the line decreased from 70 percent of the company's sales in 1910 to approximately 33 percent in 1955. The impressive growth of the motor truck division was one of the reasons for this decline in the percentage of the company's sales in agricultural equipment. Motor truck sales, which accounted for 3 percent of total sales in 1910, grew to almost 50 percent by 1957.[21]

After World War II, Harvester began to manufacture construction equipment. In 1946 the company added a line that included earthmoving equipment, power units, and related items. Sales of this division were $154 million (13.2 percent of total sales) by 1957. Thus, at this time, the firm's share in the construction equipment market was almost as great as its share in agricultural implements, not including farm tractors.[22]

UAW Local 6 and the FE: Different Trade Union Strategies

UAW Local 6 has been acknowledged as one of the most militant locals in the entire UAW.[23] It was clearly the most militant local in the UAW Harvester chain through 1952, but there were still major differences in the strategies adopted by Local 6 and the FE. The primary difference between these two unions in the immediate postwar period concerned Local 6's willingness to institutionalize collective bargaining, while the FE preferred to construct a shop floor unionism independent of the formal collective-bargaining structures. Ideological differences were also evident between the two unions, clauses in the collective-bargaining agreements, and shop floor unionism.

The UAW and the FE: Ideological and Contractual Differences

Reuther, who consolidated his control over the UAW in 1947, was committed to institutionalizing collective bargaining between the union and the large industrial companies that employed UAW members. He pursued this route through contract negotiations with the companies, as opposed to constructing a shop floor unionism independent of the formal collective-bargaining mechanisms.[24]

Reuther's strategy was to construct a system based on pattern bargaining that would deliver an increasing array of economic benefits to UAW members plus creating a private "welfare state" for workers engaged in heavy industry.[25] Left-wing Reutherites who came to dominate Local 6's administrative machinery committed themselves to institutionalize collective bargaining for Local 6. While Local 6 followed Reuther's lead, the FE was ideologically opposed to the institutionalization of bargaining. In an article in the national *FE News,* the union made its position clear:

> We regard a collective bargaining contract as an instrument to protect the workers' wages, hours, and working conditions through secure union representation. A contract is not an instrument to cover false issues of "company security."[26]

FE leadership believed that the contract should be utilized when it could be used to defend workers and abandoned when this was not so. They viewed the contract as only a temporary class truce between labor and capital, not the end of the war between these two parties.[27]

These ideological differences were manifest in different contract clauses in FE and Local 6 collective-bargaining agreements with Harvester. From 1947 to 1952, Local 6 had a five-step grievance procedure that culminated in arbitration. Local 6 could not legally strike over unresolved grievances. However, the FE's grievance procedure in the late 1940s and early 1950s permitted authorized strikes over unresolved grievances after the grievance procedure had been thoroughly utilized.[28]

In addition, different attitudes toward institutionalization resulted in different contractual provisions with Harvester concerning the control of shop floor militancy. In 1947, after the enactment of the Taft-Hartley Act, which raised the issue of a union's financial liability for the staging of wildcat strikes, the UAW negotiated an agreement with Harvester that covered the five plants it represented. The agreement stated that the company would not sue the UAW when a wildcat strike occurred if the local union posted a notice instructing workers to go back to work and to end actions that were harming plant production. If the stoppage did not end imminently, union leaders were required to take the necessary steps to end it.[29]

The FE did not sign such an agreement with Harvester. This forced the company to take responsibility for enforcing the no-strike section of the contract.[30] In addition, at least two UAW Harvester locals (Locals 6 and 57) had the following provision in their 1948 contracts that was not contained in FE collective bargaining agreements:

> In any case where an interruption of production occurs in violation of this contract, the Union agrees that it will in good faith and without delay exert itself to bring about a quick termination of such interruptions of production, and will insist that the employee involved therein return to work and to normal production promptly. To that end, the Local and the International Union will promptly take whatever affirmative action is necessary.[31]

Finally, the UAW Harvester Council committed to multiyear contracts after Reuther negotiated a five-year agreement with the auto companies in 1950. The first centralized collective-bargaining agreement signed by the UAW Harvester Council in 1950 followed the Detroit pattern of five-year agreements.[32] The FE, on the other hand, was opposed to multiyear contracts, preferring one-year agreements to keep the "rank-and-file combat ready by near-incessant contract negotiations." However, after the UAW and Harvester negotiated a five-year contract in 1950, the FE reluctantly agreed to Harvester's demands for a two-year collective-bargaining agreement.[33]

While there were differences between the UAW and the FE in ideology and contractual language, the real test of the two unions' attitudes toward the institutionalization of bargaining rested with the practice of militant shop floor unionism, and it is to this that we now turn.

Militant Shop Floor Unionism: The UAW's Tactics vs. the FE's Principles

From 1946 to 1952, both UAW Local 6 and the FE practiced militant shop floor unionism. However, Local 6's militancy was based on tactics, while the FE's was rooted in principles. The Local 6 leaders utilized shop floor militancy because they were dismayed with ineffective grievance and arbitration procedures, not because they wanted to replace these systems with other mechanisms to handle conflict at the point of production. Throughout this period, the Local 6 leadership was never interested in constructing an independent shop floor unionism along the lines of the FE. The patterns of shop floor militancy were inherently different because of Local 6's tactical use, as opposed to the FE's principled use, of shop floor militancy.

In 1946, at the Melrose Park plant, there were a number of wildcat strikes when the organizational campaign between UAW Local 6 and FE Local 103 was in full swing.[34] After the signing of a temporary "Memorandum of Agreement" between UAW Local 6 and Harvester at the end of December 1946, several wildcat strikes were held early in 1947 to register dissatisfaction with the company on the implementation of the grievance procedure and to pressurize the company to sign a collective-bargaining agreement. Since the grievance procedure did not terminate in arbitration under the "Memorandum of Agreement," it was not illegal to conduct wildcat strikes over unsettled grievances.[35] This led to the highest number of wildcat strikes in 1947, followed by a decline throughout the term of the contract.

Carl Shier, a former Local 6 shop committeeman in the late 1940s and 1950s, remembered that the sixteen wildcat strikes called in 1947 were openly organized by the leadership of the local. The designated time for a majority of the walkouts was 2:00 P.M. Shop floor leaders would hold up two fingers, indicating that the walkout would be at two o'clock. The foremen became so familiar with this procedure that when the two fingers went up, they would go to wash up early in the afternoon knowing that a strike was imminent.[36]

These events in the early years of the Melrose Park Harvester–Local 6 relationship demonstrate that shop floor militancy was used in response to actions perpetrated by the company. While the union leadership could direct the militancy into certain channels, the leaders did not create this militancy though any of their actions. Rather, the major reason for its emergence was the ineffectiveness of the grievance procedure in solving the workers' problems.

However, because of the leadership's commitment to the institutionalization of collective bargaining, the next major upsurge of shop floor militancy, in 1951–52, differed from that of 1946–47. When inherently class-conflictual issues (the cutting of both piecework prices and occupational classifications) were not resolved in 1949–50 through the grievance and arbitration procedures, the Local 6 leaders modified their 1946–47 shop floor tactics when Harvester sharpened its attacks in 1951–52. While the shop floor militancy of 1946–47 consisted primarily of wildcat strikes, in the 1951–52 period it consisted of job actions that were dubbed either "extended lunch hours" or "locker room meetings."

According to Carl Shier, these tactics were quite an effective weapon:

> A great tactic was to extend the lunch hour. Just don't come back after lunch for 10 minutes. After ten minutes, there was immediately a crisis on the shop

floor. Where were the workers? The foremen would go crazy. And they'd realize the guys weren't coming back and they would call Industrial Relations. And Industrial Relations would beep the shop committee. But it was a good tactic, it was successful.[37]

Additional insight concerning the use of this strategy is provided by Seymour Kahan, the shop committee chairman in the early 1950s:

> We used it as a trade union tactic to try to solve the problems we couldn't get solved otherwise. And we did it at a leadership level in a careful manner, so as not to expose people to discharges. For example, we insisted that the guys do not leave the plant, because that would broaden it into a full-fledged wildcat strike. We insisted that the union representatives stay on the job, because arbitrators held them to higher standard than rank and filers when it came to discipline.[38]

Thus the shop floor militancy of the 1951–52 period was different from that of the 1946–47 period in terms of control of shop floor militancy. In 1946–47, the shop committeemen openly organized wildcat strikes—actual plant walkouts —when conflictual issues could not be resolved by any other means. Such a strategy was used by the local because there were no contractual provisions against the holding of such actions. However, by the early 1950s, the control of militancy had changed because the contract explicitly forbade the holding of any job actions that interfered with production. Thus the shop committeemen could no longer openly organize shop floor actions but had to do it clandestinely to simultaneously control shop floor militancy and to pressure the company. In fact, the major strategy of the shop committeemen was to make the job actions appear to have occurred spontaneously, so that management could not hold them legally responsible for such occurrences.

According to Seymour Kahan, the "locker room meetings" would unfold in the following manner:

> We [the shop committeemen] would organize an action. The guys would go down in the locker room. I would get a call from the manager in Labor Relations because I was chairman of the bargaining [shop] committee. He'd say, "Do you know there's a wildcat strike in Department so-and-so? Do you know it's your job as chairman to get those people back to work?" And I would say, "I've got to find out what's wrong. Give me some time. I know my responsibilities under the contract." And I would have a meeting with the guys. And we would get a list of what was bothering them enough to precipitate an action. I would call the company back and say, "Okay, I can get the guys back to work, but I need a couple of things. I need a meeting immediately about these issues. And I need a guarantee that nobody's going to get disciplined." And we'd get that and then we'd send the guys back to work and we'd have a meeting. And we'd hammer out a settlement of the issues.[39]

Although the shop committee controlled shop floor militancy through the organizing of these "locker room meetings," at other times they actively discouraged worker militancy. In April 1951, for example, when there was strong sentiment among many shop stewards and rank-and-file workers for immediate action because of the piecework and classification cuts, the Local 6 leadership called for "patience" while it was preparing for a strike vote (*The Union Voice* 1951). While planning for a legalized strike, the shop committee counseled the plant's workers:

> [We] know how impatient a person can get. However, we are informing you that an officially authorized strike vote will be conducted in the immediate future. Also that your representatives are meeting this weekend with the representatives from every other UAW Harvester plant in the country. Meantime continue to see your steward and file your grievance as if the company were meeting with the Union in good faith.[40]

This indicates the preference of the Local 6 leadership for conducting legal strikes as opposed to the holding of departmental job actions in violation of the collective-bargaining agreement.

While the taking of strike votes and the organizing of job actions on the shop floor may have forced Harvester to make some immediate concessions, they did not prevent the company from continuing to cut both piecework prices and classification rates throughout the mid- and late 1950s.

However, the nature of both the grievance procedure and shop floor militancy was different in the Harvester plants where the workers were represented by the FE. Because the FE had not institutionalized collective bargaining, the union had a different attitude from that of the UAW toward the grievance procedure. Unlike the UAW, the FE believed that the grievance procedure should remain simple, nonbureaucratic, and not overly legalistic. In fact, the bureaucratization of the UAW-Harvester grievance procedure was noticed by former FE leaders when the UAW-FE merger occurred in 1955. Compared with the operation of the FE's grievance procedure, the UAW's grievance procedure was seen as being both complicated and unwieldy.[41]

James Wright, a former leader of FE Local 236 (Louisville), compared the strategies of the FE and the UAW in processing grievances:

> Our strategy [in the FE] was hit 'em, get the case for the man, get him a clean job, get his money that's due him, and go on. But the UAW had a department, they had people handling grievances, they had people over here at this desk, so that when we went into the UAW, I said, "What the hell have all you got in there? Is this an officeworkers' union, or what is this?" Hell, all we had [in the FE] was a plain old brown contract, write the grievance, we knew what we were doing. But over there in the UAW, you had a department of people to say, well, this comes under this classification, this skill is here, and all this business.[42]

Nevertheless, because of this view of the grievance procedure, the FE was not averse to abandoning it when it did not serve the union's purpose. Although the

FE's contract permitted authorized strikes during the period of the agreement after the grievance procedure had been thoroughly utilized, the FE often held shop floor job actions and/or wildcat strikes in lieu of filing grievances in order to obtain "industrial justice."[43]

This difference in the union attitudes (UAW vs. FE) toward the collective-bargaining agreement, as well as the weaker no-strike provisions in the FE contracts, resulted in the FE staging a significantly greater number of work stoppages than the UAW in Harvester plants. Although the UAW and the FE represented a comparable number of workers throughout this period, during the seven-year period from October 1, 1945, through October 31, 1952, the FE was engaged in 971 work stoppages compared with 185 for the UAW. In each of these years, the FE stoppages outnumbered the UAW stoppages by at least a two-to-one margin. From October 1, 1946, to October 1, 1947, the margin was greater than ten to one.[44] It appears that the FE preferred to hold "short intracontract stoppages," while the UAW's strategy was to hold longer, and legalized, strikes.[45]

Post-1952: The Decline of Shop Floor Militancy at Harvester

For both the FE and UAW Local 6, 1952 was a crucial year in their relationships with Harvester. In 1952 Harvester attempted to break the FE. Because of the bitter rivalry between the UAW and the FE at the time, the company's strategy was to maintain production at its UAW facilities while it battled the FE.[46] The strike resulted in a total defeat for the union. The contract that the FE signed with Harvester was one in which the union capitulated to the company on all of its initial demands.[47]

While the FE's strike in 1952 against Harvester resulted in a resounding defeat, Local 6's 1952 production standards strike against the company ended in a decisive, if temporary, victory for the Melrose Park plant workers. It was the first time that any trade union had legally struck a major corporation over production standards (both piecework and daywork) when a contract was in effect.[48] Although all of the plants in the UAW Harvester chain were experiencing these production standards problems, Local 6 was the only UAW local to conduct a legal strike against Harvester at this time.

The Local 6 strike began earlier than the FE strike and was unexpected.[49] However, it was settled more than a month before the FE strike, as Harvester decided to devote all of its energies to breaking the FE.[50]

With the defeat of the FE, Harvester implemented a policy of strict discipline for all kinds of "illegal" job actions on the shop floor that drastically reduced the number of work stoppages in both the UAW and the FE plants. Since the FE was on the defensive after its 1952 strike, it was in no position to challenge Harvester on the shop floor on a daily basis. In addition, the UAW's raids on the FE in 1953–54 were of major concern to the union. The first crack in the FE Harvester chain occurred in May 1954, when the workers at the East Moline, Illinois, plant voted overwhelmingly to disaffiliate from the FE and join the UAW.[51]

After the loss of the East Moline plant to the UAW, other FE locals continued the pattern by voting to join the UAW. The next plant to leave was Farmall, in Rock Island, Illinois. After that, the movement extended to the Chicago plants and finally to all of the FE plants. In the middle of March 1955, the FE Harvester Conference Board voted for disaffiliation with the UE and decided to join the UAW as a group.[52]

Concerning UAW Local 6, the shop floor tactics of the 1951–52 period were abandoned by the end of 1953. The institutionalization of collective bargaining led the local union leaders to abandon the use of "illegal" job actions on the shop floor. Instead of organizing these types of job actions, the Local 6 leaders pursued a resolution to the piecework and occupational classification problems through both contractual and noncontractual modifications of the grievance and arbitration procedures implemented by Harvester and UAW International.[53]

Conclusions: What Can Be Done?

UAW Local 6 and the FE differed in their attitudes toward the institutionalization of collective bargaining, as evinced in terms of ideology; contract clauses; and, most importantly, shop floor unionism. While UAW Local 6 utilized shop floor militancy in a tactical sense, the local ultimately depended on grievance and arbitration procedures for handling its shop floor problems with Harvester. However, after 1952, when Local 6 leaders actively discouraged most forms of in-plant job actions and began to exert an even tighter control over shop floor militancy, the number of grievances exceeded even that of the 1947–52 period. By the mid-1950s the grievance and arbitration procedures were less effective for handling the workers' problems than in the years before.

On the other hand, the shop floor–oriented FE based the use of its militancy on principles. The union's approach to trade unionism was much more flexible; it used whatever technique was necessary to defend the workers both on and off the shop floor. If the collective-bargaining agreement could be used to successfully defend the workers, it was used; if not, it was abandoned. Shop floor militancy was encouraged in the form of wildcat strikes, sit-down strikes, and in-plant meetings at both the departmental and plantwide levels.

The lessons from the experiences of UAW Local 6 and the FE suggest that a trade union strategy based on the institutionalization of collective bargaining ultimately confirms the gross inequality of power between capital and labor. As can be seen with Harvester, collective bargaining is but one method that capital uses in its relationship with labor. Other mechanisms include the development of certain kinds of investment strategies, the introduction of new technology, and the periodic reorganization of the labor process. To balance the power relationship between capital and labor, unions must use a wide variety of tactics in combination with the formal collective bargaining structures. In the current political climate of the 1990s, in which the state's minimal protection of labor is continually being eroded, it is suicidal not to resurrect an approach to trade unionism that increases the solidarity of the rank-and-file while simultaneously revitalizing the local union on the shop floor.

If the FE's approach to trade unionism had been generalized to the American trade union movement as a whole over the past thirty-five to forty years, it is likely that trade unions would have been more effective in organizing workers against concession bargaining in the 1980s. However, methodologically, this sort of analysis amounts to viewing history as counterfactuals. Yet, a trade union that uses the general approach of the FE would probably be more successful in terms of recognizing the fundamental antagonism between labor and capital than a union that was committed to the institutionalization of collective bargaining and to viewing the contract as "the workplace rule of law."

With the return of a limited amount of union-sanctioned shop floor militancy in the early to mid-1980s,[54] one scholar noted that these "strategies require the virtual rebuilding of local unions from the ground up" and that the ideology behind this militancy was that "a return to the status quo—or the pre-Reagan period—of collective bargaining is desirable."[55]

This is precisely the point that is missed. Militant shop floor activity must be legitimized through daily struggle so that rank-and-file participation in local unions will not atrophy as in the post–World War II years for the majority of American industrial unions. As in the case of the FE from 1946 to 1952, the institutionalization of collective bargaining will have to be transcended, or in Gramsci's words, "industrial legality as a permanent state of affairs" must not be honored. This should provide a new meaning for shop floor militancy and will rekindle a spirit in the American trade union movement that has not been seen for decades.

Notes

1. David Brody, *Workers in Industrial America* (New York: Oxford University Press, 1980), 217.

2. C. Wright Mills, *The New Men of Power—America's Labor Leaders* (New York: Harcourt, Brace, 1948), 223–24.

3. Ibid., 224–25.

4. Ibid., 225.

5. Victor L. Allen, *Social Analysis: A Marxist Critique and Alternative* (London: Longman Group, 1975).

6. The construction of Gramsci's theory of trade union bureaucratization can be found in ch. III of the author's doctoral dissertation, "A History of UAW Local 6, 1941–81: A Study in the Development of Trade Union Bureaucratization" (Minneapolis: University of Minnesota, 1990), 41–51.

7. Antonio Gramsci, *Selections from Political Writings (1910–20)* (New York: International Publishers, 1977), 105.

8. Antonio Gramsci, *Selections from Political Writings (1921–26)* (New York: International Publishers, 1978), 77.

9. Ibid., 265.

10. Ibid.

11. Richard Hyman, *Industrial Relations: A Marxist Introduction* (London: The Macmillan Press, 1975), 192–93.

12. Paul Rigg, "Miners and Militancy: A Study of Branch Union Leadership," *Industrial Relations Journal* 18, no. 3 (Autumn 1987): 189–200.

13. Mills, *New Men of Power*, 224–25.

14. Christine Edwards and Edmund Heery, "The Incorporation of Workplace Trade Unionism?" *Sociology* 19, no. 3 (1985): 345–63.

15. Alvin Gouldner, *Wildcat Strike* (Yellow Springs, OH: The Antioch Press, 1954).

16. Arlyn John Melcher, "Collective Bargaining in the Agricultural Implement Industry: The Impact of Company and Union Structure in Three Firms," Ph.D. diss. (Chicago: Graduate School of Business, University of Chicago, 1964), 66–71.

17. Ibid., 67.

18. Toni Gilpin, "The FE-UAW Conflict: The Ideological Content of Collective Bargaining in Postwar America," 1988 North American Labor History Conference, Wayne State University (October 20–22, 1988), 1.

19. Toni Gilpin, "Labor's Last Stand," *Chicago History* XVIII, no. 1 (1989): 48.

20. Ibid., 45; Melcher, "Collective Bargaining," 39–41.

21. Melcher, "Collective Bargaining," 41–44.

22. Ibid., 44.

23. David Rothstein, "Scholarly Steward Pride of Local 6, U. of Chicago," *UAW Solidarity* (Midwest Edition) 1, no. 26 (1958): 3.

24. One should refer to Toni Gilpin's paper "The FE-UAW Conflict," where this argument is made.

25. Nelson Lichtenstein, "UAW Bargaining Strategy and Shop Floor Conflict: 1946–70," *Industrial Relations* 24, no. 3 (Fall 1985): 360.

26. Gilpin, "The FE-UAW Conflict," 17.

27. Ibid., 25–26.

28. See 1947 Collective Bargaining Agreement Between International Harvester Company and UAW Local 6, UAW-CIO, 13–22; and 1948 Collective Bargaining Agreement Between International Harvester Company and UAW Local 6, UAW-CIO quoted in Gilpin, "The FE-UAW Conflict," 12–23, 25–26.

29. Gilpin, "The FE-UAW Conflict," 26–27.

30. Ibid.

31. Ibid.

32. Seymour Kahan, "Strike Reports," *The Hi-Flyer* (January 1951): 4 (Detroit: UAW Local 6 Newspaper Collection, Walter P. Reuther Library, Archives of Labor and Urban Affairs, Wayne State University).

33. Gilpin, "The FE-UAW Conflict," 17.

34. Seymour Kahan, oral history interview by author (1989).

35. Joel Seidman, Jack London, Bernard Karsh, and Daisy L. Tagliacozzo, *The Worker Views His Union* (Chicago: University of Chicago Press, 1958), 92.

36. Carl Shier, oral history interview by author (1989).

37. Ibid.

38. Kahan, oral history interview by author (1989).

39. Ibid.

40. *The Union Voice* (April 19, 1951) (Detroit: Walter P. Reuther Library, Archives of Labor and Urban Affairs, Wayne State University).

41. Gilpin, "The FE-UAW Conflict," 20.

42. Ibid.

43. Ibid., 25–26.

44. David Cole Collection, "International Harvester Company No. of Work Stoppages Due to Labor Interruptions: Man-Hours Lost, and Estimated Pay Lost," accession 5588, box 101 (October 1, 1944–October 31, 1953), folder "International Harvester Paper on Perm Umpire" (Ithaca, NY: Labor-Management Documentation Center, Cornell University).

45. Robert Ozanne, *A Century of Labor-Management Relations at McCormick and International Harvester* (Madison: The University of Wisconsin Press, 1967), 214.

46. Ibid., 219.

47. For an excellent discussion of the 1952 Harvester-FE strike, see Gilpin's "Labor's Last Stand."

48. For detailed information on this point see Annual Report to Membership, 1952, by the Executive Board and Shop Committee, Local 6, UAW-CIO, 4 (Detroit: Holgate Young Collection, box 7, folder 5, Walter P. Reuther Library, Archives of Labor and Urban Affairs, Wayne State University).

49. Norm Roth, oral history interview by author (August 15, 1989).

50. Ibid.

51. "Smashing Victory at East Moline," *The Union Voice* (May 27, 1954) (Detroit: UAW Local 6 Office Collection, Walter P. Reuther Library, Archives of Labor and Urban Affairs, Wayne State University).

52. Ozanne, *A Century of Labor-Management Relations,* 219–20.

53. For an elaboration of this argument see ch. VII, "Shop Floor Unionism: The Onset of a 'Cold War,'" "A History of UAW Local 6," 325–45.

54. See Tom Balanoff, "The Cement Workers' Experience," *Labor Research Review* 7 (Fall 1985): 5–32; and Jack Metzgar, "'Running the Plant Backwards,'" *Labor Research Review* 7 (Fall 1985): 35–43.

55. Steven Rosswurm, "In-Plant Strategies and 'The Social Contract,'" *Labor Research Review* 8 (1986): 110–13.

8

Lean and Mean: Work, Locality, and Unions

Philip Garrahan and Paul Stewart

Introduction

Current upheavals in the auto industry typify how labor organizations are being put on the defensive by changes in global economic relations. These changes have an impact on new developments in the labor process, where there are many prescriptive strategic prognoses for labor union participation. Purveyors of the new consensus invariably hold independent unions responsible for complicity with management in the errors of Fordist companies. By Fordist we mean not just mass production for mass markets, but also the corporate decision-making ethos premised on two separate interests—those of management and those of labor.

The conflictual rigidities between these interests are blamed for the failing efficiency and competitiveness of Fordist companies. Hence the new consensus, wherein the autonomy of unions is threatened by company developments driven by lean production methods. A picture of employee involvement and participation is presented by management in justification for lean production methods (LPMs). Yet in practice there is evidence to show that unions are being sidelined by incorporationist management strategies that are based on surprisingly inflexible command and control structures. Although this is a global trend identifiable in both North America and Europe, the two main auto production centers outside Japan, nevertheless there are many adaptations. Indeed, the new industrial model characterized by LPMs is proving to be as varied in its local adaptations as was Fordism, especially in the expression of labor-management relations.

In this chapter we analyze one local example of this phenomenon, drawing evidence from Nissan's investment in a giant production facility in Sunderland, in northeastern England. It is by recognizing the specific constellation of local circumstances that the apparently global inevitability of lean production methods can be reassessed by organized labor.

Lean Production Methods in the Auto Industry

The manufacture of motor vehicles by the world's auto industry is currently experiencing major management-initiated changes. These changes derive from the broadly based application of new and revised production systems, which are associated principally with Japanese LPMs in manufacturing.[1] These LPMs are so called because of their emphasis on raising productivity by reducing waste or inefficiency in the management of human and material resources. Their impact in the global auto industry is directly reflected in the ascendancy of Japanese companies in the past four decades.

In 1950 the total annual production by the Japanese auto industry was equivalent to only a few days' output by the U.S. auto industry. The "Big Three"—General Motors (GM), Ford, and Chrysler—seemed to be without rival, not just in the United States but also worldwide, in terms of the scale of their enterprise and their share of markets. However, new trends in the globalization of the auto industry progressively changed this situation. Japanese companies proved to be leaders in these new trends, so that by the end of the 1980s Japanese companies had won one-quarter of the world market. Toyota has come to challenge Ford as the world's second-largest producer of vehicles; Toyota, Nissan, Honda, and Mazda occupy four of the places at the table of the world's top ten auto producers.[2]

An additional aspect of this development was that during the 1980s Japanese companies accelerated the degree to which their production became transnational in character. Initially, in the 1960s and 1970s, Japanese companies had been successful by exporting vehicles overseas. However, the extent of this commercial success began to generate political reaction and opposition as domestic producers in North America and Europe saw their own market shares fall in line with the rise in imports from Japan. Economic recession following the oil crises further stimulated the support for protectionist economic policies, and the quickening pace toward the single European Market also placed export-led company strategies in jeopardy. A major new Japanese initiative, therefore, exemplified competition in the global auto industry from the early 1980s onward.

Beginning with an upsurge of investment into North America, the major Japanese auto companies all opened their own production facilities in the United States or joined in ventures with U.S. firms, in either the United States or Canada. This dramatic shift of production via transplants saw the Japanese share of the U.S. market grow to more than one-third by the beginning of the 1990s. This development has been followed by Nissan, Toyota, and Honda, opening plants in the United Kingdom with the aim of winning an equally substantial share of the single European Market during the 1990s.

For domestic U.S. or U.K. manufacturers, the consequence of this heightened competition are manifested in plant closures and layoffs. In the United States, GM and Ford have been responding to the combined effects of economic downturns and increased Japanese competition by anticipating the need to engage in joint ventures with Japanese companies. Chrysler has been less fortunate, and has lost third place in the U.S. market to Toyota. The only remaining British-owned high-volume producer of autos was Rover, with 14 percent of U.K. sales in 1991. It was a successor to British Leyland, and was bought by BMW after initially developing joint operations with Honda.

In the United States, interest has focused on Japanese transplants—those companies that have moved complete manufacturing systems into North America during the 1980s.[3] In the United Kingdom, there has been a tendency to refer to these changes as "Japanization."[4] Neither of these terms does full justice to the fundamental, global changes under way today. To focus only on the wholly owned Japanese car firms in the United States ignores the commonality of joint ventures between Japanese and U.S. and U.K. firms. Furthermore, it neglects the adoption of LPMs within the domestic U.S. industry as a whole, both among firms assembling vehicles and in the components industry.[5]

There are similar limitations associated with the notion of "Japanization" in the United Kingdom, since this runs the risk of referring to industrial transformation in modern capitalism in terms of the national characteristic of one particular country. While reference to a process of "Japanization" has some analytical merit, there nevertheless may be an inherent danger in the use of this term of arousing racist feelings against the Japanese people, whether they are working in their own country or abroad.

To promote understanding of why the transition to LPMs in the auto industry is taking place, it is vital to establish their origins. This will bring us to the question of adoption of the new management techniques that make lean methods of auto production so competitive. In the adoption of these techniques by management, the process of change is initiated by Japanese example. It is also increasingly reflected in the policies of many auto manufacturing concerns, whatever their national ownership. As a result, it is more accurate not to characterize LPMs as either "Japanese transplants" or "Japanization."

Those working in the American and British auto industries have been increasingly experiencing the new management techniques, and their corresponding features, in a wide variety of ways during the past decade. In practice, the impact of the current changes is identifiable in some measure in firms where auto components are being manufactured or complete vehicles assembled. Whether Japanese ownership is evident or not in these firms, extensive transformations have been occurring, and organized labor's response is just taking shape as we enter the second half of the 1990s. In this context, trade unions are struggling to get to know the nature of the management initiatives, which often seductively lay claim to the virtues of participation and empowerment in the workforce.

For the auto industry, with its traditional reliance on unskilled and semiskilled workforce, the new management techniques also seem to offer a transition to higher levels of technology and more rewarding upgrading of skills. The prospect of a concerted labor movement response in this changing situation is made all the more problematical by the hostile industrial relations climate.[6] This has been shaped by the antiunion legislation during the Reagan and Thatcher decade:

> [The] character of relationships inherent within workplace organization have been influenced by state employers' policies intended to achieve restructuring and union demobilization. Legislation has curtailed individuals' rights against employers and expanded rights against trade unions.[7]

Improving on the ways and means of understanding and thus responding to the new management techniques would raise two issues for organized labor. First, there is a need for a fuller appreciation of the range and diversity of the new management techniques and the rhetoric in which they are cloaked. Secondly, there must be a heightened awareness of the degree to which the new management techniques reflect an integrated assault by employers and the state on independent unions.

The central importance of the auto industry to modern economies and lifestyles, together with the inevitable instabilities in the industry's development, make it the prime arena for testing the new management techniques.[8] The commitment to flexibility in working practices by auto companies is more far-reaching in some cases than in others. However, once there is a company commitment to introducing flexibility, typical managerial rhetoric claims that industrial attitudes among employees will be radically revised. The rhetoric also asserts that having won the necessary changes in attitudes to work, a company's production methods should be leaner and less wasteful, and thus more efficient and more profitable.

In addition to this argument about the inefficiencies of the old ways, and the counterproductive industrial attitudes that went with them, there is another element to the rhetoric. This is the moral selling point to the effect that flexible working conditions and revised industrial attitudes together reinvigorate the experience of daily industrial activity. In doing so, flexibility supposedly humanizes the work experience by empowering workers, giving them more discretion, responsibility, task variation, and enlarged skills.[9]

Thus there is an almost revolutionary turnaround envisaged by the rhetoric of the new management techniques and used to propel LPMs. It is the Japanese auto companies that are at the forefront in implementing the new management techniques and claiming the advantages in efficiency and humanizing terms just described. The efficiency gains speak for themselves. A report by the U.S. General Accounting Office shows that a typical U.S. firm needed 4,068 workers to manufacture 200,000 vehicles a year, whereas only 2,460 workers produced the same number of vehicles annually in a Japanese transplant. As a result, first of imports and then of transplant investments in the 1980s, the Japanese companies' growing market share reflects their achievements in industrial organization and productivity. A similar degree of market penetration in the British and other European countries is commonly anticipated if the existing industry does not adopt the essentials of LPMs, an apparent source of Japanese greater efficiency.

The joint ventures that have sprung up between U.S. and Japanese firms are giving the U.S. partners the opportunity to learn firsthand about flexible working practices, the grouping of workers into teams, and the corporate emphasis on building in quality rather than subsequently rectifying production errors. Joint ventures have the attraction for Japanese firms of providing another avenue into the U.S. market. Except where such shared or joint ventures occur, the Japanese auto transplants in the United States are distinctively against union recognition. Mazda (in which Ford has a 25 percent stake) recognizes a trade union at its Michigan site. Agreements with unions have been made at NUMMI, the joint GM/Toyota venture in California, and at Diamond-Star, the joint Chrysler/ Mitsubishi venture in Illinois. The others, Honda in Ohio, Toyota in Kentucky, Nissan in Tennessee, and Subaru-Isuzu in Indiana, have located in rural, small-town areas lacking an industrial base and thus any recent experience of strong unionization.

In these instances, the Japanese transplants recruited their employees on the assumption that unions would play no part. Attempts to get recognition for the United Autoworkers' Union through ballots of these employees have failed, most visibly at Nissan's plant in Smyrna, Tennessee, in 1989. More recently, the UAW withdrew from a membership campaign at the Toyota plant in George-town, Kentucky, when the union's own polls predicted certain defeat in the anticipated ballot of the workforce. In addition to these major Japanese auto transplants, only a mere handful of the many hundreds of Japanese businesses making and supplying auto components in the United States recognize a trade union.

This evidence unequivocally connects the new management techniques with the marginalization, wherever possible, of trade unionism. The Japanese auto transplants of greenfield sites are located primarily in the upper southern states, where state restrictions have historically stood in the way of trade unionism, especially via the "right to work" principle. Notwithstanding the weighty obsta-cles, such as the extensive screening of applicants to employ those with "the right attitudes" sympathetic to the company ethos, fully one-third of the Nissan workforce in Tennessee voted for a union in 1989. Seen in this light, the election outcome at Nissan is a positive one in the UAW's campaign and marks a turning point against all the odds and in favor of trade unionism. That there is a turn toward unions at all, in an atmosphere under the control of management, un-doubtedly points to the workers' negative attitude concerning the real nature of the current transition to LPMs in the industry.

From what is known of the "lean" revolution in the U.S. auto industry, therefore, important questions emerge. These questions are worth extra emphasis given the recent major investments by Japanese companies in the United Kingdom, as a means of accessing European markets after 1992. The role of automation and its extent, the degree of genuine multiskilling that is put into practice, and the impact of team working are all matters that now demand attention. It is significant, in assessing these questions and in examining the contribution from organized labor, that the three major Japanese firms investing in the United Kingdom (Honda, Nissan, and Toyota) have chosen "greenfield" sites with limited union involvement. It is to the case of Nissan in Sunderland that we turn for evidence about the local impact of the new management techniques. The new management practices are highly developed in the Nissan plant and they provide the best available empirical evidence to test the nature of the current transformation.

Flexibility in Sunderland

The importance of these questions for northeastern England is highlighted by the area's long-term economic decline and the recent emphasis that government has placed on market-led recovery and flexible attitudes toward change.[10] This encompasses not only the abandonment of earlier postwar policies of state spending on infrastructure and regional grants for industry; it also includes the Thatcher government's antiunion legislation, support for companies such as Nissan, which have an established record of marginalizing organized labor, and an image-building exercise to boost confidence in the new way forward for the local economy. The political economy of northeastern England has been heavily characterized by a public relations and media exercise in boosting or talking up the prospects of economic recovery. In this exercise Nissan is described as the jewel in the crown of new inward investment, and Sunderland is depicted as the "advanced manufacturing capital" of the North of England.

There have, of course, been a number of government initiatives in local economic development and training. Foremost among these are the government-appointed urban development corporations, the enterprise zones, and the training and enterprise councils, which are assuming many of the functions previously done by locally elected councils.[11] In addition, a range of new, self-appointed, private-led agencies have emerged, including the Newcastle Initiative, the Wearside Opportunity, and Common Purpose. Without exception, these various government- or self-appointed bodies lay claim to a more prosperous future for this old industrial region. By contrast, independent academic research reports and published studies have titles such as "Illusions of Prosperity," "Distinguishing Fact from Hype," and "The Great North?"[12]

The interface between the global restructuring of the auto industry and the local political economy of northeastern England, just briefly described, is the context in which we examine workers' encounters with the new management techniques and relate these to the strategies that trade unions might adopt. Our purpose in this chapter is to consider the essential elements of the new management techniques as they have been put in place in the Nissan plant. Many of the company's employees have entered working life in a period of intensified recession and decline in the local economy. Long-term and especially youth unemployment have proved to be consistently worrying features of northeastern England. The average age of production workers at Nissan is twenty-seven, as this relatively youthful workforce is also one in which there is little prior experience of employment in large-scale industry.

As with the pattern in the United States, Nissan has exercised great care to establish the suitability of individuals to work for the company. Some workers have concealed union membership in their past to prevent failing at the interview stage. The company ethos—the "Nissan Way"—is foregrounded at an early stage in the recruitment and training of new employees, but the Nissan workers we interviewed were anything but a happy family working as a team. Nissan puts special emphasis on the role of team working, conjuring up all the benefits promised by the rhetoric of the new management techniques.

The Social and Industrial Relations of a New Regime of Subordination

Three connected levels of change need to be addressed: the eclipse of Fordism and the rise of lean production methods; the character of industrial relations; and union participation.

Flexible Specialization or Mass Production Refound?

It is now clear that the argument to the effect that customized production implies the demise of mass production can no longer be sustained. Most commentators recognize that only car plants producing more than a quarter million units per year are viable.

Specifically, in the British and European context, the automotive industry continues to be dependent on mass sales of standardized small and sedan models. It is still the market as opposed to customer-led sales, the predilections of flexible specialization theorists aside. One can only presume the sovereignty of the customer where assumptions, implied by the logic of the capacities of new technologies of production and their assumed organizational and social virtues, are maintained (i.e., new forms of quality circle and team working). But this latter view is difficult to sustain, because it relies on the assumption that these new social and organizational forms are something other than short-term trends.

In addition, the assumption ignores the impact of these methods on social and production relations, particularly in respect to their lack of managerial and social neutrality. In this sense, the ideology of the "management of human resources" becomes an abstraction without relevance to the necessary microsocial antago-nisms in the organization. "Resources" are components of production, "Humans" represent an anthropological abstraction without societal conflict, other than con-flict of human nature. Human resources are thus items of debit or credit as opposed to real living and "recalcitrant" labor whose own interests cannot be assumed a priori.

Employees as Participants in Change?

What is the relationship between compliance and commitment, and what is the part these play in articulating new forms of work organization? To what degree is consensus achieved through the organizational form (teamwork) of the new flexible working arrangements? Murray, Piore and Sabel, and Sayer proffer the view that worker involvement and participation are made possible through tech-nological innovation. Do we need the new forms of work organization to cope with the tough world of the auto industry today (possibly even tougher than in the past)?[13] Are workplace institutions such as teamworking founded on mana-gerial commitment to a new industrial citizenship, or, alternatively, the necessary precondition of attenuated Fordist labor processes? In the words of Tomaney, "Participation can, therefore, be seen as coerced rather than a voluntary consen-sus. Total Quality Control and Quality circles ensnare workers themselves into this system of intensification."[14] Nissan, "Facts Against Fallacies," and Wickens reject the simplistic view of the company's work organization by emphasizing that flexibility does not entail unlimited flexibility. However, both of these sources believe that the development of new cognate skills, which are the result of the new flexibilities (polyvalence) within teams, will engender reskilling.[15]

On the contrary, we argue that upskilling is not an adequate description of the change in work practices being introduced by Nissan. In this respect our argu-ment supports Elger's, that what looks like upskilling is often in reality no more than a process of task enlargement. His conclusions are based on a survey of the literature of U.K. manufacturing.[16] These developments, whether at the level of work organization (teams, *kaizen*, etc.) or the labor process (flexibility), are unlikely to ensure that workers' involvement will be transformed from compli-ance to commitment in the longer term.

In addition, there is a third issue, which would tell us why these two levels of change may require, and indeed may be substantially dependent on, radical transformation in industrial relations. The new industrial regimes are neither an automatic product of technical innovation nor an innovative social environment that could exist without extant processes of subordination in consent. As research on the U.K. and U.S. auto industries points out, new patterns of control and subordination can be developed with or without the presence of unions. In fact, it is the capacity of these new forms to construct new relations in production around existing cultural factors (e.g., union autonomy) that today testifies to the persistence of particular forms of social conflict in the auto industry. Hence an important contribution to this debate misses the point precisely because it is falsely capitalizing on the issue of environmental adaptability of the lean production methods—that is, being capable of acting as agents of local social and economic transformation.[17] It is to the role of trade unions in Nissan (U.K.) that we now turn.

Union Involvement and Participation

Organizational change and innovations are traditionally mediated by representatives of the company and the trade union. Therefore, to be able to begin operations with a raw workforce minus trade union participation represents a great bonus in the development of a corporate ideology. In this respect, the director of personnel of Nissan (U.K.) makes it clear that neither he nor Nissan is opposed to trade unions. This, of course, runs counter to the history of Nissan-union relations in Japan, where he overlooks how Nissan defeated the Japanese autoworkers' union 1953. Not only does this ignore the fact that Japanese workers have been just as much trade unionist in their collectivist identities as their British counterparts, it also allows for a glossing over of the very principle of trade union participation: negotiation of the terms and conditions of employment.

Nissan is not opposed to trade unions unless their autonomy can influence their membership. This autonomy would allow the Amalgamated Electrical and Engineering Union (AEEU) to discuss issues of seniority and mutuality with its membership independently of company interference. It would enable discussions over working practices and work methods to be considered on terms related to employee interest, which are not reducible to those delineated in advance by Nissan. Views on these issues need not be hostile. But the very fact that they are different from Nissan's, or rather, that they do not originate from Nissan, has to be guarded against.

Yet, when we consider the agreement between Nissan and the AEEU, it is clear that the company has little to fear. The agreement was signed prior to recruitment—that is, at no time have employees had any say in deciding which union should represent their interests. The three most significant clauses signing away autonomy in the determination of terms and conditions of work are as follows: "(a) To ensure the fullest use of facilities and manpower, there will be complete flexibility and mobility of employees. (b) It is agreed that changes in technology, processes and practices will be introduced and that such changes will affect both productivity and manning levels. (c) To ensure such flexibility and change, employees will undertake . . . training for all work as required by the Company. All employees will train other employees as required."[18]

The difficulty is that unions pursuing an Anglo-Saxon agenda can challenge company strategies based on the fact that they are leading to uncertainty in the organization and its environment.[19] However, through the ideology of the manufacturing system, including the social organization of the line, the set of ideological imperatives summed up as the "Nissan Way" has for the present blocked this possibility. This is vital to the creation of organizational commitment to the company's injunctions on flexibility, quality, and teamwork.

Despite Nissan's attempt to deny the possible relationship between LPMs and autonomous unions, there are many examples to indicate the contrary. In many instances in the United Kingdom and the United States, it is the unions that have been at the forefront of organizational innovation and change (*inter alia,* the Transport and General Workers' Union at GM and Rover in the United Kingdom, and the UAW at NUMMI in the United States). The sidelining of the AEEU by Nissan is fundamental to maintain control. This is essential so that when the tempo of work gets too hot, it will be difficult to define grievances except in ways sanctioned by the company.

Employee skepticism of the union is pretty clear, and trade unionists ignore it at their peril. Yet, despite the fact that the union plays such an insignificant role at Nissan, as many as 30 percent of employees are now represented by it, an indication, some might argue, of the need felt by a sizable percentage of workers for some kind of trade union, however weak it might be. Employees can hold other union cards. However, the AEEU is the sole representative of union membership under the rules laid down before initial recruitment began. Indeed, these rules show that the union has very few bargaining rights. For instance, the union cannot communicate directly with workers about membership. Interviewees have pointed out that management often makes "suggestions" about the importance of AEEU membership when the plant's low union orientation is pointed to as a sign of the union's compromised position. Illustrating this point is the following letter to employees, which was signed by the deputy managing director and the director of personnel and information systems at Nissan:

Nissan calls on all workers to join the union!

As you well know the level of union membership is lower than originally anticipated—although it is now growing. We enjoy excellent relationships within Nissan and these are greatly assisted by the formal Agreement we have with the AEU which we know is committed to the success of both the Company and the staff. AEU representatives greatly support the Company, particularly in many external forums [sic.]. We genuinely believe that with this joint commitment to success there are considerable advantages to everyone if the membership level increases. Direct benefits to employees include:

1. There may be times when you need representation.
2. The union offers legal representation free of charge.
3. The union can provide a whole range of advice to your Company Council negotiators.

4. It can provide a comprehensive financial package arranged in conjunction with the Midland Bank.
5. The AEU has set up a Nissan branch which means you can have direct control of your affairs.

We attached a membership application form and would ask that you complete this and return it to the Personnel Department who will attend to the formalities. Please remember that the long-term success of the Company, employees and the Union are tied together and we would urge your assistance to make this a three way success.[20]

This letter tells us something about why union density is so low by contrast with density levels for other producers in the same sector (in excess of 90 percent for GM, Ford, and Rover). Because 50 percent of the Company Council is nominated by management, the role of the union is circumscribed by company interests. The Company Council ensures that there is involvement but no power. At the same time, the union obtains formal recognition but is sidelined in terms of any real decisions made in the organization. The AEEU has subordinated itself entirely to the company's view of the world. The company delineates the world of those who work for Nissan, as the director of personnel says: "He who communicates is King!"[21]

The Realities of Lean Production at Nissan in Sunderland

Thus far the objective of this chapter has been to assess the social and political impact and foundation of lean production methods in the light of empirical evidence from one of the largest manufacturing companies in the world. This study of changes in the character of production in an auto firm raises a number of concerns with respect to social organization and control that are outside of our focus here. To be sure, the findings serve to reject the notion of a post-Fordist reconstruction. Further generalization of this case reveals that employee autonomy, upskilling, and knowledge enhancement are not evident according to the scenario envisaged by post-Fordism. The criteria by which any argument concerning the social nature of flexibility and lean production are to be judged should link directly to the question of power and control in the workplace. The post-Fordist thesis assumes the potential for worker empowerment around employee autonomy, upskilling, and knowledge enhancement, derived from new developments in manufacturing.

The evidence from Nissan, however, demonstrates that lean production is more demanding on workers. Job enlargement occurs because skills of manual dexterity are increased largely on a horizontal basis and vertically downward. One example of this is where line workers acquire some material handling jobs. This is a recipe for job intensification.[22] This intensification of effort requires that standard-task time is regarded as flexible on management's terms. In practice, employees are encouraged to push toward reduced time sequences. This has long been recognized as an important feature of the new production arrangements, and as Parker and Slaughter have shown, it is a central objective of *kaizen* or continuous improvement meetings.[23]

Kaizen allows the employee to become responsible for problems in product quality, and the "Neighbor Watch" code (employee peer surveillance) sustains this. "Neighbor Watch" ensures that employees up and down the line check on each other's performance, so ensuring that supervisor-directed discipline is replaced by employee-directed discipline.[24] If problems arise with the quality of someone's work, these are seen to be due to individual failing by the worker concerned—faults have nothing to do, for example, with speedups. In some respects, therefore, we can see this as constituting the groundwork for extra-technical forms of subordination, which operate through company-centered legitimization processes. Consequently, these extra-technical forms of control (i.e., teamwork, *kaizen,* and "Neighbor Watch") provide the basis for a new regime of subordination in which employees participate in their own subordination to the organization.

Conclusions

At the beginning of this chapter we argued that the concept of LPMs was a conceptually more adequate response to the rise of new management strategies in multifarious production and the control of labor associated with it in the late 1980s and 1990s. We also maintained that these variations arise out of the specificity of two overlapping and interdependent factors: (1) region-locale peculiarities and (2) labor-capital specificities. This case study has shown the importance of region-locale peculiarities of globalization, a task that has not been dealt with adequately in the literature. Most studies tend to ignore the impact of this factor.[25] Also, as significant an oversight has been a myopia regarding the salience of labor-capital specificities.[26]

There are, of course, obvious reasons for the dismissal of labor, especially where the analysis is oriented to the prescription of strategic management goals in which labor needs to lose its corporate autonomy. In the headlong rush toward the guiding light of the new global panacea for stagnation and decline, it is hardly surprising if management gurus view the richness and variety of social relations as tiresome obstacles to progress. It is strange indeed that the advocates of the LPMs can distill what is seen to be the essence of the system's success as if these were not dependent on local, not to say national, specificities. Yet it is precisely these variations in practice that mold the character of LPM adaptations. And since among these local forces for adaptation is labor, it is hardly surprising that the underlying difficulty in imposing a one-dimensional view of LPMs becomes so elusive for their advocates. Unless and until labor is brought into the equation, the fundamental point about LPMs will be missed, the fundamental point being the very context of labor-management relations and contradictions that all management strategies seek to suppress and control. What happens to employer power and control in the work organization and in the labor process? Who benefits from the new system, in what ways, and by what criteria are losses to be judged?

To begin with, we will have to look afresh at the old concerns of labor, including union independence, control of the labor process (along with the recognition of gender, race, and ethnicity), and the significance of local and national power brokers in the orientation and operation of LPMs. A proper understanding of these will be vital if labor is to begin to cast its own spells for change.

Employee autonomy, upskilling, and knowledge enhancement are important elements to be considered in managerial strategies and the way they link to new manufacturing techniques. Subordination at work enhanced by the particular form of association constitutes not employee empowerment, but rather enhancement of employer power and control. As a result, given the commitment by many workers to trade unionism, the character of union participation in the development of LPMs is crucial in understanding their existence. Labor's role is problematical because the proponents of LPMs instinctively practice a variety of labor management strategies whose common thread is to reduce or exclude the role of independent unions. All of these are consistent with the social and political foundations of LPMs, and they take several forms: (1) At Nissan in Sunderland the single-union recognition provides representation without influence, reflected in the low union membership. Although the AEEU is marginalized, the fact that a union exists indicates the company's sensitivity to a local history of prominent laborism in the mass industries. (2) By contrast, Honda (U.K.) in Swindon has been able to recruit its workforce without union recognition. This highlights Honda's confidence in being able to implement lean methods of production in an area characterized by traditionally high levels of union participation. (3) At NUMMI Fremont, the closure of the former GM plant and the joint venture with Toyota did not prevent the UAW from playing a central role in all subsequent aspects of work conditions and plant organization. (4) In the upper southern states of the United States, such as Kentucky and Tennessee, Toyota and Nissan seized the opportunity, provided by local employment conditions, to set up union-free plants.

We need to begin to draw the lessons of these variations for a new set of labor movement strategies. As we argued at the outset of this chapter, transformations in the auto industry are derived from major management initiatives that all have common global features but vary in their local specificity. LPMs are not one-dimensional technical devices without variation in responses from locale to locale and from country to country. Thus we need to elicit a positive balance sheet of those instances where labor has been able to regroup and strengthen. The outcome of this will involve transforming *management's* agenda into an *employee-* and *labor-* oriented agenda.

Notes

1. See J. Womack et al., *The Machine That Changed the World* (New York: Rawson Associates, 1990); and P. Garrahan and P. Stewart, *The Nissan Enigma: Flexibility at Work in a Local Economy* (London: Mansell, 1992).

2. P. Dickens, *Global Shift* (London: Paul Chapman, 1992).

3. See J. Fucini and S. Fucini, *Working for the Japanese: Inside Mazda's American Auto Plant* (New York: The Free Press, 1990); and E.J. Yanarella and W.C. Green, eds., *The Politics of Industrial Recruitment: Japanese Automobile Investment and Economic Development in the American States* (London: Greenwood Press, 1990).

4. N. Oliver and B. Wilkinson, *The Japanization of British Industry: New Developments in the 1990s,* 2d ed. (London: Basil Blackwell, 1992).

5. R. Florida and M. Kenney, "Transplanted Organizations: The Transfer of Japanese Industrial Organization to the U.S.," *American Sociological Review* 56 (June 1991): 381–98.

6. P. Stewart, P. Garrahan, and S. Crowther, eds., *Restructuring for Economic Flexibility* (Avebury/Gower, 1990).

7. P. Fairbrother and J. Waddington, "The Politics of Trade Unionism: Evidence, Policy, and Theory," *Capital and Class* 41 (Summer 1990): 15–57.

8. P. Garrahan and P. Stewart, "Nothing New About Nissan," in C. Law, ed., *Restructuring the Auto Industry* (London: Routledge, 1991), 143–55.

9. See P. Garrahan and P. Stewart, "Management Control and a New Regime of Subordination," in N. Gilbert, R. Burrows, and A. Pollert, eds., *Fordism and Flexibility* (London: Macmillan, 1992); and P. Wickens, *The Road to Nissan* (London: Macmillan, 1987).

10. Stewart, Garrahan, and Crowther, *Restructuring for Economic Flexibility.*

11. F. Robinson and K. Shaw, "Urban Regeneration and Community Involvement," *Local Economy* (May 1991).

12. See A. Amin and J. Tomaney, "Illusions of Prosperity," in P. Fasenfest and P. Meyer, eds., *The Politics of Local Economic Policy Formation* (London: Macmillan, forthcoming); F. Robinson, "The Great North?" (Newcastle, Eng.: Center for Urban and Regional Development Studies, Newcastle University, 1990); and I. Smith and I. Stone, "Foreign Investment in the North," *Northern Economic Review* 18 (1989).

13. See R. Murray, "Life After Henry Ford," *Marxism Today* (October 1988); M.J. Piore and C. Sabel, *The Second Industrial Divide* (New York: Basic Books, 1984); and A. Sayer, "New Developments in Manufacturing: The Just in Time System," *Capital and Class* 30 (1985).

14. J. Tomaney, "The Reality of Workplace Flexibility," *Capital and Class* 40 (1990).

15. "Information Pack," Nissan Motor Manufacturing U.K. Ltd. (1988); Wickens, *The Road to Nissan.*

16. T. Elger, "Technical Innovation and Work Reorganization in British Manufacturing in the 1980s: Continuity, Intensification, or Transformation?" *Work, Employment, and Society* (Special Issue 1990): 67–101.

17. On this issue see Florida and Kenney, "Transplanted Organizations"; S. Crowther and P. Garrahan, "Corporate Power and the Local Economy," *Industrial Relations Journal* 19 (1988): 51–59; and Garrahan and Stewart, *The Nissan Enigma.*

18. Nissan/AEU agreement (1986).

19. R. Hyman, *The Political Economy of Industrial Relations: Theory and Practice in a Cold Climate* (London: Macmillan, 1989).

20. Nissan letter to employees (April 1989). The letter refers to the AEEU as the

AEU. In 1992 the Electrical, Electronic, Telecommunication, and Plumbing Union (EETPU) merged with the AEU to form the AEEU.

21. Wickens, *The Road to Nissan.*

22. Elger, "Technical Innovation"; A. Pollert, "Dismantling Flexibility," *Capital and Class* (1988).

23. M. Parker and J. Slaughter, *Choosing Sides: Unions and the Team Concept* (London: Labour Notes/South End Press, 1988).

24. P. Garrahan and P. Stewart, "Post-Fordism, Japanization, and the Local Economy" (Sheffield, Eng.: paper presented to the CSE conference, Sheffield Polytechnic, 1989).

25. The recent work of Florida and Kenney, "Transplanted Organizations," with its emphasis on the way organizations shape their environment, is beginning to address this absence in the U.S. literature.

26. Womack et al., *The Machine That Changed the World.*

9

The Future Is Already Here: Deskilling of Work in the "Office of the Future"

Vernon Mogensen

Introduction

The introduction of the desktop computer, or video display terminal (VDT), during the 1970s and 1980s was the key technological development that made the computerized "office of the future" a reality. Corporate users, computer manufacturers, and the media proclaimed that the VDT would solve the crisis of office productivity; liberate workers from boring, repetitive work; and create new career opportunities. "New gadgetry, better jobs, less monotony—all are part of the office of the future," proclaimed *U.S. News & World Report* in 1978.[1] According to IBM's 1987 annual report, "Centralizing and automating [VDT] network operations help eliminate routine operator tasks and errors, freeing skilled operators and programmers for more productive tasks."[2] A report on office automation by Adia Personnel Services, the world's second-largest provider of contingent (part-time and temporary) office workers, even suggested that the VDT could become a tool for worker empowerment:

> Today's machines require much more human input and are capable of much more than merely performing a repetitive task. The person at the keyboard can input data, control, interpret and create patterns. If knowledge is power, then today's office workers have the ability to shape a very powerful system. And, the acquired ability to use these machines can lead to changes in the balance of power within an organization.[3]

Today, the computerized office is a ubiquitous reality. At least 25 million computer terminals, and millions of personal computers, are being used by approximately 50 million American workers, mostly in white-collar occupations.[4]

However, the introduction of the VDT to the office work process has neither freed most clerical workers from repetitive tasks nor given them new career opportunities. The VDT has helped many companies increase productivity, but the computerized office has created a new crisis—the deskilling of work and the creation of occupational safety and health hazards virtually unknown in the office. These include vision problems, high levels of stress, cumulative trauma disorders (or repetitive strain injuries), skin rashes, angina, and reproductive problems such as infertility, birth defects, stillbirths, and higher-than-normal incidences of miscarriages.

In many respects, the "office of the future" resembles the factory of the past. The introduction of the VDT has enabled managers to apply Taylorist concepts of efficiency—long a part of industrial production—to routinize the relatively inefficient methods of office work. The new office technology has been used by management to lessen its dependence on workers by incorporating what they know into computerized systems, not to liberate the worker from drudgery— although it may do that in some cases, especially where work patterns resist routinization. In many clerical operations, this objective has been achieved to the point that full-time employees have been made redundant and have been replaced by contingent workers. The computerized office has given managers new power to monitor workers' production: automatically counting keystrokes, recording work and time quotas, and collecting work quality (i.e., percentage of errors) information, all of which can be used to pit workers against each other and speed up the work process. VDT-based automation has created job loss, and has accentuated the gap between skilled and unskilled workers in the workforce. Finally, capital's ability to electronically shift work to cheaper and less organized labor markets undermines the worker's ability to organize, fight for safety and health protection, and maintain adequate wage and benefit levels.

The Crisis of Office Productivity

The United States has undergone a long-term structural shift during the twentieth century, from an industrial to an information-based economy (see Table 9.1). Eighty-nine percent of the 19 million new jobs created during the 1970s were in white-collar, information-based industries.[5] In 1993, white-collar workers outnumbered their blue-collar counterparts by more than a two-to-one ratio.

By the 1960s, existing office machines were incapable of keeping pace with the rapidly increasing volume of paperwork being produced by the emerging information economy. The pressure on business to resolve this problem was made more acute by the rapid growth of office expenses, which accounted for as much as 40 to 50 percent of all business costs by the early 1980s.[6] An advertorial in *Fortune* stated capital's problem succinctly: "The office [is] the jugular of the low productivity problem that faces business today."[7] To further complicate matters, investment was focused on the automation of factory work. Automation investment figures show that U.S. businesses spent an average of

Table 9.1

The Rise of the Postindustrial Workforce

Sector	1900 (%)	1940 (%)	1980 (%)	1993 (%)
White-collar	17.6	31.1	52.2	57.9
Blue-collar	35.8	39.8	31.7	25.5
Service	9.1	11.7	13.3	13.8
Agriculture	37.5	17.4	2.8	2.8

Sources: For 1990, 1940, and 1980, see OTA, *Automation of America's Offices*, 3. Percentages for 1993 calculated by the author from Department of Labor, Bureau of Labor Statistics (BLS), *Employment and Earnings* (January 1994), 203.

Note: This table uses the four occupational sectors as defined by the BLS: white-collar sector: "managerial and professional speciality" and "technical, sales,, and administrative support"; blue-collar sector: precision production, craft, and repair," and "operators, fabricators, and laborers"; service sector: "service occupations"; and agricultural sector: "farming, forestry, and fishing."

$12.50 per factory worker for each $1.00 invested per office worker in 1980. While factory productivity increased 85 percent during the 1970s, the small gain in office productivity (only 4 percent) was overshadowed by the doubling of operating costs.[8]

The introduction of the VDT during the early 1970s marked a turning point in capital's capability to control and rationalize the office work process along the lines of factory work. As IBM put it, computer-based automation would bring "manufacturing and production lines into the office" by having clerical "work divided [and] specialization introduced."[9] Futurist John Naisbitt was also enthusiastic about the industrialization of information production:

> We now mass-produce information the way we used to mass-produce cars. In the information society, we have systematized the production of knowledge and amplified our brain power. To use an industrial metaphor, we now mass-produce knowledge and this knowledge is the driving force of our economy.[10]

Corporate America's goal of automating the office along industrial lines is clearly illustrated by an influential *Harvard Business Review* article by Richard J. Matteis, a senior vice president at Citibank. He wrote that Citibank, like many of its labor-intensive competitors in the banking, finance, and insurance industries, was faced with an overwhelming paperwork crisis in the 1960s and early 1970s. Labor accounted for 70 percent of Citibank's costs, computer-related expenditures amounted to only 10 percent, and the remainder was due to "other expenditures." Matteis said Citibank's solution to the paperwork crisis was "to flip the ratio entirely . . . until labor and other operations costs constituted only 30 percent, while [computer] hardware and software made up the rest." He acknowledged that the "management program of controls, forecasting, and accountability" were "borrowed from production management." Even the idea for the development of VDT-based computer technology was inspired by the industrial concept of manufacturing. "In banking," he declared, "the equivalent of the machine tool is the computer."[11]

Business use of VDTs to automate office work has put many secretaries and clerical workers out of work. Cost-conscious corporations have even used VDTs to streamline the management hierarchy, whose salaries and benefits account for up to 80 percent of the typical office payroll.[12] But the biggest impact in terms of job loss and deskilling has been, and will continue to be, on clerical workers, the single largest occupational group in the labor force. The Office of Technology Assessment (OTA) projects that the "most likely outcome" of increased office automation is "slowing growth in the number of office jobs, and eventually, *an absolute reduction in the number of jobs in offices* from some peak in the 1990s."[13]

Taylorism Comes to the Office

Efforts by office managers to get a grip on the expanding volume of paperwork date back to the turn of the century. William H. Leffingwell, a management consultant and president of the National Office Management Association, pioneered the standardization of the office work process. Impressed by Frederick W. Taylor's principles of "scientific management," which broke down industrial work to its simplest parts and redesigned it in a more mechanical manner, Leffingwell and his followers sought to do the same in the office. Leffingwell applied Taylor's system of time and motion studies to eliminate superfluous steps and standardize tasks. Preaching "simplification" of work, he regarded no task as too insignificant for scrutiny, not even the "correct" method for opening an envelope and removing its contents, or the proper amount of time it should take a worker to cut a piece of paper. Dr. Harlow S. Person, the managing director of the Taylor Society, summed up this approach as follows: "The mental attitude of scientific management . . . must govern the management of clerical as well as of processing operations; in fact, desk activities *are* processing operations as surely as are activities at machine and bench."[14]

From capital's standpoint, one of Taylorism's most important benefits was that standardized production procedures increased its command over the work process. As Leffingwell made clear: "Effective management implies control. The terms are in a sense interchangeable, as management without control is not conceivable." Implying that too much was left to workers' discretion in the nonscientifically managed office, Leffingwell stated that the purpose of scientific management "is that the balance shall be very much in favor of the manager, and not against him."[15]

As a corporate ideal, Leffingwell's work had an important impact on business administration, but the problem of routinizing office work continued to bedevil office managers. The mechanization of the office during the 1920s was the development that permitted managers to start emulating the industrial work process.[16] Writing at mid-century C. Wright Mills observed the effects of Leffingwell's legacy in what he referred to as the "managerial demiurge":

> The introduction of office machinery and sales devices has been mechanizing the office. . . . Since the twenties it has increased the division of white-collar labor, recomposed personnel, and lowered skill levels. Routine operations in minutely subdivided organizations have replaced the bustling interest of work in well-known groups. Even on managerial and professional levels, the growth of rational bureaucracies has made work more like factory production. The managerial demiurge is constantly furthering all these trends: mechanization, more minute division of labor, the use of less skilled and less expensive workers.[17]

Harry Braverman remarked on the maturation of the deskilling trend in the office work process from his vantage point in the early 1970s. He noted that the mechanization of clerical work made it possible for managers to train clerical workers more quickly, thereby making them more interchangeable and expendable:

> The recording of everything in mechanical form, and the movement of everything in a mechanical way, is thus the ideal of the office manager. But this conversion of the office flow into a high-speed industrial process requires the conversion of the great mass of office workers into more or less helpless attendants of that process.[18]

Women in the "Office of the Future"

Most VDT workers in the "office of the future" are women, and as with the typewriter operators of the past, have little chance for job enrichment or career advancement. The key, but disadvantaged, role that women play in the white-collar workforce is confirmed by Bureau of Labor Statistics (BLS) data for 1993—71.3 percent of all women workers are employed in the white-collar sector, where they constitute a majority (56.4 percent) of the workforce. But the post-industrial economy perpetuates the gender-based, two-tier employment pattern, with women filling most of the lower-paid positions. The single largest group of working women (26.8 percent) is concentrated in clerical occupations. Women office workers earn only $0.76 for each $1.00 a male coworker makes, and since women constitute 80 percent of the clerical workforce, employers' labor costs are kept artificially low. These trends are expected to continue as the number of women entering the workforce increases.[19]

A good example of sex-typing of women's work is provided by the positions of typist and secretary, which were considered to be prestigious positions held by men until the 1880s. But as the typewriter came into widespread use, these positions were downgraded into low-paying, dead-end jobs, filled by women. By 1910 one-third of the 2 million typewriters in use were operated by women, and by 1930 the transition was virtually complete with 95.6 percent of all typing and stenography jobs being performed by women.[20]

This structural pattern of women's employment is being continued in the "office of the future." Women are the production workers of the new information age economy. They account for 90 percent of all VDT workers. A 1985 poll conducted for Honeywell, Inc., revealed that women were twice as likely as men to be assigned to jobs that require VDT work for more than half the workday.[21] The extent to which women's work, low pay, and VDT work are intertwined is shown in Table 9.2.

The VDT-using occupations shown in Table 9.2 reveal the structural bias of office work. First, all the occupations where women predominate have median annual earnings well below the 1993 national average of $24,076.[22] Conversely, women represent a minority of workers in the highest-paying occupation: editors and reporters. Second, it illustrates the structural pervasiveness of the practice of pay inequity. Despite the fact that women constitute the overwhelming majority of workers in all but one of these occupations, they were paid less than men in 1993.[23] Third, with the exception of editors and reporters, all these jobs were low-status, highly automated, and involved routinized work procedures that provided little room for employee creativity or variation. For example, some directory assistance telephone operators are expected to take no more than twenty-four seconds per call. At this rate, they may handle as many as twelve hundred calls a day. This involves a continuous process of repetitive motions at the VDT which creates physiological stress and can lead to the development of painful cumulative trauma disorders.[24]

Ironically, the deskilling of much of white-collar work is occurring at a time when more Americans are going to college to increase their occupational skills. The U.S. Department of Labor has found that "hundreds of thousands of jobs," including secretarial, book-keeping, clerical, data, and word processing positions, "once creditably performed without a college degree, are going to college graduates as employers take advantage of an oversupply of them."[25] This situation has created a seller's market that helps business keep its labor costs low.

Safety and Health Hazards in the "Office of the Future"

The reorganization of office work to meet the capabilities of the VDT has created stressful working conditions. With much of the creativity and variety transferred to the computerized system, the worker is left to perform repetitious, simplified tasks, which lead to heightened levels of stress on the job. As with the assembly line, the computerization of office work without regard for the human factor has created new job hazards. According to the National Institute of Occupational Safety and Health (NIOSH):

Table 9.2

Selected Occupations Where VDTs Are in Widespread Use (1993)

Occupation	Number (000)	% of women's earnings	Median annual pay, women ($)	Men (%)
Data entry keyers	502	82.3	17,888	96.1
Editors and reporters	208	46.2	29,848	73.9
Financial records clerks	1,546	88.7	19,760	82.4
General office clerks	491	82.7	18,200	96.9
Records processing clerks*	624	81.7	19,552	82.0
Secretaries	2,881	99.0	20,072	n/a
Telephone operators	167	88.6	20,072	n/a
Transportation ticket and reservation agents	172	71.5	21,684	n/a

Source: BLS, *Employment and Earnings*, 244–45; percentages calculated by the author.
*Includes order, personnel, library, file, and records clerks.
n/a= men's earnings not available.

This is a serious concern since the persons who design systems such as these, and thereby the work activities of VDT operators, are typically computer scientists and systems analysts who have no concept of the human element in such a work process. *This leads to a dehumanization of the work activity that is similar to that produced by the introduction of assembly lines in manufacturing industries.* In fact, such offices become *"paper factories"* with clerical assembly lines in which the work content is simplified to increase "thru-put" and capitalize on computer capabilities. This leads to jobs that produce boredom and job dissatisfaction. As such, the machinery becomes a source of misery rather than a helpful tool as it is for the professionals using the VDTs.[26]

Finding that the stress levels of clerical workers using VDTs were higher than those of either clerical workers not using VDTs or professionals using VDTs, NIOSH concluded that "The comparison of the working conditions for the various groups demonstrates that those working conditions that led to the stress problems reported by the clerical VDT operators are not entirely related to the VDT use, *but are also related to the entire work system that goes along with using VDTs.*" Stress due to VDT work has become so prevalent in the computerized office that a new term, "technostress," was coined to describe it.[27]

NIOSH's findings have been substantiated by business surveys of employee attitudes toward the new office technology. A survey of two thousand secretaries by Minolta Corporation found that 50 percent were frustrated by a lack of responsibility on the job, and 40 percent felt that they were overqualified for the job.[28] Kelly Services, the nation's largest supplier of temporary secretarial and office workers, polled 504 corporate secretaries and found that level of education also influences stress. Those secretaries with the highest education reported the least amount of job satisfaction and were the least capable of preventing work-related stress from affecting their personal lives.[29]

The health hazards faced by VDT workers fall into two categories: those that are ergonomic-related problems, and those thought to be related to the non-ionizing radiation emitted by the VDTs flyback transformer. Ergonomic problems include eye strain; blurred vision (the most commonly cited complaint among VDT workers) due to bright lighting, which creates screen glare; increased levels of stress (higher than those experienced by air traffic controllers in one NIOSH study), which contribute to heart attacks and nervous breakdowns; and musculo-skeletal pains known as cumulative trauma disorders (repetitive strain injuries), which accounted for 60 percent of all reported VDT-related injuries and illnesses in 1991. Hazards thought to be associated with the non-ionizing radiation include skin rashes, angina, and reproductive problems such as infertility, birth defects, stillbirths, and higher-than-normal incidences of miscarriages. Preliminary studies in Europe show that pulsed, 60 Hz, extremely low-frequency fields—like those emitted by VDTs—can interfere with the immune system's defenses, altering cell structure and promoting leukemia, lymphoma, and brain cancer.[30]

Many of these problems can be alleviated by redesigning the workplace using ergonomic knowledge. Unlike the Taylorist/Leffingwell system, which adapts the worker to the requirements of the technology, ergonomics is the science of adapting the workplace to the needs of the worker. Lighting levels can be lowered and screens used to reduce glare, while detachable and split keyboards, and adjustable desks and chairs permit workers to adapt each workspace to individual comfort needs. Workers should be given vision tests before commencing VDT work and periodically thereafter. In addition, jobs need to be restructured to give workers periodic rest breaks—every two hours, or after one hour if the pace is intense—and alternative non-VDT work that utilizes employees' creative abilities. These recommendations were made by NIOSH and provide a good starting point for collective bargaining and organizing efforts.[31]

Under pressure from labor, NIOSH has conducted some investigations into the ergonomic problems, but computer manufacturers and corporate users of VDTs have utilized their influence to block federal studies of the non-ionizing radiation problem. Likewise, the Occupational Safety and Health Administration (OSHA) has been constrained from promulgating protective standards for VDT workers by the last three administrations' higher priority of maintaining the confidence of the industry that is the engine of the post-industrial economy. After years of delay, OSHA recently announced the release of a draft regulation on repetitive strain injuries. However, in the present deregulatory climate, it may be years before a final regulation is promulgated, if at all.[32]

VDT Work in the Two-Tier Post-industrial Economy

Corporations have used the VDT to further institutionalize and widen the gap between the two tiers of the office workforce. For some, such as executive secretaries, time saved by automation has been filled with more rewarding tasks, but for most it has meant heavier workloads. Substantiating this trend was the Louis Harris survey of office workers that found that, despite the introduction of VDTs, the percentage of office workers who felt they were overworked rose from 42 percent to 49 percent between 1978 and 1989. It also reported that the percentage of office workers who used VDTs for more than five hours a day jumped from 25 percent in 1988 to 32 percent in 1989.[33] Additional evidence that workloads have increased came from the Data Entry Management Association (DEMA), which reported that the average VDT operator made 11,934 keystrokes per hour in 1988, a jump of almost 500 keystrokes from the year before.[34] These findings contradict the claim that VDTs free office workers to do more meaningful work.

VDT-based office automation has not resulted in new opportunities for advancement to management positions for office workers. IBM said that secretaries and clerical employees would have "their job status raised" as a result of the computerization of office work.[35] But after more than a decade of office automation, secretarial and clerical earnings still lag behind (see Table 9.2). The Louis Harris survey also belies IBM's claims. It found that those who use VDTs for more than five hours a day

> tend to be less educated than office workers overall (37% are college graduates compared with 46% overall). They are more likely than average to be women (61% to 53%), and show distinctly lower levels of personal income (73% report their own income as falling in the $35,000-or-less category, compared with 62% of office workers overall in this income group).[36]

Nor did IBM's rosy prognostication prove to be true for data entry workers. John Maxwell Hamilton, a World Bank official, explains why: "In the data-entry business, one of the essential ingredients is a dependable supply of low-wage workers."[37] The result of this corporate policy, says Faye Duchin, director of New York University's Institute for Economic Analysis, is that "It remains a dead-end job where the worker is even more specialized" than before the arrival of the computer.[38]

The Minolta survey of secretaries found that two-thirds doubted that they stood a fair chance of career advancement and commensurate salary increases. The Kelly Services survey of corporate secretaries revealed that there was very little room for career advancement to management positions. "When asked what new positions or careers open up as a result of word processing, very few name positions which could be considered middle level management or higher," the

Kelly survey reported. "When asked to identify new decision-making responsibilities that they see as a result of word processing, most name duties which are essentially the same as the traditional tasks done before the introduction of automated equipment," it added.[39]

The Kelly survey also found that secretaries under twenty-five suffered "more stress and a low level of job satisfaction" and were "inclined to find meeting deadlines and being overworked to be very stressful." Overall, it reported, "Stress is a very real problem for many secretaries, as indicated by the large number (80 percent) who claim that their job is stressful." The high levels of occupational stress suffered by secretaries and clerical workers is due in large part to the fact that VDTs have not lessened their work burdens as office automation advocates expected. The Kelly survey found that increasing numbers of secretaries spent more time tied to their VDTs; 58 percent spent more than half their time using VDTs during any given workweek; 40 percent of the under-twenty-five secretaries were using their VDTs for 70 percent of the day, and 30 percent said that "all" the secretaries did word processing. Most agreed "that word processing equipment is in use for a large portion of each day."[40]

VDT use has also altered the secretarial work pattern. Managers can either dictate messages via the telephone or the VDT's electronic mail network to the word processing pool. Now most corporate secretaries work for three to as many as thirteen superiors. Moreover, the job requirements of secretaries who use VDTs have been increased without commensurate pay raises. They are now expected to know an increasing variety of software programs, but many secretaries whose jobs "have been upgraded" are not rewarded with pay raises.[41] The Kelly report found that while 88 percent believed that their new computer skills would merit pay increases, only 30 percent had actually received one as a result. Moreover, the median annual earnings for secretaries in 1993 was only $20,072, $4,000 below the median for all full-time workers. Perhaps the most telling commentary on being a secretary in the "office of the future" was that 55 percent of those who were polled in the Kelly survey would not recommend the job to their daughters.[42]

Using VDTs to Make Full-Time Office Workers Expendable

By hiring more contingent workers and by parceling out tasks to those working at home and abroad, corporations are lessening their dependence on permanent employees. VDT-based automation has deskilled office work to the point that employers can easily replace their full-time employees with contingent workers. This development has made it possible for management to use office personnel as low-cost, interchangeable parts for which they have only the minimum responsibility. As the OTA put it: "When back-office work (the routine processing of standardized data or text) is rationalized and deskilled, investment in training is minimal, and the value of experience and continuity is also minimal."[43]

The permanent labor bill (salary and benefits) is the single largest component in the cost of doing business for information industries. The automating ability of VDTs, coupled with slow economic growth, have prompted the corporate trend toward "lean staffing" in an effort to maintain profit margins. "Even if temporary and contract workers receive higher wages than permanent employees doing the same work," though OTA noted that this is not the case for "lower level clerical workers," they "are usually a bargain for the employer . . . because [he or she] pays only for actual productive work hours." In other words, in a market environment, VDT-based office automation enables employers to avoid paying for such overhead items as Social Security, workers' compensation, medical and dental benefits, or pension plans. These economic advantages resulted in 20 percent annual growth rates for the temporary service business during the mid- to later 1980s, with 60 percent of its business coming from clerical work.[44] It is likely that employers will continue to hire women, who constitute 82.1 percent of the nation's half million part-time clerical workers and 75 percent of temporary workers, to fill the vast majority of these low-wage, dead-end jobs.[45] If corporate reliance on contingent employees continues to increase, it is likely to have a dampening effect on efforts to close the wage and career advancement opportunity gap between men and women.

Computer networks linking VDTs across the country and around the world have enabled managers to reinvent and expand the office's locale. Employers such as Blue Cross/Blue Shield, Control Data Corporation, Mountain Bell, and the State of California are farming out data entry tasks to part-time workers in pilot projects. Forty-five thousand workers, or 25 percent of all clerical home-workers, were estimated to be telecommuting in 1986. If telecommuting's potential is realized, millions of workers could become homeworkers in the next ten to twenty years.[46] Employers tout the advantage of working at home: the time and money saved by not having to commute, and the convenience and flexibility of working at home. Mothers are told that they can be both home-maker and homeworker. But homework also saves the employer considerable office expenses—since many of these employees are part-timers, they do not qualify for benefit packages such as health and dental care and pension plans— and relieves them from any day-care responsibilities. Moreover, many of these telecommuters must lease their terminals from their employer and take personal responsibility for any health hazards that might arise. Homework also makes labor organizing efforts that much more difficult, if not impossible.[47]

The Globalization of Office Work

VDTs are giving corporations a truly global reach. With the aide of satellite signals, employers are now beaming work to back offices in the Caribbean, Ireland, India, Hong Kong, South Korea, Taiwan, China, and Singapore. At least forty companies involved in banking, insurance, publishing, and transportation in the United States, Japan, and the United Kingdom are engaged in the practice.[48] Companies such as Kansas City, Missouri–based Saztec International, Inc., act as service bureaus for corporate clients by electronically shipping their data entry work to both home and offshore workers. Wages as low as 10 percent of the U.S. rate make it far cheaper for American employers to have two data processors do the same job overseas to catch mistakes than to do the work in the United States with one worker. Moreover, there are no unions to push wage rates up or to protest against poor working conditions.[49]

The offshore office, just like its onshore counterpart, is modeled on the industrial work pattern. As the *New York Times* declared, the "New technology lets services follow the [global] route taken by manufacturing."[50] In business parlance the process of exporting work to an offshore office is referred to as "office sharing." From management's perspective it represents the best of both worlds. Adapted from the industrial practice of "production sharing," "office sharing" combines, in the words of Kevin P. Power, a Washington-based international business consultant, "the higher labor skills and technology available in the developed countries for the manufacture of materials and components with lower-cost labor available in developing countries for processing and assembly operations to produce finished goods for the market." Writing in the *Wall Street Journal,* he emphasized the advantages to U.S. corporations faced with shifting competition in exporting work to low-wage countries: "Application of the office sharing concept in developing countries can revitalize companies in banking, insurance, publishing and other industries facing rising operating costs and increasing competition." Power argues that "The application of office sharing to these economies can provide employment within a relatively short period of time, diversifying the skills of the labor force and familiarizing it with computer technology."[51]

But, as the following examples show, "employment within a relatively short period of time" is made possible only by virtue of the fact that word and data processing jobs are deskilled occupations, not the sophisticated programming jobs that would truly familiarize the offshore labor force "with computer technology." In the early 1980s, Satellite Data Corporation set up back office operations in Barbados to take advantage of its cheap and plentiful labor supply. Based on an interview with Satellite Data's chairman, George R. Simpson, *Business Week* reported that "The average pay for Caribbean data-entry personnel is about $1.50 an hour . . . compared with up to $9 an hour in New York. This low-cost labor will more than offset the $10,000 monthly charge for the satellite channel, he says, and allow him to realize a 50 percent after-tax profit—three times the domestic industry average." Simpson was so ecstatic about the low labor bill and high profit margins that he exclaimed, "We can do the work in Barbados . . . for less than it costs in New York to pay for floor space."[52]

In 1983, American Airlines moved its ticket processing jobs from Tulsa, Oklahoma, to Barbados. It found that the same work could be performed in

Barbados by non-union women for one-third the pay of U.S. workers, and that the government was willing to include generous tax incentives to ensure the move. "With technology where it is now," a corporate official explained, "we had no reason to keep this operation in America."[53] The new subsidiary, AMR Caribbean Data Services, soon branched out to do work for insurance and medical companies. One of the reasons for AMR Caribbean's success at attracting outside business was their policy of keeping clients' names confidential. As one of its executives explained: "If you were an insurance company and were firing data-entry people in the States, would you want anyone to know you were hiring them in the Caribbean?"[54]

Power concluded with the opinion that "Office sharing holds the potential to be a powerful development tool in bridging the technological gap that exists between industrialized and developing nations." But the more likely prospect of the globalization of work is the strengthening of corporate domination over Third World workers.[55] The ability to disperse computer-based work beyond local and national borders via satellite is an enormous aid to multinational corporations in their efforts to find the cheapest labor markets and foil union organizing attempts.

Controlling Workers through Computer Monitoring

Sophisticated computer technology gives employers the power to monitor their employees' behavior and productivity. The systematic use of employee monitoring techniques has been a factor in the office since William H. Leffingwell adapted Frederick Taylor's system of work measurement to clerical work at the turn of the century. What is significant about the VDT is that it permits employee monitoring and work measurement on a scale unheard of before the age of computer technology. As William R. McAlister, vice president of Xytec Corporation, a manufacturer of computer monitoring devices, put it, they are "much more thorough 'than [the results] that used to be gotten by some guy with a clipboard jotting things down.' "[56]

The spread of VDTs in the workplace and the increasing availability of cheaper and more sophisticated computer technology have made employee monitoring a pervasive phenomenon. Estimates indicate that 4 million to 10 million of the then 15 million VDT workers were being monitored in 1987. At this rate, 27 to 67 percent of the VDT workforce was being monitored.[57] Among the many companies monitoring their employees are Blue Cross/Blue Shield, Equitable Life Assurance, MCI Telecommunications, NYNEX, the *New York Times,* and the *Washington Post.*

Basically, the process of computer monitoring works as follows. Specially programmed computer systems count the keystrokes each VDT operator makes, including the number of mistakes, time spent per assignment, and the amount of idle time between tasks. VDT operators are expected to keep pace with the fastest 10 percent in the office. Employee productivity figures are posted at the end of each week on a bulletin board as a means of peer pressure to induce the slower operators to work faster. Those who can't are warned, exhorted to work faster, and are docked a percentage of their pay. Many VDT operators are pieceworkers whose pay is directly linked to their productivity. This has the effect of disciplining workers and speeding up the work, just as the assembly line does in the factory. "In the worst sites, centralized [word processing] . . . is designed as an industrial assembly line, emphasizing line counts and time spent on line."[58] Nine to 5: The National Association of Working Women, reports that VDT workers are given more work to do per day than their counterparts in non-automated offices.[59]

In many offices VDT operators are not allowed to take breaks without management's permission. When they are permitted to go, the computer tells them how much time an employee took. Managers can stimulate workers, with subliminal messages to "work faster" to their less productive operators, or "I love my job" to those who dislike their work.[60] Computer programs can also monitor employees' telephone conversations for key words and phrases that indicate signs of union or political activities, drugs, or personal problems. Directory assistance operators and airline reservation agents are among those who are monitored to ensure that they don't spend more than the allotted time with each caller.[61]

Professionals are also being monitored, a sign that the extension of management's control of the workplace is not limited to word and data operators. According to the OTA's report, *The Electronic Supervisor,* management's monitoring of VDT work

> is increasingly being directed to higher level, more skilled technical, professional, and managerial positions. Even the most complex work has its routine elements, and given sufficient analysis, those elements can be identified, grouped together, and counted. The jobs of commodities broker, computer programmer, and bank loan officer . . . could lend themselves to monitoring.[62]

The effect of the automation and monitoring of many professional tasks is to level out the work hierarchy, making the job characteristics of many professional groups less distinct from those of clerical workers.

Many corporate managers maintain that monitoring gives them more data on employees from which they can make better-informed decisions on meeting production quotas. Managers also say that the data collected on an employee's work and personal life help them determine if each person is right for the job and guards against theft of corporate services. The Equitable Life Assurance Society goes so far as to claim that "workers like the objectivity" of computer monitoring, and maintain that "any stress" they feel "is self-imposed."[63] But the information that can be collected provides management with a powerful tool for controlling workers. The American Civil Liberties Union reports that employers have subjectively used and distorted data to harass employees, especially those engaged in union activity and those with alternative lifestyles.[64]

Employers have attempted to redefine what the monitoring debate is about by arguing that the issue is productivity, not invasion of privacy. Knowing that the power to define terms determines how issues are debated, they prefer euphemisms such as "work measurement" for the more onerous-sounding "computer monitoring," "incentives" for "piecework," and "service observation" for "surveillance of employee telephone conversations."[65]

The irony of computer monitoring and its attendant piecework/incentive pay system is that it usually fails to achieve its stated goal: increased productivity. A DEMA poll of data entry managers revealed that "statistical results showed that *incentive programs do not necessarily improve employee performance.*"[66] Instead, computer monitoring increases employee stress, anxiety, and turnover, which lower morale and productivity. In a survey of its members at Southern New England Bell, the Connecticut Union of Telephone Workers found that 75 percent of VDT operators who were monitored suffered from muscle aches, headaches, and dizziness. At Bell Canada, keystroke monitoring of individuals' productivity resulted in high levels of job-related stress; 66 percent of the operators studied reported "high" or "very high" stress levels. The results were so alarming that, under union pressure, Bell Canada was induced to switch to group keystroke monitoring.[67]

Conclusions

In many respects, the VDT-automated clerical workplace more closely resembles the factory of the past than the "office of the future." Automation is helping to produce a two-tier labor force with a white-collar elite of highly skilled, educated, and privileged workers and a lower but much larger pool of unskilled, less educated, and underprivileged workers. The declining status of the working and middle classes is illustrated by the fact that 80 percent of Americans suffered losses in inflation-adjusted income from 1977 to 1988.[68]

Workplace hazards have long served as an issue around which labor has organized. As business uses VDTs to automate and routinize clerical jobs, the distinctions between assembly line and office work blur. Computer monitoring and the VDT-related health hazards are not aberrations of the system; they are outcomes of management's efforts to make workers adapt to the capabilities of the technologically driven work process. Labor should stress that a better use of office computers' potential requires that companies utilize the creative talents of workers by giving them more responsibility.[69] It also makes for a healthier and more productive workforce. But unions must guard against such a move degenerating into an exploitative "reform."

There are lessons to be learned from the organizing and lobbying failures of the 1980s. The Service Employees International Union (SEIU), the Newspaper Guild, the Communications Workers of America, the American Federation of State, County, and Municipal Workers, and the Teamsters mounted attempts to organize office workers during the 1980s. Despite the much-publicized but small victory at Equitable in Syracuse, organized labor's efforts have been sporadic and have lacked full-scale coordination. In 1981, 9 to 5 and the SEIU joined together to form Local 925, the first union local created to address the needs of the female white-collar workforce. However, their failure to organize Blue Cross/Blue Shield workers during the 1980s—an ostensibly friendly target, since they did much business with labor—illustrates the difficulty of the challenge and the need to mount an effectively coordinated national organizing drive.

Labor's drive to secure occupational safety and health protections for VDT workers was stymied by a combination of corporate opposition and the antilabor policies of both the Reagan and Bush administrations, within the context of structural shifts in the economy such as chronic recession and the globalization of labor markets. Although Clinton's support for labor has been lukewarm at best, unions should exploit the opportunity to lobby OSHA for the promulgation of repetitive strain injury and comprehensive VDT safety and health regulations. Labor's lobbying effort has come closer to success at the state and local levels of government, securing initial support in Suffolk County, New York; New York City; San Francisco; and in a number of states. These initial gains at the state level were blocked by a combination of corporate lobbying and public officials wary of imposing new regulations on a booming economic sector during a time of sluggish growth. Suffolk County and San Francisco passed laws regulating VDTs in the workplace but were blocked by corporate suits on the grounds that occupational safety and health policymaking is the exclusive domain of state and federal governments. However, the initial successes at the state and local levels indicate the opportunity for grassroots coalition building. Success will take the energy of a social movement backed by the political resources of the AFL-CIO. With the globalization of capital and the export of work, organized labor must form tighter alliances with foreign workers and their unions. Without such an effort, domestic attempts are bound to fail, since work can be readily exported.[70]

Many of the problems now facing white-collar workers in the new information age economy are those that have traditionally led industrial workers to organize. Workplace issues that affect women as well as men will dominate labor's agenda into the next century. Comparable worth, reproductive and ergonomic hazards of VDT work, parental leave, day care, and national health insurance are issues around which the AFL-CIO could launch nationally coordinated and funded organizing, collective-bargaining, and legislative drives. The persistence of these problems provides organized labor with a new opportunity to organize office workers. Given that many of these workers are wary of labor unions, associational unionism, loosely structured professional groups that offer a variety of benefits to workers, may serve as a stepping-stone to eventual full-scale organization. With only 13.8 percent of clerical workers organized and an estimated 50 percent of the U.S. workforce using VDTs by 1997,[71] organized labor must address the needs of the office worker. Here lies organized labor's chief challenge for the 1990s and beyond.

Notes

1. "Office 'Miracles' That Electronics Is Bringing," *U.S. News & World Report* (September 18, 1978): 76–78. Also, "The Office of the Future," *Business Week* (June 30, 1975): 48–70; "Computers Are Changing Newsrooms Across Nation," *New York Times* (February 19, 1976), 50; Michael Zisman, "Office Automation: Revolution or Evolution?" *Sloan Management Review* 19 (1979): 1–17; John J. Connell, "The Future Office: New Technologies, New Career Paths," *Personnel* (July-August 1983): 23–32; *Computerworld's* special report on office automation (September 28, 1981): and "Previewing Office of Future," *Industrial Union Department Digest* 6 (November/December 1984).

2. International Business Machines Corporation, *1987 Annual Report* (Armonk, NY: IBM, 1988), 17.

3. *The Impact of Office Automation: 84/85 International Survey* (Menlo Park, CA.: Adia Personnel Services, n.d., circa 1985), 22.

4. "Computers in the Office," in Department of Commerce, Bureau of the Census, *Statistical Abstracts of the U.S.,* 110th ed. (Washington, DC: U.S. Government Printing Office, 1990), 944–45; and Bob Baker, "Assembly Line Stress in Offices," *Los Angeles Times* (June 13, 1991): A1.

5. David L. Birch, "Who Creates Jobs?" *The Public Interest* (Winter 1981): 9.

6. "The 'Automated Office' Is Thriving," *Office Management* (May 1983): 13.

7. "Information Processing and Tomorrow's Office," *Fortune* (October 8, 1979): 32. A special advertising section prepared by International Data Corporation, a market research company.

8. SRI International, Information Systems Management Department, Office Automation Program, *Office Automation: Consulting and Research* (Menlo Park, CA.: n.d.), 2. Also, Wassily Leontief and Faye Duchin, *The Impacts of Automation on Employment, 1963–2000: Final Report* (New York: The Institute for Economic Analysis, New York University, 1984); and Marvin Kornbluth, "The Electronic Office: How It Will Change the Way You Work," *The Futurist* (June 1982): 37.

9. Quoted in Craig Brod, *Technostress: The Human Cost of the Computer Revolution* (Reading, MA: Addison-Wesley, 1984), 45–46.

10. John Naisbitt, *Megatrends* (New York: Warner Books, 1982), 16.

11. Richard J. Matteis, "The New Back Office Focuses on Customer Service," *Harvard Business Review* (March–April 1979): 146–59.

12. "Changing 45 Million Jobs: The Speedup in Automation," *Business Week* (August 3, 1981): 62.

13. U.S. Congress, Office of Technology Assessment (OTA), *Automation of America's Offices* (Washington, DC: U.S. Government Printing Office, 1985), 33, 55; emphasis in original.

14. Foreword to William H. Leffingwell, *Office Management: Principles and Practice* (New York: McGraw-Hill, 1925), vi.

15. Ibid., 35, 36.

16. OTA, *Automation of America's Offices*, 9; also, Margaret Lowe Benston, "For Women, the Chips Are Down," in Jan Zimmerman, ed., *The Technological Woman* (New York: Praeger, 1983), 46–47.

17. C. Wright Mills, *White Collar* (New York: Oxford University Press, 1951), 226–27.

18. Harry Braverman, *Labor and Monopoly Capital: The Degradation of Work in the Twentieth Century* (New York: Monthly Review Press, 1974), 347.

19. For statistics on women in the workforce, see Department of Labor, Bureau of Labor Statistics (BLS), *Employment and Earnings* (January 1994), 203, 243. Percentages calculated by the author. For future projections, see Department of Labor, Women's Bureau, "Women and Workforce 2000," Fact Sheet No. 88–1 (January 1988).

20. Margery W. Davies, *Women's Place Is at the Typewriter* (Philadelphia: Temple University Press, 1982), 51–53, 102.

21. *Indoor Air Quality: A National Survey of Office Worker Attitudes,* public opinion poll for Honeywell, Inc., 1985, cited in "Numbers Worth Knowing," *VDT News,* (May/June 1987): 2. Despite the computer's widespread use by women workers, the BLS does not report statistics on the number of women who use VDTs.

22. BLS, *Employment and Earnings,* 243; percentages calculated by the author.

23. While men's earnings were not available for secretaries, transportation ticket and reservation agents, and telephone operators, the fact that women's median was below the total median for each occupation suggests that men are paid considerably more than they.

24. Testimony of Morton Bahr, president, Communications Workers of America, in U.S. Congress, House of Representatives, Committee on Government Operations, *Dramatic Rise in Repetitive Motion Injuries and OSHA's Response: Hearing before the Employment and Housing Subcommittee,* 101st Cong., 1st sess. (June 6, 1989): 36.

25. Louis Uchitelle, "Surplus of College Graduates Dims Job Outlook for Others," *New York Times* (June 18, 1990): A1. See also Elizabeth M. Fowler, "Graduates Find Tighter Job Market," *New York Times* (July 10, 1990): D19.

26. Michael J. Smith et al., *An Investigation of Health Complaints and Job Stress in Video Display Operations* (Cincinnati: National Institute of Occupational Safety and Health, 1981): 13; emphasis added.

27. Ibid., 13; emphasis added. On the development of technostress, see Brod, *Technostress.*

28. Anne-Marie Schiro, "Secretaries' Poll on Computers," *New York Times* (March 14, 1983): 18.

29. Kelly Services, "Poll Says Secretaries Think Automation Makes Work Less Stressful," press release (Troy, MI), 2.

30. Paul Brodeur, *Currents of Death: Power Lines, Computer Terminals, and the Attempt to Cover Up Their Threat to Your Health* (New York: Simon & Schuster, 1989), chs. 33–45; "VDT Use Linked to Increased Miscarriage Risk," *VDT News* (July–August 1988): 1.

31. The NIOSH recommendations are listed in U.S. Congress, House of Representatives, Committee on Education and Labor, *OSHA Oversight—Video Display Terminals in the Workplace: Hearings before the Subcommittee on Health and Safety,* 98th Cong., 2nd sess., 1984, 212. Many of these reforms have been won by European unions on both the collective bargaining and political levels.

32. The literature is voluminous; a selected sample follows: *Video Display Terminals in the Workplace;* American Medical Association, "Council Report: Health Effects of Video Display Terminals," *JAMA* 257 (March 20, 1987): 1508–12, and "Health Effects of Video Display Terminals: An Update," presented by George H. Bohigian, M.D. (April 1989); David Charron, *Health Hazards of Radiation from Video Display Terminals: Questions and Answers* (Hamilton, ON: Canadian Centre for Occupational Health and Safety, 1988); Bob DeMatteo, *Terminal Shock: The Health Hazards of Video Display Terminal Workers,* 2d ed. (Toronto: NC Press, 1986); Mary Sue Henifin, "The Particular Problems of Video Display Terminals," in *Double Exposure: Women's Health Hazards*

on the Job and at Home, ed. Wendy Chavkin (New York: Monthly Review Press, 1984), 69–80; Joel Makower, *Office Hazards* (Washington, DC: Tilden Press, 1981); National Research Council, Committee on Vision, *Video Displays, Work, and Vision* (Washington, DC: National Academy Press, 1983); *Potential Health Hazards of Video Display Terminals* (Cincinnati, OH: NIOSH, 1980); Michael J. Smith et al., *Electronic Performance Monitoring and Job Stress in Telecommunications Jobs* (Madison, WI: University of Wisconsin, Department of Industrial Engineering and the Communications Workers of America, 1990); Jeanne M. Stellman and Mary Sue Henifin, *Office Work Can Be Dangerous to Your Health* (New York: Pantheon Books, 1983); *The VDT Book: A Computer User's Guide to Health and Safety* (New York: New York Committee for Occupational Safety and Health, 1987).

33. *Office Environment Index: 1989 Detailed Findings* (Grand Rapids, MI: Steelcase, 1989): 63, 65.

34. "DEMA Tenth Annual Member Statistical Compensation Survey," *DEMA* (June 1989): 4. Some VDT operators punch more than twenty thousand keystrokes per hour. Also Peter T. Kilborn, "Automation: Pain Replaces the Old Drudgery, *New York Times* (June 24, 1990): 11.

35. Quoted in Brod, *Technostress,* 45–46.

36. *Office Environment Index,* 63.

37. John Maxwell Hamilton, "A Bit Player Buys into the Computer Age," *New York Times,* "Business World" (December 3, 1989): 24.

38. Trish Hall, "A Changing World for Secretaries," *New York Times* (April 27, 1988): D1.

39. Minolta survey cited in Schiro, "Secretaries' Poll," 18. Kelly Services, "American Secretaries Say They Are Satisfied with Current Jobs: Yet Less Than Half Would Advise Daughter to Pursue Secretarial Career," press release (Troy, MI, 1984), 2.

40. Kelly Services, "Tomorrow's Secretary: Computer-Wise and Ambitious," 2; "Poll Says Secretaries," 1; "Tomorrow's Secretary," 1; and "Romance Growing Between Secretaries and Word Processing, but Love Does Not Necessarily Bring More Money," 3, press releases (Troy, MI, 1984).

41. Hall, "Secretaries," D1.

42. Kelly Services, "Romance Growing,"2, and "American Secretaries," 1–2. For secretaries' median annual earnings see BLS, *Employment and Earnings,* 244.

43. Vary T. Coates, "Office Automation Technology and Contingent Work Modes," in Department of Labor, Women's Bureau, *Flexible Workstyles: A Look at Contingent Labor,* Conference Summary (Washington, DC: Department of Labor, Women's Bureau, 1988), 31. Part-time workers are those who are on the company payroll but work for only a portion of the week. Temporary workers are outsiders who are provided by an agency to fill a company's particular need for a specific period of time.

44. Ibid., 30.

45. For part-time workers see BLS, *Employment and Earnings,* 201. For figures on temporary workers, see Mary Murphree, Women's Bureau, Department of Labor (telephone interview, July 16, 1990).

46. Testimony of Kathleen Christensen, director, Project on Home-Based Work, City University of New York Graduate Center, in U.S. Congress, House of Representatives, Committee on Government Operations, *Pros and Cons of Home-Based Clerical Work: Hearing Before the Employment and Housing Committee,* 99th Cong., 2nd sess. (February 26, 1986), 22. For future projections see Gene Darling, "The 'New' Homework: Still the Same Old Story?" Labor and Occupational Health Program, *Monitor* (October–December 1988): 3–7.

47. See the congressional hearing *Pros and Cons of Home-Based Clerical Work.*

Also, Vincent E. Giuliano, "The Mechanization of Office Work," *Scientific American,* (September 1982): 163, 247. For a more skeptical view see Philip Mattera, "High-Tech Cottage Industry: Home Computer Sweatshops," *Nation* 236 (April 2, 1983): 390–92.

48. OTA, *Automation of America's Offices,* ch. 8, "Off-Shore Office Work"; "U.S. Clerical Work Sent Overseas," *Monitor* (October–December 1988): 5.

49. Hamilton, "A Bit Player," 22–23, 25; Coates, "Office Automation," 32.

50. Steve Lohr, "The Growth of the Global Office," *New York Times* (October 18, 1988): D1.

51. Kevin Power, "Now We Can Move Office Work Offshore to Enhance Output," *Wall Street Journal* (June 9, 1983): 32.

52. "The Instant Offshore Office," *Business Week* (March 15, 1982): 136E.

53. "Work Sent Overseas," *Monitor,* 5.

54. Hamilton, "A Bit Player," 24.

55. Power, "Move Office Work Offshore," 32. The computer manufacturing industry (e.g., Texas Instruments, Hewlett-Packard) is also exporting jobs to such low-wage locales as Malaysia (the world's leading producer of computer chips) and the Philippines. Workers, who toil for long hours under harsh conditions, have been harassed and denied their rights to organize unions. The U.S. government is required by law to monitor workers' rights, but has not done so in the case of these two allies. See Denis MacShane, "Dreaming of the Forty-Hour Week," *Nation* (May 15, 1989); and "Deficits Begin at Home," *Nation* (April 23, 1990): 552.

56. Paraphrased and quoted in "Monitoring Workers by Computer," *Business Week* (August 9, 1982): 62F.

57. The low estimate of 4 to 6 million comes from Office of Technology Assessment, *The Electronic Supervisor: New Technology, New Tensions* (Washington, DC: U.S. Government Printing Office, 1987): 32. The high estimate comes from the *Los Angeles Times* (July 28, 1987): 1, cited by Karen B. Ringen, "Electronic Monitoring," in *Liberty at Work: Expanding the Rights of Employees in America* (New York: American Civil Liberties Union [ACLU], 1988): 9.

58. Ronald Rice et al., "The Survival of the Fittest: Organizational Design and the Structuring of Word Processing," cited in Heidi I. Hartmann, Robert E. Kraut, and Louise A. Tilly, eds., *Computer Chips and Paper Clips: Technology and Women's Employment* 1 (Washington, DC: National Academy Press, 1986): 143. Also, Lawrence M. Schleifer, "Effects of VDT/Computer System Response Delays and Incentive Pay on Mood Disturbances and Somatic Discomfort," paper given at International Symposium on Work with Display Units (Stockholm, Sweden, May 12–15, 1986).

59. *The 9 to 5 National Survey on Women and Stress* (Cleveland: 9 to 5: The National Association of Working Women, 1984).

60. Jesse Wing, "Subliminal Messages," in ACLU, *Liberty at Work,* 40–43; Chuck Fogel, "The Electronic Boss: How Management is Using the Latest Technology to Control Employees in the Workplace," (UAW) *Solidarity* (July 1987): 11–14.

61. Nine to 5: The National Association of Working Women, *Computer Monitoring and Other Dirty Tricks* (Cleveland: 9 to 5, 1986); Karen Nussbaum, "Outlaw Monitoring; It Abuses the Worker," *USA Today* (July 11, 1986): n.p.; Gary T. Marx and Sanford Sherizen, "Monitoring on the Job: How to Protect Privacy as Well as Property," *Technology Review* (November–December 1986): 63–72; Gary T. Marx, "The Company Is Watching You Everywhere," *New York Times,* (February 15, 1987): 21; Bahr, *Repetitive Motion Injuries Hearing,* 36.

62. OTA, *The Electronic Supervisor,* 29.

63. "Big Brother in the Workplace," The MacNeil/Lehrer News Hour (December 28, 1983) (New York: Journal Graphics Transcripts, 1983); see James O'Brien's remarks, 9–13.

64. ACLU, *Liberty at Work,* 9–11.

65. Ibid., 9; OTA, *The Electronic Supervisor,* 1; "Statistical Compensation Survey," *DEMA,* 2.

66. "Statistical Compensation Survey," *DEMA,* 2; emphasis in original.

67. Fogel, "The Electronic Boss," 14; 9 to 5, *Computer Monitoring;* Nussbaum, "Outlaw Monitoring." For the New England Bell survey see Fogel, "The Electronic Boss," 13; "Bell Canada Counts Group, Not Individual, Keystrokes," *VDT News* (November–December 1989): 8.

68. On the development of the two-tier workforce see *The Future of Work: A Report by the AFL-CIO Committee on the Evolution of Work* (Washington, DC: AFL-CIO, 1983): 8. On declining incomes, see Urban Institute, *Challenge to Leadership* (Washington, DC: Urban Institute, 1990).

69. Shoshana Zuboff, *In the Age of the Smart Machine: The Future of Work and Power* (New York: Basic Books, 1988): esp. "Office Technology as Exile and Integration," 124–73. Also, Larry Hirschhorn, *Beyond Mechanization* (Cambridge, MA: MIT Press, 1984).

70. For a broader treatment of the VDT issue see Vernon Mogensen, *Office Politics: Video Display Terminals and Occupational Safety and Health Policymaking in the Postindustrial Era* (New Brunswick, NJ: Rutgers University Press, 1995).

71. For percentages of organized clerical workers see BLS, *Employment and Earnings,* 249. For future estimates of VDT use see *VDT News* (May–June 1987): 2.

10

Management Resistance to Change: A Case of Computer Information Systems

Elaine Bernard

Introduction

The mass-production model has existed to varying degrees in factories, services, and offices through most of the twentieth century. It is characterized by an extensive division of labor, a clear separation between the planning and the execution of work, the resulting deskilling of production workers, and a drive by management to minutely monitor and control all aspects of work. Today, it is argued, "new production models" are emerging with the increased application of information technologies in the workplace. These production systems can be seen as somewhat analogous to continuous processing.[1] While continuous processing is not a new means of organizing work, its extension into new areas of manufacturing, and more significantly into services and information processing, is new. Continuous processing in the service and information handling sectors reduces the unproductive duplication characteristic of mass production, resulting in the merging of formerly distinct stages and significantly condensed procedures.

Lately much has been written about the death of the mass-production model and its replacement with new production models.[2] The nature of this change is one of the major themes in discussions about the transformation of work organization and the implications for industrial relations.[3] The research presented in this chapter reviews the transition to these new production models and, more particularly, the social consequences of the new technical systems that are being introduced. It looks at the introduction of computer information systems in five organized workplaces in the public sector in British Columbia. Each of these examples of new production models exhibited evidence of an underlying tension between the control of the work process and the control of workers. In contrast with the more traditional portrayal of workers resisting technological change, this study observes management resistance to change, wherein management refused to accept some of the social consequences that the new technical systems seem to promote. In the work sites studied, managers attempted to assert traditional models of social control in the face of the more flexible possibilities offered by the new technology.

The five cases look at industries or services in the process of moving from batch systems of information collection and processing to on-line systems and direct source entry. The cases are comprised of the Corporation of the Municipality of Burnaby, Canadian National Railways (CNR), the Insurance Company of British Columbia (ICBC), the British Columbia Ferries Corporation (BC Ferries), and the British Columbia Land Titles Office (LTO). The following summaries sacrifice details for broad observations that show that all case studies exhibit evidence of the tension between control of work processes and control of workers within new production models.

Case Summaries

Municipality of Burnaby

The Corporation of the Municipality of Burnaby began reassessing its computer needs in the early 1980s. Management initiated the conversion in order to meet the growing information needs of a large municipality. Its ambitious Strategic Plan for Information Management called for the phasing out of Burnaby's existing computer systems (which consisted of isolated computers in Engineering and Finance), and their replacement with a cluster of computers capable of running an electronic, integrated, direct-source-entry, local-area-network, management information system for the entire municipality.

The union in Burnaby, the Canadian Union of Public Employees, felt completely locked out of the discussions and decision making around this major change. With little worker input in the design, faulty assumptions were made by management about the quality of existing information that would underpin the new system, and after many delays and major changes, the proposed system was totally revised and still is not operative.

At the time of the study, most workers in the municipality had heard about the plans for the new computer system, but few specifics about individual jobs were known. Questionnaires and interviews with Burnaby workers revealed both positive and negative expectations for the new computer system. On the positive side, there was the expectation for more information as a tool in doing one's job. This was linked to having greater individual independence and eliminating the tedious and repetitive parts of the job. For the workers, the "management" in management information system refers to the workers themselves. They view the system as a tool to aid them in managing their work and resources.

One concern expressed by a number of interviewees highlighted the problem of "upgrading errors." In the cases of mapping and licenses, for example, new applications started from existing information held by the municipality. Manual records in mapping and licensing are widely considered to have a significant number of errors. Workers were concerned about the vulnerability and accuracy of electronically maintained records. Concerns for database security were not limited to management, but failure to involve workers familiar with the records into the discussion meant that planning proceeded with little recognition of the doubtful quality of existing data.

By the completion of this research none of the developmental goals had been reached. Each year the plan was revised reflecting a "more realistic and experience-based estimating process." Unexpected costs associated with installing new computers, hiring new staff, and the failure to easily transfer information from the existing databases to the new computer system increased costs and extended the timeline of the project. Also, the top–down approach to system design, with no input from the workers affected by the changes, resulted in expensive failures and delays.

Canadian National Railways

At Canadian National Railways (CNR), the research was limited to the organization and movement of freight traffic, including the administrative work performed by railyard clerks. Research focused on the interaction of two groups—the clerks in the Canadian Brotherhood of Railway, Transport, and General Workers (CBRTGW), and the running trades organized by the United Transportation Union (UTU)—within a rail system becoming progressively integrated and centralized through increasing reliance on information technology.

Computers first made their appearance on CNR in the accounting department at the head office. This coincided with the arrival of centralized traffic control. Keypunch cards were first used in the early 1970s, to record information on cars and their location. The cards, which reflected the train manifest, would be run on the computer to provide a list, and travel with the train to its destination. Cards would be left for each car at the point where it set out. Later in the 1970s, the railway was closed for forty-eight hours, with no movement of cars allowed. During this time, the information of all cards was entered into terminals, along with their location at the time. Since that time there have been two "worlds"— the real, physical world where cars arrived (or didn't arrive), and the shadow computer world of the TRACS system, integrated with the yard inventory system (YIS). While the unions could still conceive of rail computerization in terms of "EDP units operated by clerks" as late as 1977, with on-line databases and data capture at source, the distinction between the tasks individual clerks inherited from the precomputer age will disappear.

Since the early 1960s, one could detect the movement of control away from operating crews and toward computer-dependent workers or managers. This exemplified a broad trend in rail technological change and promoted a highly centralized computer-based system of information and control. As traditional union work disappears, including "information" work done by the clerks (collection and manipulating data), questions arise as to what new work will be in the bargaining unit and who will do it. For example, historically "top" management decided when and where trains go. Today this work is done with the aid of the computer. Management should not input data, this is CBRTGW work, although this arrangement is a "courtesy," not supported by any contractual or legal obligation. As data are collected automatically, at the source, this "courtesy" will not even be open as a choice for management.

The transfer of work from one highly demarcated rail union jurisdiction to another has proceeded slowly, but is expected to accelerate substantially as existing and planned computer information and control systems become integrated. New jobs will not correspond to the previous work organization upon which the unions' jurisdictions are based. Thus far changes have been minor and piecemeal—for example, getting yardmasters to do "clerks' work" in "moving" cars within the yard on the TRACS/YIS system. Union activists in both unions believe that amalgamation of job duties between the two groups is next to impossible. Yet it is hard to imagine that separate job classifications will be maintained to perform redundant work, inputting or extracting data that have been incorporated into the work of others. Also, the few jobs we foresee remaining after the present stage of computerization are likely to be held by nonunionized workers. While today, protection of one's job appears as a jurisdictional issue between unions (even if both unions agree on "whose" work it is), in the near future the focus of job protection will be defined in terms of defending service levels and claiming management work for the unit.

Insurance Company of British Columbia

Our study at the Insurance Company of British Columbia (ICBC) organized by the Office and Technical Employees Union, Local 378, focused on the new Autoplan Processing Service (APS) department. ICBC is a crown corporation and the sole agency for auto insurance in the province. The APS department receives policy changes over the telephone from Autoplan agents throughout the province and updates the computer database. In ICBC the technical system is changing from a batch input system toward data capture at source. At the time of the study, the new technical system of interactive on-line processing had already been introduced.

The new APS job is an amalgamation of five previous tasks and is performed in an industrial-style assembly-line process: data capture, data entry, financial reconciliation, editing, and confirmation. Most important are human relations and listening skills, being able to solve problems, and knowing where to get information. The APS representative has access to an expanding number of databases, including some linked to outside agencies such as the police and the Motor Vehicle Branch. Due to the wide range of tasks and possible problems, it is difficult to monitor worker performance. The system is constantly being customized, and worker suggestions for improving it, based on firsthand experience, are actively encouraged. There is partial dedication of a "customer base" (a geographical grouping of agents) to each APS representative, allowing for personalization of service. High job satisfaction is reported due to the personal contact and problem-solving aspects of the job.

Many APS representatives like the potential that electronic measurement of their work offers, but want it to be a tool for self-evaluation. However, at present it is used by supervisors to develop abstract measures of productivity; and everything the APS representative does has his or her identity on it, leaving a traceable audit trail.

The process involved attempts to standardize inherently nonstandard work. "Confirmation," for example, might take two minutes or two hours, depending on the particulars of the transaction and the necessity for background research. Workers feel that in this situation, supervisory monitoring acts to reduce quality in the name of quantity. They face conflicting pressures of correcting problems before they get into the computer, which reduces their all-important quantity statistics. As their work becomes routinized, exceptional calls have been transferred to the Technical Inquiry Unit.

Clerical interview subjects were unanimous in describing supervision in the APS as regimented and unproductive. Workers are prevented from talking to each other, and from social interaction in general; and are subjected to dress codes; pressured on absenteeism; and have received negative, not positive, feedback on their work.

ICBC workers are very receptive to the new labor process and technical progress and computerization but argue it should be used to benefit people. The social system at the ICBC has not kept pace with the technical system. There is a reliance on the computer to "catch errors," which includes any worker response that is exceptional. There is a trend, once the new system is in place, to separate exceptional from routine tasks—for example, in the re-creation of the Technical Inquiry Unit to handle exceptions.

BC Ferries

The British Columbia Ferries Corporation (BC Ferries) is a crown corporation formed to operate provincial government coastal passenger and vehicle ferry service. In 1976, management consultants prepared a review of BC Ferries' revenues and expenses. Among its recommendations for improvement of its financial health were increased management control through obtaining and using more information. Intelligent use of information (assuming it is being captured accurately) can overcome many of the built-in inflexibilities of running a ferry service. Yet both management and union perceive that computers are fairly marginal to the running of the corporation. We found that the use of computers is becoming more sophisticated, integrating the various departments and putting new kinds of information in the hands of managers and workers. This has begun in the administrative area but is rapidly spreading through personnel functions, reservations, and inventory control, to the management of voyages and vessels.

Crewing of vessels, for example, is needed on a 24-hours-a-day, 365-days-a-year basis, to allow for provision of service and regular ship maintenance. Within each department, deck, engine room, and in catering, there is a multitude of job classifications, special licenses and tickets (for personnel), and variable cross-skilling among different crew members. Federal government regulations set unbending minimum levels for crewing, relative to different passenger loads. Thus, every absence must be replaced. Manning clerks can receive word of absence at the last minute, or even during a shift. They must juggle an immense amount of information as to who is qualified for which jobs, who with more seniority should be upgraded for the day, who lives how many minutes from the terminal, and information on "manning pool" (regular employees who can only be used for their particular classified position) and three categories of "casuals" (who can be used for any job they are qualified for). Other contingencies can occur—for example, whether the general rule against "short turnarounds" can be ignored in particular cases, or whether it is advisable to allow for overtime or bring in another employee.

The computerized personnel system, once fully implemented, will help clerks answer inquiries from crew members—for example, on how much accumulated time off they have in their account. This task is very difficult to accomplish manually in "real time." Crew members complain that personnel clerks are too tied to their computer terminals and fail to deal properly with their questions. This would change when the system is fully implemented, and this becomes a priority of the clerks' job. Clerks felt that computerization has led to a greater demand for workers to analyze information. Their expectation is for the computer to "take over" staffing functions, including those that are difficult to do manually, such as locating an available chief officer in different terminals. They believe they would be less involved in recording and manipulating each crew member's assignments and time, take on a "monitoring" and "inquiring" role, and continue to utilize their informal skills and practices to ensure efficient personnel functioning.

The public information and reservations functions of BC Ferries have been computerized for three years and are being redesigned. The first manual processing system was described by one manager as "little bits of paper going all over the office." It had a low accuracy level and lacked interactive capability. Reliability of the system was low, reservations were mistakenly filed or were unrecorded, and sailings would be overbooked before reservations agents were aware of it (reflecting a lack of "real time" information).

Computerization has meant that the reservations clerk (and others) can access the file by the name, the license plate number of the vehicle, and several other keys. The manifest can get printed at any time, at the terminal itself. Information on the system covers all BC Ferries terminals. It receives traffic updates and information on sailing cancellations from the four major terminals (normally entered on the computer by terminal staff, but telephoned in exceptional circumstances). Routine inquiries have been removed from the system and put on a tape machine. As the information/reservation computer system has taken on more complex work, and as new routes have been added to the system, the skill requirements have increased for reservations clerks. They are now involved in highly interactive work, using different screens to solve the ever-changing problems that passengers present. Some of the fragmentation seen in the old manual system has disappeared.

It is an open question at BC Ferries to what extent the current computer system adequately re-creates the "tacit knowledge" of the worker or provides computer tools to allow those tacit skills to be utilized. With no central database, the model being used by the Systems Department emphasizes "systems development by the user rather than the profession." While management and systems developers ultimately conceive of the network as a management information system, with workers entering transactions and management running control, inquiry and report-generating functions, some of the new functions are blurring the once clear lines in the division of labor between the work of management and that of employees. At the current stage there is great reliance on the informal, social aspects of work, and supervision has remained rather "loose," being performed "manually," not through electronic monitoring.

BC Land Titles Office

The Torrens system of land title has been in place in British Columbia since before Confederation. Like other systems of land title, its essential purpose is to provide for clear ownership of, and interests in, land. Its four principles are indefeasibility, registration, abolition of notice, and assurance. Once registered in the Land Titles Office (LTO), a land title cannot be defeated in law; to be valid, the title must be registered in the central agency; sellers have no obligation to provide separate notice to other than the central agency; and the state financially supports the agency to pay for errors. The Torrens system places heavy responsibility on the operating agency, the LTO, and provides only limited powers for correction of error. Applications are date-stamped and serial-numbered to establish priority, but "indefeasibility" does not begin until after they have been "examined" and "registered."

With its large and varied indexes and need for accuracy and speed, the LTO was an obvious but difficult choice for computerization. It was a model of system design among the cases studied, particularly given a serious and ongoing involvement of the "users." A veteran of thirty-five years, an examiner, and a land titles clerk were directly involved in the design and implementation process. This use of land titles expertise has extended to the creation of "computer coordinator" positions in each office as they have gone on line. This type of involvement is regarded as central to the high quality of design. While formally the BC Systems Corporation (BCSC) consultants relegate the end user to a passive informant of the systems experts, LTO implementation has emphasized user involvement at a very early stage, slowed down the design process to permit user review of projected designs, and allowed the office to develop a system that has revealed few serious mistakes, and is still capable of evolving with further user experience.

The Automated Land Title Office System (ALTOS) is among the most complex information management systems that the BCSC has created, yet it is also easy to use. As mentioned above, one of its design criteria was flexibility. The system (embracing technical and social aspects) "learned," from its own experience, a key component of cybernetic systems. Criticisms expressed by users at various stages have been eliminated with subsequent system updates—for example, a new billing system was introduced. Several new transactions were added in response to demands from the public and staff, and there is a recognition that there is no one best way to do LTO work. Experience is likely to lead to further modifications, but there is little evidence toward having the computer make decisions for the examiner.

The computer coordinators are crucial to gathering information for the system, and the need for enhancements. In addition to a provincial computer coordinator, there are local computer coordinator positions in the seven regional offices. Despite the name, the position is not a technical one. People in these positions do not necessarily have computer expertise. Rather, they are an extension of the process of direct involvement of people with land titles expertise in ALTOS design and implementation. One coordinator noted that they do not know how to program, but know "how it should be done." Another mentioned as the main requirement for the job, existing technical knowledge of the land titles system. They "don't have to know about bits and bytes."

Registrars praised their coordinators, but there was a difference in perception between what the registrars thought the coordinators were doing, and what the coordinators described as their work activities. The registrars saw the job as mostly technical, the work of people who knew how to keep the computer running. The coordinators view themselves as having people skills. They have taken on a role in workplace organization that reflects operational changes produced by computerization. This is not appreciated by the registrars, who are unaware of the organizational changes implied by seemingly "neutral technical" decisions. Registrars may find themselves with considerably less power as ALTOS strengthens the director's office through interoffice searches on a centralized database and as computer coordinators become a force in running the offices.

In line with the user-driven approach, the system was seen as improving the existing (manual) system, not eliminating it. The systems development team of computing specialists from BCSC, along with land titles knowledge workers, "made no attempt to program human logic into the system, the computer doesn't understand the law, we still need your head." This is central in understanding the positive and negative aspects of ALTOS design and operation, that the essence of the LTO is human judgment, which computerization ought to (and largely does) support and enhance. As much as they could, the design team reproduced the existing format and sequence of steps in examining and registering a title. Among the benefits was ease of teaching a system that relied on existing skills and procedures.

The work process in the LTO prior to computerization, as now, is extremely complex. Since computerization, a number of stages in the process have been eliminated, with the examiner having directly absorbed the work of the title preparers and comparers, since titles are now prepared on the examiner's computer. While the computer system was modeled closely on the existing manual system, it has significantly altered this system. Computerization involved the absorption of support work into the core function of legal judgment, and this eliminated several job tasks. Although the format remained the same, the introduction of "segments" to a title, only one of which comes upon the screen at a time, has meant new work practices for the examiners. The skills of the examiner are now more abstract and analytical, given that there is no single piece of paper to refer to and that several screens must be integrated mentally by the examiner. Coordinators suggest that the consolidation of tasks could lead to junior clerks taking over the work of examiners, but the process so far is in the other direction, preserving the skilled positions at the expense of the more routine jobs. As long as the LTO provides an essentially interpretive, legal service, this is likely to remain the case; if it were to become a simple recording service, the reverse might occur. It is open to speculation how many examining-related support jobs such as microfilming, cashier, vault, phone/mail, and photocopying in "survey" will remain.

The New Production Model and the Old Social Regime

The research confirmed empirically that mass production is giving way to "new production models." Mass production, whether in factories or offices, meant the existence of multistage production, with the need to move materials between the stages. Continuous processing tends to eliminate much of this material handling in information production. Data are being entered or captured where they first arise. In the next generation of systems being planned and implemented, these data will be used to reconfigure operations before problems or bottlenecks occur.

New Work and Skills

The cases in this study exemplify the move toward direct source capture information systems, as distinct from the isolated use of computers to undertake batch transactions only. In this new environment it is no longer easy to make computerization fit a simple deskilling thesis. Both skilling and deskilling are taking place, often at the same work site. For example, our case studies show:

1. some capture of data at source;
2. "piping" of data between previously separate functional units, leading to greater organizational integration, and eliminating data "ownership" by particular departments;
3. the capability to extract summary and ad hoc reports from databases, with most routine data handling being absorbed by the machine;
4. a dynamic process of "system learning" wherein technical and human components evolve over time.

These developments, in particular the removal of the workers from direct involvement in the production and handling of data, have expanded existing skills and developed new ones:

1. monitoring for exceptional events and handling unexpected contingencies to flexibly achieve system goals and build on existing tacit knowledge, negotiation, and personal relationships;
2. judgment and analytical skills;
3. holistic system skills;
4. abstract skills that involve dealing with informational representations of reality.

These changes in skills and the nature of work promote at least a minimal level of workplace discretion and control by workers. Similarly, technical systems that require workers to perform work traditionally attributed to management functions of analyzing, interpreting, and decision making might be a partial explanation for middle management's resistance to labor process changes with new technology.

At the Insurance Company of British Columbia, CNR, BC Ferries, and the BC Land Titles Office, data are being entered "in the field" by clients of the organization. The immediate effect of this source data entry is the partial removal of workers from direct involvement in the labor process. Workers are coming to perform an "auditing" function of machine watching for exceptions.

While workers no longer "physically" move materials or data, "routine" decisions are being taken over by the computer. Discretionary decisions—ones that are out of the ordinary—are left to workers. Far from representing "automatic" systems that are "untouched by human hands," the new computer systems require workers who understand the entire process, including the reasons behind the separate stages of the old system. These workers, experienced in the manual system, relied on that experience to set off "triggers" when visually reviewing material or information. Such "tacit knowledge," which cannot easily be absorbed by computers at present, is still needed, but now on a broader scale, under computerization. The resultant need for close attention is exemplified by the LTO system, where accuracy must be nearly total, or by CNR's TRACS system, where misinformation can cause the loss of a car and/or a derailment. No longer concerned about regular and nonproblematic data transactions and transfers, these workers become "troubleshooters" and will also require query systems to do their jobs properly. The logic of the new system suggests a work process wherein a worker will not only troubleshoot after-the-fact problems, but also anticipate bottlenecks and resolve them ahead of time.

In what way does this differ from traditional "management" work? These technical developments implicitly question dysfunctional supervisory systems and divisions of labor that are throwbacks to the mass-production model. This may explain why at BC Ferries and the Municipality of Burnaby, "end-user computing," where information of one's choice can be derived from databases, is extolled but artificially conceived of as only a management tool.

Re-Taylorization

Proponents of the "new production models" argue that the real potential of the new information technology is in the reintegration of work and the expanded flexibility in operations and information use. In practice this study indicates a continuing attempt to restrict flexibility and integration, with management pressure for the labor process continuing to be organized in a neo-Taylorist fashion. One of the earmarks of Taylorism is the separation of the planning and execution of work, and the discouragement of worker initiative to change or improve on the process. With both BC Ferries and the Municipality of Burnaby, workers view the centralized database as a management tool to aid senior management control costs and personnel.

The most successful implementation of new technology in this study was designed with major worker input to augment the knowledge of workers, such as the very successful LTO application. A comparison of the ICBC case, where the new system integrated five previously relatively boring, separate jobs into a new APS job, and LTO, shows that re-Taylorization is a conscious management choice, not an inherent attribute of systems. In the ICBC case, Taylorist attitudes among managers were clearly demonstrated in their strict supervisory style.

Another aspect of re-Taylorization is the management preference for the model over the real world. In both the CNR and Municipality of Burnaby studies, workers pointed out numerous flaws in the computer models and management dependence on flawed models with weak validation systems. In the case of the Municipality of Burnaby, the new mapping computer system is even using error-ridden, paper-based maps as the basis for their new system.

Management Resistance to Change

A driving force behind the re-Taylorization of work may be the middle management concern that the new systems challenge their authority and role in the labor process. This new model of work organization, with the "augmented knowledge worker" at its center accessing information from a variety of sources, is a challenge to management authority. The supervisory and work allocation role of middle management can be taken over by information systems. The logic of integrated systems such as the inventory system at BC Ferries, or APS at ICBC, or LTO, is that the worker will be responsible for the entire system. Managers are becoming increasingly aware of this encroachment and are asserting their authority in an unnecessary or counterproductive manner.

Middle management has not been informed about the impact and implications of the new systems and rarely was informed much in advance of the line staff. In some cases consultants used middle management for input, but in most cases, such as at BC Ferries, it was discovered that they have incomplete knowledge of their own department's technical systems, and of computer issues, leaving them as the odd ones out.

Managers expressed the view that workers will resist any changes. This was not supported in this study. In questionnaires, the overall attitude to technological change by workers was positive. Even in offices where a majority of employees thought there would be "some job loss," the response was still overwhelmingly positive about the benefits of new technology. In offices where changes had taken place and workers complained about many problems with the new systems, they still overwhelmingly rejected the proposal "to go back to the way things were before." Workers expressed the view that the main roadblock to a successful implementation of the new system was management.

Resistance by management to flexible design and utilization of information systems underlines an important dynamic of new production models that needs to be studied by workers and their organizations. Management resistance is a manifestation of the continued rejection of workplace democracy and a tendency to utilize computers to the extent that they can enhance management's control over workers and the work process. Contrary to the claims of proponents of the new information technology that the computer revolution will automatically lead to job enhancement, and increase skills and worker responsibility, new technology has become a "contested terrain" on which workers seek to control work processes and management seeks to control workers.

Notes

1. L. Hirschhorn, *Beyond Mechanization* (Cambridge, MA: MIT Press, 1984), 41–47.

2. On this point see K. Dohse, U. Jurgens, and T. Malsch, "From Fordism to Toyota-ism? The Social Organization of the Labor Process in the Japanese Automobile Industry,"

Politics and Society 14 (1985): 2; L. Hirschhorn, *Beyond Mechanization*; H. Kern and M. Schumann, "Limits of the Division of Labor: New Production Concepts in West German Industry," *Economic and Industrial Democracy* (1987): 8; H. Kern and M. Schumann, "New Concepts of Production in German Plants," in P. Katzenstein, ed., *Industry and Politics in West Germany: Toward the Third Republic* (Ithaca, NY: Cornell University Press, 1989); M. Piore and C. Sabel, *The Second Industrial Divide* (New York: Basic Books, 1984); J. Womack, D.T. Jones, and D. Roos, *The Machine That Changed the World* (New York: Rawson Associates, 1990); and S. Zuboff, *In the Age of the Smart Machine: The Future of Work and Power* (New York: Basic Books, 1984).

3. See C. Heckscher, *The New Unionism* (New York: Basic Books, 1988); R. Hyman and W. Streeck, eds., *New Technology and Industrial Relations* (New York: Basil Blackwell, 1988); T. Kochan, H. Katz, and R. McKersie, *The Transformation of American Industrial Relations* (New York: Basic Books, 1986); and T. Rankin, *New Forms of Work Organization: The Challenge for North American Unions* (Toronto: University of Toronto Press, 1990).

11

Legal Challenges Against Plant Closings:

Eminent Domain, Labor, and Community Property Rights

David Schultz

*Well, we're living here in Allentown,
and they're closing all the factories down.
Out in Bethlehem they're building time,
filling out forms, standing in line.*
—"Allentown," Billy Joel

Introduction

Throughout the 1980s and 1990s numerous writers have charted the evolution of the American economy as businesses have divested assets, merged, downsized, or completely closed facilities.[1] Many thought that with the close of the Reagan and Bush era, the election of Clinton would produce an administration more favorable to labor and sympathetic to the problems of plant closings. Unfortunately, the passage of NAFTA and GATT would indicate that the forces in the 1980s that encouraged plant closings and job loss overseas will not stop and perhaps will continue to accelerate.

The results of these business decisions and political economic policies do not bode well for communities devastated by major plant closings and job losses. The impacts of these closings have been discussed at length elsewhere and are known to include such symptoms as chronic unemployment; reduced income; loss of savings and other property; and physical and mental health problems such as alcoholism, physical abuse, divorce, and even suicide.[2]

A business decision to close a facility has a tremendous impact on both individuals and communities. Sometimes this impact will remain localized, resulting in a loss of jobs, an increased demand for city services at a time of a shrinking tax base, outmigration of population, and a general loss to community pride. At other times the decision will be felt across a region or a nation if the employer is large enough and chooses to relocate out of state or out of country. For example, Harrison and Bluestone indicate that during the 1970s and 1980s, the results of this outward shift (overseas or out of state) were the erosion of union membership, the loss of millions of jobs, shifts of billions of U.S. corporate investments abroad, a net increase in the value of U.S. imports of goods previously produced in America,[3] and an increase in the income gap between the rich and the poor in this country.

Yet when faced with the prospect of an employer leaving, a community may feel entirely unable to affect that business decision.[4] In recent years, however, several options have become available to challenge business decisions to close plants. One option typically chosen by unions is to attempt to negotiate settlement on the closing with the employer.[5] The usefulness of this option is limited because it is generally available only in unionized settings, and even then negotiations normally lead to a handful of actual agreements.[6]

Another method to affect a plant closing decision is to adopt legislation regulating the closing process. Typically, plant closing legislation, such as the federal WARN law, would require advance notification for either a major layoff or a complete closing.[7] The goal here is to cushion or lessen the disruption individuals and communities experience when jobs are lost. Unfortunately, these statutes usually require only a few months' notice and the payment of limited economic benefits, if any, to affected workers. Furthermore, they do not directly address the impact of the closing on the health of the whole community. Finally, companies avoid compliance with these laws either by ignoring them or by engaging in gradual layoffs that fall outside the requirements of plant closing legislation.

While these options may cushion the impact felt by employees, neither option can actually prevent a plant closing, compensate the community as a whole for the economic losses that flow from these types of business decisions, nor augment the ability of workers and the community to bargain with businesses. In short, these options fail to address the power imbalances in the negotiating positions among capital, government, and labor. There are, however, two additional options that have been recognized by unions. The first option involves the use of eminent domain power to halt a plant closing. The second option is via claiming infringement of the community's property rights.

This chapter attempts to explain how these two options can be used as proactive tools to fight against plant closings. Three case studies are presented here to show how local unions conducted themselves as catalysts and joined with their community to encourage local officials to take a more active and offensive stance against plant closings.

The Use of Eminent Domain

The Midkiff Case

The concept of eminent domain refers to the inherent authority of the government to take private property for public use as long as just compensation is paid to the owner for the taking.[8] This authority is available to the federal government[9] and to all fifty states by virtue of their respective constitutions. Typically, only roads, sewer systems, and other public utility projects and public institutions, such as schools, prisons, and state hospitals meet the "public use" test.[10] However, while eminent domain has generally been used to support corporate interests, it is also open to union and municipal use to defend their interests. This is particularly true today, for the definition of public use has expanded so that any acquisition would meet the test if it serves a public purpose, confers a benefit on the public, or furthers the state's police powers.[11] This expansion of public use would even accommodate the acquisition of a company's assets under certain conditions. A brief review of recent eminent domain litigation supports this contention.

In 1954, the U.S. Supreme Court, in *Berman* v. *Parker*,[12] unanimously held constitutional Washington, DC's, use of eminent domain, pursuant to statutory authority,[13] for the public use of acquiring commercial property for an urban renewal project. While hardly newsworthy today, the *Berman* decision was quite remarkable when announced. The expansion in the public use definition came as the Court noted that "[the] concept of public welfare is broad and inclusive . . . [and] . . . the power of eminent domain is merely the means to the end." Notably, the Court also found that the means used to exercise eminent domain could include utilizing an entity of private enterprise or the authorization to take private property for its resale or lease to the same or other parties. In this regard, and especially important here, the Court said:

> [T]he means of executing the project are for Congress and Congress alone to determine, once the public purpose has been established. The public end may be as well or better served through an agency of private enterprise than through a department of government—or so the Congress might conclude. We cannot say that public ownership is the sole method of promoting the public purposes of community redevelopment projects.[14]

While *Berman* illustrates the use of eminent domain to benefit society as a whole, other recent decisions approve its use to benefit narrower interests in the hope that they will eventually serve the broader, public interest. This concept is important because it supports using eminent domain to prevent a business closing even though it would appear to benefit only employees. In fact, given the ripple effect of unemployment in the economy, preventing closings benefits the entire public.

With *Berman* as its base, numerous court decisions have expanded upon the public use concept. Cases illustrating this include the decisions in *Poletown Neighborhood Council* v. *City of Detroit*,[15] *City of Oakland* v. *Oakland Raiders*,[16] and *Hawaii Housing Authority* v. *Midkiff*.[17] In *Poletown* the court upheld the City of Detroit's use of its eminent domain authority to level a city neighborhood and relocate its residents in order to accommodate the desire of General Motors Corporation to build a new assembly plant. The eminent domain authority was exercised pursuant to the Michigan Economic Development Corporations Act,[18] a statute similar to that at issue in *Berman*. The act declares:

> There exists in this state the continuing need for programs to alleviate and prevent conditions of unemployment, and the legislature finds that it is accordingly necessary to assist and retain local industrial and commercial enterprises, including employee-owned corporations, to strengthen and revitalize the economy of this state and its municipalities. . . . Therefore, the powers granted in this act constitute the performance of essential public purposes and functions for this state and its municipalities.[19]

With the City of Detroit's stated object and this statute before it, the court asked whether the proposed condemnation was for the primary benefit of the public or the private user. It answered by holding that the public would be the primary beneficiary, reasoning that "the most important consideration in the case of eminent domain is the necessity of accomplishing some public good which is otherwise impracticable, and . . . the law does not so much regard the means as the need."[20] In *Poletown* the court recognized that the needs that would be served by upholding this use of eminent domain included the alleviation of "the severe economic conditions facing the residents of the city and state, [and] the need for new industrial development to revitalize local industries, the economic boost the proposed project would provide."

Particularly notable about this decision is its expansive definition of public use. Generally, the court has approved the taking of private property for numerous economic and usually pro-business purposes. However, there are also circumstances in which the government may properly take a business's private property to serve the larger public goal of general economic welfare by either redistributing business assets or placing limits on corporate power to serve not business but community interests that include the working and middle classes. Thus there is no reason why eminent domain could not be used against businesses to serve broader community interests.

That is precisely what occurred in the *Oakland Raiders* case, where the City of Oakland was allowed to use its eminent domain power to seize all the business assets, real and personal, of the Raiders' football franchise. Eminent domain was used to take over a private business to serve the greater economic needs of the general public.

In *Oakland Raiders,* the coliseum that the team played in was leased by the team owners from a public, nonprofit city-county corporation. Upon failure to reach a settlement on an option to renew the lease, the team announced its intention to remove itself to Los Angeles. To prevent this, the City of Oakland commenced an eminent domain action to acquire all the property rights associated with the team, including players' contracts, team equipment, and television and radio contracts. The franchise owner argued against the city's action on two grounds: (1) that the law of eminent domain did not permit the taking of intangible property not associated with realty (here, the team's network of intangible contractual rights), and (2) that the taking contemplated by the city cannot, as a matter of law, be for any public use within the city's authority.

In reversing the trial court's grant of summary judgment in the team's favor, the California Supreme Court rejected both of the team's arguments, concluding that "the acquisition and, indeed, the operation of a sports franchise may be an appropriate municipal function."[21] The court stated, in response to the team's arguments, that "intangible assets are subject to condemnation" and that the subject acquisition could meet the public use test when it is defined as "a use which concerns the whole community or promotes the general interest in its relation to any legitimate object of government." Perhaps in recognition of the City's argument that "the factual circumstances surrounding the construction of the Oakland Coliseum and the integration of the past use of the stadium with the life of the City of Oakland in general will readily demonstrate the 'public' nature of the use contemplated here," the court noted that "[i]t is not essential that the entire community, or even any considerable portion thereof, shall directly enjoy or participate in an improvement in order to constitute a public use." Although it may appear that by retaining the team only the fans and those deriving direct economic gain (i.e., vendors) benefit from this use of eminent domain, in reality the community as a whole benefits economically and culturally and in this manner the public use requirement is served.

The goal sought to be served by the use of eminent domain in the *Oakland Raiders* case is indistinguishable from the goals that would be served by using that power to prevent a plant shutdown. Furthermore, the taking of an ongoing business enterprise, in the form of a football franchise, to serve these goals is, again, indistinguishable from taking, for example, a manufacturing plant to serve the same purposes.

Another case that exemplifies the expanded definition of public use is *Hawaii Housing Authority* v. *Midkiff*.[22] In *Midkiff* the issues revolved around the constitutionality of the Land Reform Act[23] enacted by the Hawaii legislature in 1967. The purpose of the act was to reduce the perceived social and economic evils inherent in the then existing large feudal land estates traceable to the early high chiefs of the Hawaiian Islands. To achieve this purpose the act created the Hawaii Housing Authority,[24] whose mission was, by use of a land condemnation scheme, to take title to the real property from the lessors, condemn it, compensate the lessors for the taking, and then sell the property to the lessees inhabiting the land at the time it was condemned. The process was instituted only after it was determined by the authority that the acquisition of the tract would effectuate the public purposes of the act.

In this particular case, the authority determined that taking the land held by the lessors would effectuate the act's purposes and directed the lessors to negotiate the sale of the land to its lessees. When these negotiations failed, the authority ordered the lessors to submit to the compulsory arbitration required by the act. Rather than comply with the order the lessors filed suit in federal district court, asking that the act be declared unconstitutional. The U.S. Supreme Court unanimously reversed a lower court of appeals decision and upheld the use of eminent domain for this purpose.[25] The Court noted and dispelled the court of appeals' concern that "[s]ince Hawaiian lessees retain possession of the property for private use throughout the condemnation process, . . . the act exacted takings for private use." In response to this concern the Court stated:

> The mere fact that property taken outright by eminent domain is transferred in the first instance to private beneficiaries does not condemn that taking as having only a private purpose. The Court long ago rejected any literal requirement that condemned property be put into use for the general public. "It is not essential that the entire community, nor even any considerable portion, . . . directly enjoy or participate in any improvement in order [for it] to constitute a public use." [W]hat in its immediate aspect [is] only a private transaction may . . . be raised by its class or character to a public affair.[26] (citations omitted)

The *Midkiff* ruling, as well as the rulings in the *Oakland Raiders* and *Poletown* cases, endorse the use of eminent domain as a tool to redistribute private resources within society to accomplish certain widely drawn public purposes. The cases exemplify the expansive interpretation now given the public use requirement and signal the appropriateness of now using eminent domain to prevent plant closings. Such a use is clearly within the spirit, if not the letter, of these cases. These cases have led legal commentators[27] and community activists[28] to conclude that eminent domain could be used by municipalities as a tool, bargaining chip, or strategy to prevent a plant closing. Against this case law backdrop, we turn then to the first two of three case studies indicating how unions, armed with the legal resources of eminent domain, can challenge plant closings.

The Steel Valley Authority

The Steel Valley Authority (SVA) is a quasi-public agency that represents various economic development interests of ten communities in and around Pittsburgh, Pennsylvania. It was organized in response to the general erosion,[29] during the late 1970s and early 1980s, of the manufacturing base in the tri-state region of eastern Ohio, western Pennsylvania, and northern West Virginia. Threatened by the erosion of the manufacturing base of this region, local union, church, and grassroots political activists banded together in 1979 to form the Tri-State Conference on the Impact of Steel (Tri-State). In 1984, when the U.S. Steel Corporation announced its plans to close its Duquesne, Pennsylvania, blast furnaces, Tri-State called for the formation of the SVA to combat the closure. When the ten municipalities banded together, the SVA was born.

The SVA concept was first proposed at a Tri-State meeting held late in 1983. Out of this meeting came a published proposal titled *Rebuild Steel*.[30] The proposal ambitiously called for the establishment of a "TVA for Steel" program that would seek a workable and socially responsible plan to save the domestic steel industry. This would be accomplished by the creation of the SVA, which would acquire abandoned or soon-to-be-abandoned steel mills in the area.[31] The major difference between the TVA and the SVA would be that the latter would be neither federally funded nor federally controlled. In fact, the aim of the SVA would be for local community control.

To accomplish these goals Tri-State stated that "[t]he power of 'eminent domain,' inherent in the sovereign state of Pennsylvania, must, therefore, be delegated to the 'Steel Valley Authority.' " Both SVA's incorporation[32] and its use of the eminent domain power rested on the Pennsylvania Municipal Authorities Act.[33] This act defines the power of any authority incorporated under it, including the SVA, to engage in economic development. The parameters of the act are very broad. It permits an authority to undertake various kinds of projects, including the acquisition, construction, improvement, maintenance, and operation of structures or facilities. The purposes of these projects may include efforts to *retain* or develop existing industries and the development of new industries. Furthermore, the delegated powers may be exercised to acquire and hold any form of property. An authority may sell, lease, transfer, or dispose of all or part of a project to a third party, or it may operate the project itself. The act also grants authorities power to contract with any municipality, corporation, or public authority of Pennsylvania or any adjoining state, on such terms as the authority shall deem proper, for the construction and operation of any project that is partly in Pennsylvania and partly in an adjoining state.

Based on the clear authority and mandate of the Municipal Authorities Act, the SVA has formulated a basic operational outline. At present it does not contemplate operating industrial development projects in the sense of managing facilities.[34]

Instead, the SVA intends to coordinate industrial development managed by third parties. This coordination may be carried out in two ways. First, the SVA could "retain or develop existing industries"[35] by acting as a broker between owners of a presently operating facility and a third party. Second, the SVA could acquire abandoned facilities for the "development of new industries" and then sell or lease them to other operators.[36] Under the first option, when a party is interested in acquiring an existing industrial facility whose present owner is not willing to sell, the SVA could condemn the property and then transfer it to the buyer. The SVA would thus "force" a sale of the structure or facility at fair market value as determined in an eminent domain proceeding.[37]

Thus the SVA power to use eminent domain to fight plant closings is substantial. As noted above, the recently expanded definition of public use resulting from the *Berman, Poletown, Oakland Raiders,* and *Midkiff* cases supports the conclusion that local, quasi-governmental entities can constitutionally exercise granted eminent domain powers for the public use purpose of broadly or discretely enhancing the local economy. Furthermore, other quasi-governmental agencies established pursuant to the Pennsylvania Municipal Authorities Act have had their exercises of eminent domain power upheld under Pennsylvania law.[38]

The SVA has not, however, actually used its eminent domain power to acquire property, despite its legal authority to do so. This is due in large part to the financial constraints of exercising the power (see the conclusions below). Nevertheless, it has been noted that even a threat of using eminent domain can be an effective tool in keeping a plant where it is. "Threatening to take a facility may avoid the problem of determining and paying just compensation, while securing the desired result of keeping business in the community. In order for this tactic to work in the long run, the public authority must at least appear to have the ability and the intent to take the property."[39]

For example, in the fall of 1982, Nabisco Brands Food Company announced its intention to close a plant in Pittsburgh that employed 650 people.[40] A coalition of various community groups, led by numerous labor groups, pushed local officials to threaten the use of eminent domain should the company attempt to close the plant. Less than a month after the threat was initially voiced, the company announced that the plant would remain open.

The widely publicized case of Morse Cutting Tool Company provides another example of the effectiveness of threatening to exercise eminent domain, although the Morse case represents a more formalized threat than that voiced in the Nabisco case.

Morse Cutting Tool

The threat of resort to eminent domain power saved the Morse Cutting Tool factory in New Bedford, Massachusetts. The threat was voiced by the mayor of New Bedford on June 2, 1984, as a final attempt by a frustrated city and its citizens to keep a large employer in the community. Fewer than three months later the company was in the hands of a new owner, who promised to keep it in New Bedford. While New Bedford did not actually have to exercise its eminent domain power, the Morse Cutting Tool case illustrates how the threatened exercise of the power may work as an effective tool of industrial policy to fight plant closings.

The first plant of its kind in the country, Morse Cutting Tool was organized in 1864 as a family firm in New Bedford.[41] In 1941, while the company was still family-owned, it was unionized by the United Electrical Workers' Union.[42] In its more than fifty-year involvement at Morse Cutting Tool, the local has gone on strike only twice, once in 1976, and again in 1982. It is the events that unfolded following the conclusion of the second strike that laid the groundwork for the mayor's eventual threat to take over the company through eminent domain.

"After the Morse family sold the plant in 1946, two successive owners operated the company until 1968, when Gulf + Western bought the plant. . . . Though conditions at Morse outwardly remained the same for the next 13 years . . . events in 1981 began to spell trouble for the future of the plant."[43] In 1981, "Gulf + Western Board chairman Charles Bluddorn announced at the conglomerate's annual meeting . . . that despite record earnings, 'We are going to propose a six-month freeze on all wages at G + W and a reduction of bonuses.'"[44] "In January of 1982, corporate management told [the New Bedford union local] that unless they agreed to meet four conditions, production would be shifted to Super Tool in Michigan, where the local had already granted concessions."[45] Several days later G + W management presented new terms to the union's officials, demanding substantial wage and benefit concessions.

Despite a 415 to 7 union membership vote in favor of a strike, the union leaders did not want to wage a long, defensive strike. They decided to take the offensive, enlist community and local political support, and make G + W's disinvestment at Morse rather than wage concessions the real issue.[46]

To substantiate the disinvestment theory, the union hired a private consultant to investigate G + W's policies:

> What emerged was a picture of systematic corporate disinvestment. Since 1968, Gulf + Western had drained capital from Morse, using its profits to feed other operations. [The consultant] found that in the years 1977–82, G + W invested less than $800,000 in new equipment for its New Bedford operation, far less than its competitors were investing in rival plants.[47]

Armed with data indicating that the real source of Morse's problems was its disinvestment policy, and not high wages and low productivity, the union went on strike. The strike lasted thirteen weeks and resulted in a slight union victory— wages were nominally increased. Several days into the strike the City of New Bedford raised its first "trial balloon" on the use of eminent domain when it resolved "[t]hat we do everything possible within the jurisdiction of the City Council to insure Morse Cutting Tools will survive in New Bedford under the present or alternative ownership."[48]

After the strike ended, everyone in the community thought that the fight to save Morse Cutting Tool had been won, when, in fact, it had only begun. After the strike only two hundred of the five hundred prestrike Morse employees were called back to work.[49] Then, exactly one year after the strike ended, Gulf + Western announced, in August of 1983, its plans to divest itself of much of its manufacturing sector. One month later G + W announced its plans to sell Morse Cutting Tool. By the spring of 1984 the union, with help from the State of Massachusetts (and Governor Dukakis), was actively seeking a buyer for Morse.

At about this time the City of New Bedford formally stepped in. On June 4, 1984, in a major news conference and address to the City Council, the mayor announced the city's plan to seize Morse through its eminent domain power and sell it to a buyer who would commit to keep it in New Bedford and modernize it. Noting first the long relationship between the city and the company, the mayor stated that "[i]t's a two-way street. We have been interwoven with private business for quite some time. We've got a company here that plans to abandon the city. It is not our intent to run [Morse], we are looking to save it and the jobs in the community."[50]

Shortly after this press conference, on August 24, 1984, G + W backed down and sold Morse Cutting Tool to a buyer who would agree to the two conditions set by the city.

Even if a buyer had not been found for the company, the city was convinced of its authority to proceed with its threatened use of eminent domain. The city relied in this regard on the conclusions drawn in a report prepared for the union local by the Institute for Public Representation (IPR)[51] of Washington, DC. During its search for a solution to the crisis at Morse, Local 277 learned that the IPR was researching the legal ramifications of using eminent domain to prevent plant closings. The union asked the IPR to produce a brief, examining the legal justification for the city of New Bedford to take over the Morse plant.[52] The brief[53] that was prepared concluded that "the City of New Bedford can use its eminent domain powers to condemn the Morse Cutting Tools plant."[54] Since the city's goals in acquiring the plant were to prevent unemployment, preserve jobs, and maintain a healthy local economy (all proper public purposes under the recent public use definitions[55]), the IPR reasoned that, based on at least two authorities, such a taking would be permissible. Those sources of authority were the Home Rule Amendment to the Massachusetts Constitution[56] and the Economic Development and Industrial Corporations Act.[57]

Pursuant to the latter act, a municipality may organize an economic development and industrial corporation for the general purpose of enhancing local economic development and the well-being of communities. To accomplish these goals the act establishes the corporation's power to acquire property through eminent domain for numerous economic development purposes.[58] Based on their analysis of these sections and relevant case law and other authority,[59] the IPR concluded that the city had the authority to acquire the real property elements of the Morse plant.

The second source of authority for New Bedford to proceed was the Home Rule Amendment. This amendment grants cities and towns powers not denied them by express or clearly implied state legislation or by state constitutional provisions.[60] Of particular importance in the Morse case is the amendment's apparent authorization of ordinances that allow condemnation of personal and intangible property.[61]

Despite its apparent authority to do so, New Bedford was not forced to test the correctness of the IPR's eminent domain conclusions because, as noted, the Morse plant was purchased by a private investor who promised to keep it in town. As in the case of Nabisco, some commentators believe, however, that New Bedford's threatened use of eminent domain helped push Gulf + Western into a position where it was more amenable to an offer from this investor.[62] The Morse case shows that, although as yet not entirely tested and upheld in a court of law, the uses of eminent domain espoused here appeared credible enough to some to force G + W to alter its behavior.

However, the most important limitation on this use of eminent domain is the requirement that the company be paid for what is taken. Because of this limitation, eminent domain should not be viewed as either the sole or most important economic development tool in a community's arsenal. It is only one tool and perhaps should not be used in every case of an attempted shutdown. Its use is an important policy choice that must be made on a case-by-case basis.

There may be many cases where it is simply not financially feasible to keep a company in a community. Sometimes a plant is closed because of changes in consumer preferences, and in others the plant may be closed because it simply cannot continue profitably. Decisions regarding which business to save depend in part on local economic needs, local expectations of potential profitability of maintaining the business, and other, perhaps noneconomic goals. As is well known, many profitable businesses are closed simply because their investors were either dissatisfied with their return on investment, or intended to escape from unions. Given these considerations, each community will have to embark on an assessment of concerned corporate entities before deciding whether to pursue the option of eminent domain.

Community Property Rights

Another innovative tool that could be used to prevent a plant closing is for a community to assert the existence of a property right in a business that would make unilateral decisions against the community's economic well-being. This type of property right would not be based exclusively on the traditional legal conceptions of property but also on the contractual metaphors that depict property rights in terms of either social or mutual reliance relationships.

The above approach has been taken in several recent cases. In each, some variation of a breach of contract, promissory estoppel, or contractually implied property right argument was pursued. The last of three case studies illustrates these arguments in action.

United Steelworkers

In *United Steelworkers of America* v. *U.S. Steel Corp.*,[63] the local union filed a lawsuit seeking to keep the defendant's plant open and operating. The basis of the plaintiff's claim was alleged promises made by an employee of the defendant to keep the plant open as long as it remained profitable. At issue were statements made by the plant manager over an in-house recorded message system. This system stored recorded messages and allowed employees to later hear these messages on the system. Some of the statements made included, for example: "With your help, this effort will continue and if and when there will be a phase-out depends on the plant's profitability."[64]

The plaintiffs alleged that, in response to and in reliance on such statements, they "made a sincere and forceful effort to increase productivity, or 'yield,' primarily by waiving those formal technicalities of their labor contract that contributed to easing working conditions, but detracted from productivity."[65] The accounting reports supported the plaintiffs' contention: "[T]he gross profit margin for 1977 was $24,899,000.00, that for 1978 was $41,770,000.00, that for 1979 was $32,000,000.00 and the projected gross profit margin for 1980 . . . was $32,396,000.00."[66]

Late in 1979 U.S. Steel announced its plans to close the plant. In December 1979, the plaintiffs filed for, and were granted in February 1980, a temporary restraining order. Trial on the merits began in March 1980. In their complaint, the plaintiffs suggested four theories in support of injunctive relief: violation of antitrust statutes, breach of contract, promissory estoppel, and property right. The latter three theories will be addressed here.

The court noted that the breach of contract and detrimental reliance claims were based on the telephone messages recorded by the plant manager. Applying Ohio contract law, the court concluded that the contract at issue must have been a unilateral "promise exchanged for an act" contract, the message being the promise, the act being making the company profitable.[67] Finding that these facts did not give rise to a contract, the court noted:

> [At] the time the alleged promise was made by the company, the workers did not immediately execute the contract in full—profitability would have to be achieved over a long period of hard work. This means that the contract would not come into existence until the workers had fully performed their side of the contract by making the plant profitable. "[A unilateral] contract does not come into existence until one party to it has done all that is necessary on his part."[68]

The court then addressed the plaintiffs' promissory estoppel arguments. The court began its analysis of this argument by noting the elements of a promissory estoppel claim and then shifted gears by properly noting that "the formation of a proper contract requires that the employee of the corporation who makes a promise must have the authority to enter into the contract."[69] Thus, for the court the issue became whether the plant manager had the authority to make these types of promises on behalf of the company. Applying the concept of agency in the promissory estoppel context, the court stated that "[t]he lack of a technical power of agency in any of the company's spokesmen does not relieve the company from a binding promise if it should reasonably have expected the statements of the spokesmen to be relied on detrimentally by the workers." The court found that no such reasonable reliance existed. In support of this conclusion the court reasoned:

> [A] reasonable understanding of all the statements . . . would suggest that national company management wanted to close the plant for lack of profitability and that the call for increased worker productivity was a plan [the plant manager] was presenting as a final effort for the workers to sway national management opinion. Mr. Kerwin's [the plant manager's] plan was courageous and well conceived, but it did not represent a promise made by the corporation on which the workers should reasonably have relied.[70]

Finally, the court addressed the community right theory. This theory had actually been suggested by the court itself during the pretrial conference. At the conference the court requested the parties to brief "[t]he possibility of the relationships between the steel industry and surrounding community generating a property right."[71] With regard to this suggestion, the court stated at the conference:

> Everything that has happened in the Mahoning Valley has been happening for many years because of steel. Schools have been built, roads have been built. Expansion that has taken place is because of steel. And to accommodate that industry, lives and destinies of the inhabitants of that community were based on that institution: steel.
>   But what has happened over the years between U.S. Steel, Youngstown, and the inhabitants? Hasn't something come out of that relationship, something that out of which—not reaching for a case on property law or a series of cases but looking at the law as a whole, the Constitution, the whole body of law, not only contract law, but tort, corporations, agency, negotiable instruments—taking a look at the whole body of American law and then sitting back and reflecting on what it seeks to do, and that is to adjust human relationships in keeping with the whole spirit and foundation of the American system of law, to preserve property rights.[72]

Despite this initially encouraging signal to the plaintiffs, the district court ultimately found "no legal basis for the finding of a property right"[73] because "[u]nfortunately, the mechanism . . . to recognize this new property right is not now in existence in the code of laws of our nation." The court deemed itself bound to so rule even though it also felt that "U.S. Steel should not be permitted to leave the Youngstown area devastated after drawing from the lifeblood of the community for so long." The court then concluded its community property right discussion by noting that either the state or federal legislature was the proper forum in which the right should be formally recognized.

Unfortunately, on appeal, the Sixth Circuit Court of Appeals affirmed[74] all parts of the district court's opinion except the antitrust matter. Yet despite the court's reluctance to recognize community property rights asserted in the *United Steelworkers* case, there are grounds to conclude that these rights will eventually be recognized by the judiciary. Most notable in this regard was the district court's query in *United Steelworkers,* offered after reflection on the long-term relationship between northeastern Ohio and U.S. Steel, whether something had not come out of that relationship to preserve property rights.[75] This statement, and its reaffirmation in the appellate court's opinion, suggest that both courts truly felt disturbed by the resolution of the matter. Both courts, in a seemingly *apologetic tone,* stated that under the current state of the law they felt constrained to hold as they did.[76] Both courts also stated their belief that the formulation of public policy on great issues such as plant closings was clearly the responsibility of the legislatures of the states or of the Congress of the United States.[77] This is an arguable conclusion.

While there is no denying that had the *United Steelworkers* courts held in the various plaintiffs' favor, it would have signaled a clear departure from traditional contract or property concepts, still it is elementary that in many cases when the court wishes to do what it knows to be the right thing, it reasons by analogy from existing precedent. In the case of plant closing, this may be imperative because:

> [T]hus far, it is obvious that traditional contract theory and legislative plant closing proposals cannot be expected to afford optimum worker and community protection when a major local employer decides to relocate or shut down. It is therefore necessary for advocates to explore novel approaches to creating and saving community jobs.[78]

One commentator has recently argued (while acknowledging the relative novelty of his argument) that the *United Steelworkers* courts could have held in the plaintiffs' favor based on already existing law! In "The Reliance Interest in Property,"[79] author Joseph William Singer argues that contrary to the *United Steelworkers* decisions, continued and sustained relationships can, in their own right, give rise to property rights. While acknowledging that the *United Steelworkers* courts would have had to recognize "substantial change in the law" in granting the union's claims, Singer asserts, nonetheless, that "contrary to the conclusions of the judges in this case, precedent for the creation of property rights of the kind asserted by the union does exist."[80] Singer notes that the legal system already contains a variety of doctrines that recognize the sharing and shifting of various property interests in situations that should be viewed as analogous to plant closings. "These currently enforceable doctrines encompass the full range of social relationships, from relations among strangers, between neighbors, among long-term contractual partners in the marketplace, among family members and others in intimate relationships, and finally, between citizens and the government."[81] These relationships have given rise to "reliance interests in property," which have resulted in specific legal rules about, for example, adverse possession, prescriptive easements, public rights of access to private property, tenants' rights, equitable division of property on divorce, and welfare rights.[82] What is most notable about all these relationships is that

> At crucial points in the development of these relationships—often, but not always, when they break up—the legal system requires a sharing or shifting of property interests from the "owner" to the "nonowner" to protect the more vulnerable party to the relationship. The legal system requires this shift, not because of reliance on specific promises, but because the parties have relied on each other generally and on the continuation of their relationship. Moreover, the more vulnerable party may need access to resources controlled by the more powerful party, and the relationship is such that we consider it fair to place this burden on the more powerful party by redistributing entitlements.[83]

Singer continues this argument by cautioning the courts that "[c]onsideration of competing interests in access to resources and past reliance on relationships granting such access should be a central component of any legal determination of how to allocate lawful power over those resources."[84] Based on all of these already legally recognized rules and principles Singer concludes that the *United Steelworkers* courts "had access to enforceable legal rules based on principles that could have been seen as applicable precedent for extension of existing law by creation of this new set of entitlements."[85]

There are no apparent reasons why these principles would not be applicable in most, if not all, cases of plant closings. In these cases there has usually been a continuous and mutual relationship where severance most often leaves one party "vulnerable." In any particular case the strength of the property claim would be contingent on the duration and degree of involvement in the relationship. These property rights do not need a legislative construction; they can be created by the judiciary in the same way that other property and property-like interests have been.

Thus, while the United Steelworkers lost their battle, there is reason to believe that someday a community property right could be judicially recognized, or legislatively enacted if unions organize for its support in much the same way that they lobbied for plant closing legislation. This struggle will take time and cooperation with local communities, which are generally powerless to fight a plant closing or recoup its long-term investment in city services to support a specific local business. However, recognition of a community property right will eventually put communities in a better position to negotiate the conditions of both a company's entrance to and exit from a community.

Conclusions

Since the 1970s America's economy has been deindustrializing as private businesses and multinationals have abandoned domestic reinvestment in lieu of relocating overseas. This economic transformation has brought with it a great deal of localized and national hardship. In some cases it has brought whole communities to their economic knees. In other cases a limited number of individuals within a community have faced the same result. However, communities need not remain powerless, and there may be tools available to communities to slow and alter the balance of power in this process.

To accomplish these goals labor unions and communities have two potential tools at their disposal if they can enlist support from local governments. First, using or threatening to use a municipality's eminent domain power to gain control of corporate assets is one way to alter the balance of power, giving localities greater bargaining power to deal with companies. Regardless of the specific authority granting this power, this chapter has shown how many states, such as California, Massachusetts, and Pennsylvania, have broad eminent domain powers that can be used to purchase the assets of a business that intends to either close altogether or simply leave town. The law in these states is representative of statutes that can potentially invoke the use of eminent domain in fighting against plant closings. Once acquired, business facilities can then be operated by the municipality itself, the workers of the company, or by a new private entity.

Yet there is no need to limit the use of eminent domain to reactive situations premised on a company's notice to leave. Instead, eminent domain could be used as an alternative to other types of incentives for economic development (such as property tax breaks and IRBs) that cities provide to businesses to encourage relocation or expansion. More importantly, eminent domain can be a proactive and preemptive tool to acquire corporate assets as a means to gain greater control. Eminent domain, as an offensive tool, can be used to redistribute wealth and power in a community and give workers and residents of a locality a greater sense of economic control over their lives.

Despite the utility of employing municipal powers of eminent domain to prevent plant closings, inherent in such use is the problem of providing just compensation. The traditional measurement of just compensation is the fair market value of the property taken,[86] with fair market value defined as what a willing buyer would pay a willing seller. As envisioned by Tri-State and the SVA, for example, the money to provide the required compensation would come either through the act's bonding authority provision,[87] or from a variety of other sources, including union pension fund investment in federally guaranteed bonds; federal and state loan guarantees; direct investment by local, state, and federal government; tax-exempt municipal and industrial bonds; tax credits; worker contributions; and guaranteed purchase agreements for the plate and structural steel to be used in infrastructure rebuilding.[88]

A credible threatened use of eminent domain appears to be compromised by a just compensation requirement. If the acquisition of a plant appears difficult because of inability to raise money, an alternative method of valuation can replace the test of fair market value, as follows:

> Commentators on international law have suggested that just compensation is a social as well as a technical issue. According to this view, the fair market value of a facility may be affected by how that facility has been operated. Some have suggested that the following factors should be considered in determining the amount of compensation: the circumstances of the original investment (for instance, whether the company secured its initial position through force or fraud); whether the company has extracted substantial profits from the community; whether a facility's operations have caused environmental damage over the years; and whether the taking is pursuant to a broad program of economic and social reform. These factors can dramatically affect the amount of compensation required in an eminent domain proceeding.[89]

After all, the fair market test, as the rule for just compensation, is not carved in the U.S. Constitution. This rule was judicially crafted over time and did not exist in the early days of the American republic.[90] In fact, it was not until well into the nineteenth century that just compensation for developed property was required, and it was not until late in the nineteenth century that the U.S. Supreme Court started mandating rules of just compensation requirements for states.[91] Thus fair market value compensation for corporate assets seized in an eminent domain action may not be essential, and other mitigating factors regarding a company's relationship to a community could substantially lower the amount of compensation in an eminent domain proceeding. Moreover, it is possible to devise a set of modifying compensation rules through legislative action.

A more promising avenue that unions and municipalities could explore to avoid the just compensation issue is the legal argument that between a company and the community in which it resides certain community property rights have arisen. This empowers the municipality to control the business's ability to make unilateral decisions that harm the town. The existence of this right, though currently unrecognized, could someday give rise to a claim for compensatory relief based on concepts of contract, implied contract, or equitable or promissory estoppel. Cities such as Norwood, and Ypsilanti, Michigan, in 1993, for example, sought this route, contending that some type of implied or expressed contract generated through municipal tax concessions or support for a company was created.[92] While lower court decisions ruled in favor of local governments, these decisions were unfortunately overturned on appeal. However, despite these losses, contractual metaphors in the law seem relevant to the problem of plant closings, and continued litigation of this issue may eventually produce significant victories and precedents. Labor should adopt the strategies of other groups, such as the NAACP and the ACLU, developing a conscious strategy of litigation to pursue test cases that would be most favorable to establishing community property or contractual rights. In sum, a proactive labor strategy for the 1990s and beyond should include litigation to use the law to achieve desired objectives. Citizens have the right to expect their governments to assure greater stability and predictability in their relations with local business firms. Up to now, businesses have enjoyed a "privileged status" in American politics.[93] Unions should lead the way in the 1990s and act as catalysts to encourage communities and local governments to use eminent domain and community property rights as general strategies to fight arbitrary corporate power. In the past, many municipalities, such as Oakland, California, and Minneapolis/St. Paul, Minnesota, and groups such as the Plant Closures Project and the Working Group on Economic Dislocation, have pursued eminent domain options as one means to enhance community power over private businesses.

By reaching out to the larger community, labor can solicit new support, enrich its membership, and fight against arbitrary corporate power by turning the table on all fronts, against capital, including these legal means.

Notes

1. See, e.g., M. Skidmore, *A Look at Four Plant Shutdowns in Minnesota*, a report published by the Center for Urban and Regional Affairs, University of Minnesota; "Look What Happened to Pensions When a Tractor Plant Closed," *Machinist* 28 (March 22, 1973): 12; A. Alanen, "Economics and Environmentalism in a Company Town," paper presented at the 1977 annual meeting of the Rural Sociological Society, a copy of which is available from the New York State School of Industrial and Labor Relations at Cornell University. See also Comment, "The Use of Eminent Domain to Prevent an Industrial Plant Shutdown: The Next Step in an Expanding Power?" *Alabama Law Review* 49, (1984): 95; Perry, "Iron Mills, a Dearth of Hope Are Features of Ohio's Steel Towns," *Wall Street Journal* (January 20, 1983): 1; "When Arco Left Town," *New York Times* (July 25, 1982), sec. 3, 1; "Once an Industry Hot Spot, Chester, Pa., Hits Bad Times," *Wall Street Journal* (January 26, 1981), 23; Barker, "There Is a Better Way," *Labor Law Journal* 32 (1981): 453–54; Barry Bluestone and Benett Harrison, *The Deindustrialization of America: Plant Closings, Community Abandonment, and the Dismantling of Basic Industry* (1982), 276.

2. See, e.g., Barry Bluestone and Bennett Harrison, *The Great U-Turn: Corporate Restructuring and the Polarizing of America* (1988), 51–65; see also Kasl, Gore, and Cobb, "The Experience of Losing a Job: Reported Changes in Health, Symptoms, and Illness Behavior," *Psychosomatic Medicine* 37 (1975): 106; H. Brenner, "Estimating Social Costs of National Economic Policy: Implications for Mental and Physical Health and Clinical Aggression," report prepared for the Joint Economic Committee, U.S. Congress, 1975.

3. Harrison and Bluestone, *The Great U-Turn*, 20–27.

4. See J. Portz, *The Politics of Plant Closings* (1990), 1–13, for a discussion of the different tactics communities may take toward a plant closing.

5. While it is not the purpose of this chapter to pursue this option in detail, the option is most often exercised pursuant to the National Labor Relations Act 29, *U.S.C.* secs. 158(d) and 158(a)(5), as amended. See also *First National Maintenance Corp.* v. *NLRB,*

452 U.S., 666 (1981); *Textile Workers of America* v. *Darlington Manufacturing Co.,* 380 U.S., 263 (1965); G. Haas, *Plant Closures: Myths, Realities, and Responses* (1985), 236–39.

    6. See Comment, "Eminent Domain: The Ability of a Community to Retain an Industry in the Face of an Attempted Shut Down or Relocation," *Ohio N.U.L. REV.* 12 (1985): 231, 232, n. 5, which states that "less than a quarter of the American workforce is unionized, and of those, only 13 percent of 400 sampled contracts placed any limitation of closings or relocations"; Rhine, "Business Closings and their Effects on Employers—the Need for New Remedies," *Labor Law Journal* 35 (1984): 268; for cases finding contract provisions that bar runaway shops see National Lawyers Guild, *Employee and Union Member Guide to Labor Law* (1984), ch. 4.01, n. 2.

    7. See, e.g., *U.S.C.A.* 29, sec. 2101–9, West Supp. (1989), representing the recently passed federal plant closing notification law; *Massachusetts General Laws Ann.*, ch. 149, sec. 182, West Supp. (1989); *Massachusetts General Laws Ann.*, ch. 151A, secs. 71A-G, West Supp. (1989); *Wisconsin Stat. Ann.* 109.07, West Supp. (1988); see also "Plant Closing Legislation" in A. Aboud, ed., *Key Issues* (Ithaca, NY: New York State School of Industrial and Labor Relations, Cornell University, 1984), 27.

    8. See, e.g., *United States* v. *Reynolds,* 397 U.S., 14 (1970); *United States* v. *Jones,* 109 U.S., 513 (1883); *Kohl* v. *United States,* 91 U.S., 367 (1875); see also Nichols, "Eminent Domain," sec. 1.13(1) (1985).

    9. *U.S. Constitution,* Amendment V. This amendment is made applicable to the states as well through "the fourteenth amendment to the United States Constitution, [which] throws the protection of the federal courts over an individual whose property is sought to be taken by a state without compensation." See Nichols, "Eminent Domain," sec. 8.1(2).

    10. See generally *Burnquist* v. *Cook,* 220 Minn. 48, 19 N.W. 2d, 394 (1945); *State* v. *Severson,* 194 Minn. 644, 261 N.W., 469 (1935); *Knapp* v. *State,* 125 Minn. 194, 145 N.W., 967 (1914).

    11. David Schultz, "The Public Use," and Nichols, "Eminent Domain," ed. Julius L. Sackman and Russell Van Brunt (New York: Matthew Bender, 1993); see also David Schultz and David Jann, "Business and Plant Closings: The Expansion of the 'Public Use' Doctrine in Eminent Domain," and Nichols, "Eminent Domain."

    12. 348 U.S., 26 (1956).

    13. District of Columbia redevelopment Act of 1945, 60 Stat. 790, *D.C. Code,* sec. 5–701–19 (1951); discussed in Berman, 348 U.S., 28–29.

    14. Ibid., 33–34.

    15. 410 Mich., 616; 304 N.W. 2d, 455 (1981).

    16. 31 Cal., 3d 656; 646 P. 2d, 835; 183 Cal. Rptr., 673 (1982).

    17. 467 U.S., 229 (1984).

    18. *Mich. Comp. Laws Ann.*, secs. 125.1601–36 (1974).

    19. Ibid., sec. 125.1602.

    20. "Poletown," 410 Mich., 633; 304 N.W. 2d, 459.

    21. *City of Oakland* v. *Oakland Raiders,* 31 Cal. 3d, 656, 664; 646 P. 2d, 835, 843; 183 Cal. Rptr., 673, 681 (1982); in this decision the court remanded the case to the trial court for a full trial on the merits. The subsequent history of the case includes three dismissals, the last at *City of Oakland* v. *Oakland Raiders,* No. 76044, slip., op., California Superior Court, Monterey County (June 16, 1984).

    22. 467 U.S., 229 (1984).

    23. *Hawaii Review,* stat. secs., 516.1–.182.

    24. Hereinafter the authority.

    25. *Hawaii Housing Authority* v. *Midkiff,* 467 U.S., 229 (1984).

26. Ibid., 243–44.

27. See, e.g., Comment, "Eminent Domain as a Tool to Set Up Employee-Owned Businesses in the Face of Shutdowns," *Antioch Law Review*. 4 (1986):271 (hereinafter "Eminent Domain and Employee-Owned Businesses"); "Industrial Plant Shutdown," and comment, "Retain an Industry." For an alternative viewpoint, arguing that these types of uses of eminent domain would violate the commerce clause, see Note, "The Commerce Clause Limitation on the Power to Condemn a Relocating Business," *Yale Law Journal* 96 (1987): 1343.

28. Local community action groups that have pressed eminent domain arguments in their efforts to prevent plant closures include, e.g., The Plant Closure Project, 433 Jefferson St., Oakland, CA 94607; and The Seattle Work Center, an organization discussed by Lewiston and Wise, "Locked Out by Lockheed," *Dollars and Sense* (December 1987): 17.

29. See Harrison, "When Workers Become Entrepreneurs," *Technology Review* (July 1989): 19. In this article Harrison states that "[b]etween 1977 and 1982, shrinking steel firms laid off about 100,000 workers in the tri-state region. . . . Local officials estimate that there are still 25,000 to 30,000 former industrial workers out of work in the Mon Valley alone."

30. A copy of *Rebuild Steel* is available from the William Mitchell College of Law, *Law Review* office.

31. *Rebuild Steel*, 8–9.

32. Articles of incorporation for the SVA were filed with the secretary of the Commonwealth of Pennsylvania on November 15, 1985; a certificate of incorporation was issued on January 31, 1986.

33. 53 Pennsylvania *Cons. Stat. Ann.*, secs. 301–22, Purdon (1974) (hereinafter the act).

34. Hornack and Lynd, "The Steel Valley Authority," New York University Review of Law and Societal Change 15, no. 1 (1986–87): 118–19.

35. Pursuant to 53 Pennsylvania *Cons. Stat. Ann.* sec. 306A(a)(17).

36. Hornack and Lynd, "Steel Valley Authority": 118–19.

37. Ibid.; see Pennsylvania Eminent Domain Code, 26 Pennsylvania *Cons. Stat. Ann.* secs. 1–101–903, Purdon Supp. (1986).

38. See, e.g., *In re 49.0768 Acres by Rostraver Township Airport Authority*, 427 Pa. 1, 233 A. 2d, 427 (1967); *Truitt* v. *Borough of Ambridge Water Authority*, 389 Pa. 429, 133 A. 2d, 797 (1957).

39. Hornack and Lynd, "Steel Valley Authority": 123.

40. Ibid.: 123–24.

41. Doherty, "The Struggle to Save Morse Cutting Tool: A Successful Community Campaign," Labor Education Center, Southeastern Massachusetts University (1986), 2.

42. Swinney, "Labor Community Unity: The Morse Strike Against Disinvestment and Concessions," *Labor Research Review* 1 (1982): 5.

43. Doherty, "Struggle to Save Morse," 2.

44. Ibid., 3.

45. Swinney, "Labor Community Unity," 5–6.

46. Doherty, "Struggle to Save Morse," 7. In fact, "[b]ecause labor and management disagreed over the basic issues underlying their dispute, the strike at Morse received extensive media coverage, locally, regionally and nationally." Doherty cites, for example, an article that appeared in the *Providence Journal Bulletin* on June 27, 1982, that stated that "[i]f the UE can keep the debate on this level it may have some powerful allies. The issue will not be a narrow one of labor versus management, but the much broader one of community versus conglomerate."

47. Swinney, "Labor Community Unity," 7. "The study found that G + W invested less than $800,000 in new equipment for the Morse plant in the five years between 1977

and 1982. From 1978 to 1982 (four years), $1.5 million was invested in Union Trust Drill in Athol, and from 1979 to 1982 (three years), more than $5 million was invested in new equipment in Greenfield Tap and Die—two of Morse's chief competitors, also located in Massachusetts," (Doherty, "Struggle to Save Morse," 6).

48. Swinney, "Labor Community Unity," 12.

49. Doherty, "Struggle to Save Morse," 13.

50. Ibid., 14.

51. Hereinafter the IPR. The IPR is a public interest firm and law school clinical education program that was founded by the Georgetown University Law Center and the Ford Foundation in 1971. The IPR provides legal services to groups and individuals who are unable to obtain effective legal representation on matters that have a significant impact in connection with issues of broad public importance.

52. Doherty, "Struggle to Save Morse," 17.

53. The brief is titled "Power of New Bedford, Massachusetts, to Acquire the Morse Cutting Tool Plant Through Eminent Domain" (May 18, 1984), hereinafter "New Bedford Brief"; a copy of this brief may be obtained either from the *Law Review* office, William Mitchell College of Law, or from the IPR at Georgetown University.

54. "New Bedford Brief," 4.

55. See supra sec. II.

56. *Massachusetts Constitution*, Articles of Amendment, art. II (1966).

57. *Massachusetts General Laws Ann.*, ch. 121C, West (1986) (hereinafter the act).

58. Ibid., sec. 5(L).

59. The brief cites, e.g., Opinion of the Justices to the Governor, 373 Mass. 904, 907; 369 N.E. 2d, 447, 449 (1977), "Reducing unemployment and stimulating the economy are public purposes." Opinion of the Justices to the House of Representatives, 368 Mass. 880, 885, 335 N.E. 2d, 362, 365 (1975), " 'The reduction of unemployment and alleviation of economic distress,' as well as the '[s]timulation of investment and job opportunity . . . are proper public purposes' "; *Allydon Realty Corp.* v. *Holyoke Housing Authority*, 304 Mass. 288, 292; 23 N.E. 2d, 665, 667–68 (1939); *Machado* v. *Board of Public Works*, 321 Mass. 101, 103; 71 N.E. 2d, 886, 887–88 (1947).

60. *Massachusetts Constitution*, Articles of Amendment, art. II, sec. 6.

61. The New Bedford Brief pursues a long and detailed analysis of various related statutes and case law to arrive at this conclusion, an analysis that cannot be repeated in detail here. See "New Bedford Brief," 20–33.

62. Doherty, "Struggle to Save Morse," 17.

63. 492 F. Supp., 1 (1980).

64. Ibid., 5.

65. Ibid., 8.

66. Ibid., 6.

67. Ibid., 5–6.

68. Ibid., 4.

69. *United Steelworkers*, 492 F. Supp., 5; *Bradford Belting Co.* v. *Gibson*, 68 Ohio Supp. 442; 67 N.E. 888 (1903).

70. Ibid., 6.

71. Ibid., 9.

72. *United Steelworkers* v. *United States Steel Corp.*, 631 F. 2d, 1264, 1279–80 (1980). The appellate court's statement of these matters is quoted here because, even though originally made by the district court, the appellate court's opinion more fully repeats the statements than did the district's court's opinion.

73. *United Steelworkers*, 492 F. Supp., 10.

74. *United Steelworkers* v. *U.S. Steel Corp.*, 631 F. 2d, 1264 (1980).

75. As noted in the appellate court's opinion, *United Steelworkers* v. *U.S. Steel Corp.,* 631 F. 2d, 1264, 1280 (1980).

76. Ibid., 1279–82; *United Steelworkers of America* v. *U.S. Steel Corp.,* 492 F. Supp. 1, 9–10 (1980).

77. 631 F. 2d, 1282; *Nebbia* v. *New York,* 291 U.S. 502 (1934); 492 F. Supp., 10.

78. Comment, "Eminent Domain: The Ability of a Community to Retain an Industry in the Face of an Attempted Shut Down or Relocation," *Ohio N.U.Law Review* 12 (1985): 231, 233–34.

79. *Stanford Law Review* 40 (1987): 611.

80. Singer, "The Reliance Interest in Property," *Stanford Law Review* 40 (1987): 611, 621.

81. Ibid., 622–23.

82. Ibid., 622.

83. Ibid., 623.

84. Ibid., 622.

85. Ibid., 621.

86. See *United States* v. *Miller,* 317 U.S. 369, 374 (1943).

87. 53 Pennsylvania *Cons. Stat. Ann.* sec. 306B(i) Purdon (1974).

88. "Rebuild Steel," supra n. 45, 10.

89. Hornack and Lynd, "Steel Valley Authority," 122–23; L. Henkin et al., *International Law* (1980): 752, 754, 757.

90. M. Horwitz, *The Transformation of American Law: 1780–1860* (1977), 31–63.

91. *Chicago, Burlington, and Quincy Railroad Company* v. *Chicago,* 166 U.S., 226 (1897).

92. *Ypsilanti* v. *General Motors Corporation,* 1993 WL, 132385 (Michigan Circuit Court).

93. C. Lindblom, *Politics and Markets* (1977), 170–89, 356.

Selected Bibliography

Aglietta, M. 1979. *The Regulatory Crisis of Capitalism.* London: New Left Books.

Albers, Jens. 1945. *Social Security Participants of Social Insurance Systems.* Mannheim: Report 4. HIWED Project.

Allen, Victor L. 1975. *Social Analysis: A Marxist Critique and Alternative.* London: Longman Group.

Amin, A., and Tomaney, J. forthcoming. "Illusions of Prosperity." In P. Fasenfest and P. Meyer, eds., *The Politics of Local Economic Policy Formation.* London: Macmillan.

Araghi, F.A., and Bina, C. 1991. "Production, Market Exchange, and Alienation." *Journal of Economic Democracy* 1, no. 3 (July–September): 311–17.

Aronowitz, Stanley. 1973. *False Promises: The Shaping of American Working Class Consciousness.* New York: McGraw-Hill.

———. 1983. *Working Class Hero: A New Strategy for Labor.* New York: Adama Books.

Arrow, Kenneth J. 1994. "Methodological Individualism and Social Knowledge." *American Economic Review* 84, no. 2 (May): 1–9.

Aschauer, David A. 1990. *Public Investment and Private Sector Growth: The Economic Benefits of Reducing America's "Third Deficit."* Washington, DC: Economic Policy Institute.

Balanoff, Tom. 1985. "The Cement Workers' Experience." *Labor Research Review* 7 (Fall): 5–33.

Baran, Paul A., and Sweezy, Paul M. 1966. *Monopoly Capital.* New York: Monthly Review Press.

Barkan, Joanne. 1992. "End of the Swedish Model?" *Dissent* 39, no. 2.

Barlett, Donald L., and Steele, James B. 1992. *America: What Went Wrong.* Kansas City, MO: Andrews & McMeel.

———. 1994. *America: Who Really Pays the Taxes?* New York: Touchstone.

Barnet, Richard J., and Cavanagh, John. 1994. *Global Dreams: Imperial Corporations and the New World Order.* New York: Simon & Schuster.

Bell, Daniel. 1974. *The Coming of Post-Industrial Society.* New York: Basic Books.

Beneria, Lourdes. 1989. "Gender and the Global Economy." In Arthur MacEwan and William K. Tabb, eds., *Instability and Change in the World Economy.* New York: Monthly Review Press, 246–47.

Beneria, Lourdes, and Roldan, Martha. 1987. *The Crossroads of Class and Gender: Homework, Subcontracting and Household Dynamics in Mexico City.* Chicago: University of Chicago Press.

Benston, Margaret Lowe. 1983. "For Women, the Chips Are Down." In Jan Zimmerman, ed., *The Technological Woman*. New York: Praeger.

Berberoglu, Berch. 1987. *The Internationalization of Capital*. New York: Praeger.

————. 1992. *The Legacy of Empire: Economic Decline and Class Polarization in the U.S.* New York: Praeger.

Berle, A.A., and Means, G.C. 1932. *The Modern Corporation and Private Property*. New York: Macmillan.

Bernard, Elaine. 1982. *The Long Distance Feeling: A History of the Telecommunications Workers Union*. Vancouver: New Star Books.

————. 1991. *Technological Change and Skills Development*. Australia: Deakin University Press.

Bina, Cyrus. 1985. *The Economics of the Oil Crisis*. New York: St. Martin's Press.

————. 1988. "Internationalization of the Oil Industry: Simple Oil Shocks or Structural Crisis." *Review: Journal of Fernand Braudel Center* 11, no. 3 (Summer): 329–70.

————. 1989. "Competition, Control and Price Formation in the International Energy Industry." *Energy Economics* 11, no. 3 (July): 162–68.

————. 1990. "Limits of OPEC Pricing: OPEC Profits and the Nature of Global Oil Accumulation." *OPEC Review* 14, no. 1 (Spring): 55–73.

————. 1992. "A Prelude to Internationalization of the Postwar Economy." *Journal of Economic Democracy* 2, no. 2 (January–March).

————. 1993. "The Rhetoric of Oil and the Dilemma of War and American Hegemony." *Arab Studies Quarterly* 15, no. 3 (Summer): 1–20.

————. 1994a. "Farewell to the Pax Americana." In H. Zangeneh, ed. *Islam, Iran, and World Stability*. New York: St. Martin's Press, 41–74.

————. 1994b. "Oil, Japan, and Globalization." *Challenge* 37, no. 3 (May–June): 41–48.

————. 1994c. "Towards a New World Order." In H. Mutalib and T. Hashmi, eds., *Islam, Muslims and the Modern State*. New York: St. Martin's Press, 3–30.

————. 1995. "On Sand Castles and Sand Castle–Conjectures: A Rejoinder." *Arab Studies Quarterly* 17, nos. 1–2: 167–71.

Bina, C., and Davis, C. 1990. "The Transnationalization of Capital and the Decline of the U.S. Labor Movement. " A paper presented at the ASSA meetings, Washington, DC (December).

————. 1993a. "Transnational Capital, the Global Labor Process, and the International Labor Movement." In B. Berberoglu, ed., *The Labor Process and Control of Labor*. Westport, CT: Praeger, 152–70.

————. 1993b. "Labor and the World of Coercive Competition." A paper presented at the Allied Social Science Associations (ASSA) meetings, Anaheim, CA (January).

Bina, C., and Yaghmaian, B. 1988. "Import Substitution and Export Promotion Within the Context of the Internationalization of Capital." *Review of Radical Political Economics* 20, nos. 2–3: 234–40.

————. 1991. "Postwar Global Accumulation and the Transnationalization of Capital." *Capital & Class* 43 (Spring): 107–30.

Birch, David L. 1981. "Who Creates Jobs?" *The Public Interest* (Winter).

Bluestone, Barry, and Harrison, Bennett. 1982. *The Deindustrialization of America: Plant Closings, Community Abandonment and the Dismantling of Basic Industry*. New York: Basic Books.

Boddy, R., and Crotty, J.R. 1975. "Class Conflict and Macro-Policy: The Political Business Cycle." *Review of Radical Political Economics* 7, no. 1 (Spring): 1–19.

Botwinick, Howard. 1993. *Persistent Inequalities: Wage Disparity Under Capitalist Competition*. Princeton, NJ: Princeton University Press.

Bowles, Samuel; Gordon, David M.; and Weisskopf, Thomas E. 1983. *Beyond the Waste Land.* Garden City, NY: Anchor/Doubleday.

————. 1986. "Power and Profits: The Social Structure of Accumulation and the Profitability of the Postwar U.S. Economy." *Review of Radical Political Economics* 18, nos. 1 and 2: 132–67.

————. 1990. *After the Waste Land: A Democratic Economics for the Year 2000.* Armonk, NY: M.E. Sharpe.

Boyer, R. 1979. "Wage Formation in Historical Perspective: the French Experience." *Cambridge Journal of Economics* 3, no. 2 (June): 99–118.

Braverman, Harry. 1974. *Labor and Monopoly Capital: The Degradation of Work in the Twentieth Century.* New York: Monthly Review Press.

Brecher, Jeremy, and Costello, Tim. 1991. *Global Village vs. Global Pillage: A One-World Strategy for Labor.* Washington, DC: International Labor Rights Education and Research Fund.

Brenner, H. 1975. "Estimating Social Costs of National Economic Policy: Implications for Mental and Physical Health and Clinical Aggression." A report prepared for the Joint Economic Committee, U.S. Congress.

Brenner, Robert. 1977. "The Origins of Capitalist Development: A Critique of Neo-Smithian Marxism." *New Left Review* 104 (July–August): 25–92.

Brodeur, Paul. 1989. *Currents of Death: Power Lines, Computer Terminals, and the Attempt to Cover Up Their Threat to Your Health.* New York: Simon & Schuster.

Brody, David. 1980. "The Uses of Power I: Industrial Battleground." In *Workers in Industrial America: Essays on the Twentieth-Century Struggle.* New York: Oxford University Press.

Brown, Clair, and Reich, Michael. 1989. "When Does Union-Management Cooperation Work? A Look at NUMMI and GM–Van Nuys." *California Management Review* 31, no. 4: 26–44.

Bryan, R. 1985. "Monopoly in Marxist Method." *Capital & Class* 26.

Burkett, Paul. 1986. "A Note on Competition Under Capitalism." *Capital & Class* 30.

Center on Budget and Policy Priorities. 1994. *The New Fiscal Agenda: What Will It Mean and How Will It Be Accomplished?* Washington, DC: U.S. Government Printing Office.

Chamberlain, Neil W. 1948. *The Union Challenge to Management Control.* New York: Harper & Brothers.

Chomsky, Noam. 1989. *Necessary Illusions: Thought Control in Democratic Societies.* Boston: South End Press.

Chomsky, Noam, and Herman, Edward. 1979. *The Washington Connection and Third World Fascism* (Boston: South End Press).

————. *After the Cataclysm: Post-War Indochina and the Reconstruction of Imperial Ideology.* Boston: South End Press.

Clarke, Tom, and Clements, Laurie, eds. 1977. *Trade Unions Under Capitalism.* London: Fontana Collins.

Clements, Laurie. 1991. "The Politics of Privatization: Public It's Ours, Private It's Theirs." In Margaret Hallock and Steve Hecker, eds., *Labor and the Global Economy.* Eugene: Labor Education and Research Center, University of Oregon.

————. 1994. "Privatization American Style: 'The Grand Illusions.' " In Thomas Clarke, ed., *International Privatization: Strategies and Practices.* Berlin: deGruyter.

Clifton, James. 1977. "Competition and the Evolution of the Capitalist Mode of Production." *Cambridge Journal of Economics* 1, no. 2: 137–52.

Cole, Robert E. 1971. *Japanese Blue Collar.* Berkeley: University of California Press.

Cypher, James M. 1979. "The Internationalization of Capital and the Transformation of Social Formations: A Critique of the Monthly Review School." *Review of Radical Political Economics* 11, no. 4.

————. 1995. "NAFTA Shock: Mexico's Free Market Meltdown." *Dollars and Sense* 198 (March–April): 22–25, 39.

Dantico, Marilyn, and Jurik, Nancy. 1988. "The Effect of Privatization on Women and Minority Workers." In *The Privatization/Contracting Out Debate*. Washington, DC: AFSCME.

Davidson, Alexander. 1989. *Two Models of Welfare State in Sweden and New Zealand 1888–1988*. Uppsala, Sw.: Uppsala University Press.

Davis, Mike. 1986. *Prisoners of the American Dream*. New York: Verso.

DeMatteo, Bob. 1986. *Terminal Shock: The Health Hazards of Video Display Terminal Workers*, 2d ed. Toronto: NC Press.

Denby, Charles. 1989. *Indignant Heart: A Black Worker's Journal*. Detroit: Wayne State University Press.

Dickens, P. 1992. *Global Shift*. London: Paul Shopmen.

Dohse, K.; Jurgens, U.; and Malsch, T. 1985. "From Fordism to Toyotaism? The Social Organization of the Labor Process in the Japanese Automobile Industry." *Politics and Society* 14, no. 2.

Donahue, John D. 1989. *The Privatization Decision: Public Ends, Private Means*. New York: Basic Books.

Dore, Ronald. 1987. *Taking Japan Seriously*. London: The Athlone Press.

Eiger, Norman. 1986. "Education for Workplace Democracy in Sweden and West Germany." In R.N. Stern, ed., *The Organizational Practice of Democracy*. New York: John Wiley & Sons.

Einhorn, Eric S., and Logue, John. 1989. *Modern Welfare States*. New York: Praeger.

Esping-Anderson, Gosta. 1985. *Politics Against Markets: The Social Democratic Road to Power*. Princeton, NJ: Princeton University Press.

Fairbrother, P., and Waddington, J. 1990. "The Politics of Trade Unionism: Evidence, Policy and Theory." *Capital and Class* 41 (Summer): 15–56.

Fairris, David. 1990. "Appearance and Reality in Postwar Shopfloor Relations." *Review of Radical Political Economics* 22, no. 4: 17–43.

————. 1991. "The Crisis in U.S. Shopfloor Relations." *International Contributions to Labour Studies* 1, no. 1: 133–56.

————. forthcoming. *Shopfloor Matters*. New York: Routledge.

Fine, Ben. 1978. Rejoinder, "On the Origin of Capitalist Development," *New Left Review* 109 (May–June): 88–91. 1980.

————. 1980. *Economic Theory and Ideology*. London: Edward Arnold.

————. 1982. *Theories of the Capitalist Economy*. New York: Holmes & Meier.

————. 1990. "Scaling the Commanding Heights of Public Enterprise Economics." *Cambridge Journal of Economics* 14: 127–42.

————. 1992. *Women's Employment and the Capitalist Family*. New York: Routledge.

Freeman, R.B., and Medoff, J.L. 1984. *What Do Unions Do?* New York: Basic Books.

Frobel, Folker; Heinrichs, Jurgen; and Kreve, Otto. 1977. *The New International Division of Labor: Structural Unemployment in Industrialized Countries and Industrialization in Developing Countries*. New York: Cambridge University Press.

Fucini, J., and Fucini, S. 1990. *Working for the Japanese: Inside Mazda's American Auto Plant*. New York: The Free Press.

The Future of Work: A Report by the AFL-CIO Committee on the Evolution of Work. 1983. Washington, DC: AFL-CIO.

Garrahan, P., and Stewart, P. 1991. "Nothing New about Nissan." In C. Law, ed., *Restructuring the Auto Industry*. London: Routledge, 143–55.

————. 1992a. "Management Control and a New Regime of Subordination." In N. Gilbert, R. Burrows, and A. Pollert, eds., *Fordism and Flexibility*. London: Macmillan.

————. 1992b. *The Nissan Enigma: Flexibility at Work in a Local Economy.* London: Mansell.

Glick, Mark, and Ehrbar, Hans. 1990. "Long-Run Equilibrium in the Empirical Study of Monopoly and Competition." *Economic Inquiry* 28 (January): 151–62.

Goodman, John B., and Loveman, Gary W. 1991. "Does Privatization Serve the Public Interest?" *Harvard Business Review* (November–December).

Gordon, David. 1988. "The Global Economy: New Edifice or Crumbling Foundations?" *New Left Review* 168.

Gordon, David; Edwards, R.C.; and Reich, M. 1982. *Segmented Work, Divided Workers.* New York: Basic Books.

Gore, Al. 1993. *Creating Government That Works Better and Costs Less: The Report of the National Performance Review.* New York: Plume Books.

Gormley, William T., ed. 1991. *Privatization and Its Alternatives.* Madison: University of Wisconsin Press.

Graham, Cosmo, and Prosser, Tony. 1991. *Privatizing Public Enterprises: Constitutions, the State, and Regulation in Comparative Perspective.* Oxford, Eng.: Clarendon Press.

Guile, Bruce R., and Brooks, Harvey. 1987. *Technology and Global Industry: Companies and Nations in the World Economy.* Washington, DC: National Academy Press.

Hanami, Tadashi. 1979. *Labor Relations in Japan Today.* Tokyo: Kodansha International.

Hanke, Steve H., ed. 1987a. *Privatization and Development.* San Francisco: Institute of Contemporary Studies.

————. 1987b. "Prospects for Privatization." *Proceedings of the Academy of Political Science* 36, no. 3.

Harrington, Michael. 1989. *Socialism: Past and Future.* New York: Arcade Publishers.

Harrison, Bennett. 1994. *Lean and Mean: The Changing Landscape of Corporate Power in an Age of Flexibility.* New York: Basic Books.

Harrison, Bennett, and Bluestone, Barry. 1988. *The Great U-Turn: Corporate Restructuring and the Polarizing of America.* New York: Basic Books.

Hartmann, Heidi I.; Kraut, Robert E.; and Tilly, Louise A., eds. 1986. *Computer Chips and Paper Clips: Technology and Women's Employment* 1. Washington, DC: National Academy Press.

Hatch, Richard C. 1990. "Manufacturing Modernization: Strategies That Don't Work, Strategies That Do." *The Entrepreneurial Economy Review of the Corporation for Enterprise Development* 9, no. 1 (Autumn).

Haworth, N., and Ramsay, H. "Grasping the Nettle: Problems in the Theory of International Labor Solidarity." In P. Waterman, ed. *For a New Labor Internationalism.* The Hague: ILERI.

Heckscher, C. 1988. *The New Unionism.* New York: Basic Books.

Herding, Richard. 1972. *Job Control and Union Structure.* Rotterdam: Rotterdam University Press.

Hilke, John C. 1992. *Competition in Government-Financed Services.* New York: Quorum Books.

Himmelweit, Susan. 1984. "The Real Dualism of Sex and Class." *Review of Radical Political Economics* (Special Issue: The Political Economy of Women) 16, no. 4 (Spring): 167–83.

Hirschhorn, Larry. 1984. *Beyond Mechanization.* Cambridge, MA: MIT Press.

Hobbes, Thomas. n.d. *The Leviathan.* Oxford, Eng.: Michael Oakshot.

Hoover, Kenneth, and Plant, Raymond. 1989. *Conservative Capitalism in Britain and the United States.* London: Routledge.

Howe, Carolyn. 1986. "The Politics of Class Compromise in an International Context: Considerations for a New Strategy for Labor." *Review of Radical Political Economics* 18, no. 3: 1–22.

Hyman, R., and Streeck, W., eds. 1988. *New Technology and Industrial Relations.* New York: Basil Blackwell.

Jackson, P.M., ed. 1987. *Policies for Prosperity: Essays in the Keynesian Mode.* Cambridge, MA: MIT Press.

Jenkins, Rhys. 1987. *Transnational Corporations and Uneven Development.* New York: Methuen.

Karvonen, Lauri. 1991. "A Nation of Workers and Peasants." In L. Karvonen and J. Sundberg, eds., *Social Democracy in Transition.* Brookfield, VT: Dartmouth Publishing.

Keeran, Roger. 1980. *The Communist Party and the Auto Workers' Unions.* Bloomington: Indiana University Press.

Kern, H., and Schumann, M. 1987. "Limits of the Division of Labor: New Production Concepts in West German Industry." *Economic and Industrial Democracy* 8.

Klingel, Sally, and Martin, Ann. 1988. *A Fighting Chance: New Strategies to Save Jobs and Reduce Costs.* Ithaca, NY: ILR Press.

Kochan, T.; Katz, H.; and McKersie, R. 1986. *The Transformation of American Industrial Relations.* New York: Basic Books.

Kotz, D.M.; McDonough, T.; and Reich, M. 1994. *Social Structures of Accumulation: The Political Economy of Growth and Crisis.* New York: Cambridge University Press.

Kuhn, James. 1961. *Bargaining in the Grievance Settlement.* New York: Columbia University Press.

Kurzer, Paulette. 1991. "The Internationalization of Business and Domestic Class Compromises: A Four-Country Study." *Western European Politics* 4, no. 4 (October).

La Botz, Dan. 1991. *A Troublemaker's Handbook.* Detroit: Labor Notes.

Laux, Jeanne Kirk, and Appel Molot, Maureen. 1988. *State Capitalism: Public Enterprise in Canada.* Ithaca, NY: Cornell University Press.

Laxer, James. 1989. *The Decline of the Super-Powers: Winners and Losers in Today's Global Economy.* New York: James Lorimer.

Lembcke, Jerry. 1988. *Capitalist Development and Class Capacities.* Westport, CT: Greenwood Press.

Leontief, Wassily, and Duchin, Faye. 1984. *The Impacts of Automation on Employment, 1963–2000: Final Report.* New York: Institute for Economic Analysis, New York University.

Levenstein, Harvey. 1981. *Communism, Anticommunism, and the CIO.* Westport, CT: Greenwood Press.

Lever-Tracy, C. 1984. "The Paradigm Crisis of Dualism: Decay or Degeneration?" *Politics and Society* 13, no. 1 (1984).

Lichtenstein, Nelson. 1982. *Labor's War at Home: The CIO in World War II.* Cambridge, Eng.: Cambridge University Press.

Linowes, David. 1988. *Privatization: Towards More Effective Government.* Report of the President's Commission on Privatization.

Lipietz, Alain. 1982. "Toward Global Fordism," *New Left Review* 132.

Lipsett, Seymour M. 1963. *Political Man.* New York: Heinemann, Mercury Books.

Livernash, E. Robert. 1967. "Special and Local Negotiations." In John T. Dunlop and Neil W. Chamberlain, eds., *Frontiers of Collective Bargaining.* New York: Harper & Row.

LO Congress Report. 1986. *The Trade Union Movement and the Welfare State.* Stockholm: LO.

McNally, David. 1991. "Beyond Nationalism, Beyond Protectionism: Labor and Canada-U.S. Free Trade Agreement." *Capital & Class* 43 (Spring): 236–38.

Macobby, Michael. 1991. *Sweden at the Edge: Lessons for American and Swedish Managers.* Philadelphia: University of Pennsylvania Press.

MacShane, Denis. 1990. "Dreaming of the Forty-Hour Week." *Nation* (May 15).

Marglin, Stephen A. 1974. "What Do Bosses Do?: The Origins and Functions of Hierarchy in Capitalist Production." *Review of Radical Political Economics* 6 (Summer): 60–112.

———. 1990. "Losing Touch: The Cultural Conditions of Worker Accommodation and Resistance." In F.A. Marglin and S.A. Marglin, eds., *Dominating Knowledge*. Oxford: Clarendon Press, 217–82.

Markovits, Andrei S. 1986. *The Politics of the West German Trade Unions*. Cambridge, Eng.: Cambridge University Press.

Markusen, Ann. 1985. *Profit Cycles, Oligopoly and Regional Development*. Cambridge, MA: MIT Press.

———. 1988. "Planning for Industrial Decline: Lessons from Steel Communities." *Journal of Planning Education and Research* (Spring): 2–12.

Marsh, Robert M. 1992. "The Difference Between Participation and Power in Japanese Factories." *Industrial and Labor Relations Review* 45, no. 2: 250–57.

Marx, Karl. 1973a. *Capital* III. New York: International Publishers.

———. 1973b. *Grundrisse*. New York: Vintage Books.

———. 1977. *Capital* I. New York: Vintage Books.

———. 1981. II. New York: Vintage Books.

———. 1987. "Trades' Unions, Their Past, Present and Future." In Simon Larson and Bruce Nissen, eds., *Theories of the Labor Movement*. Detroit: Wayne State University Press, 36–37.

Marx, Karl, and Engels, Friedrick. 1975. *Selected Correspondence*, 3d rev. ed. Moscow: Progress Publishers.

Mason, Patrick L. 1992. "The Divide and Conquer and Employer/Employee Models of Discrimination: Neoclassical Competition as a Familial Defect." *Review of Black Political Economy* 21, no. 2.

———. 1995. "Race, Competition, and Differential Wages," *Cambridge Journal of Economics*, 19, no. 4 (August): 545–65.

Mattera, Philip. 1983. "High-Tech Cottage Industry: Home Computer Sweatshops." *Nation* 236 (April 2).

Maurice, Marc; Sellier, François; and Silvestre, Jean-Jacques. 1986. *The Social Foundations of Industrial Power*. Cambridge, MA: MIT Press.

Meidner, Rudolph. 1978. *Employee Investment Funds*. Boston: George Allen & Unwin.

Metzgar, Jack. 1985. "Running the Plant Backwards." *Labor Research Review* 7 (Fall): 35–43.

Miliband, Ralph. 1969. *The State in Capitalist Society: The Analysis of the Western System of Power*. London: Weidenfeld & Nicholson.

Mills, C. Wright. 1951. *White Collar*. New York: Oxford University Press.

Mins, L.E., ed. 1937. *Founding of the First International: A Documentary Record*. New York: International Publishers.

Mogensen, Vernon. 1995. *Office Politics: Video Display Terminals and Occupational Safety and Health Policymaking in the Post-industrial Era*. New Brunswick, NJ: Rutgers University Press.

Moody, Kim. 1988. *An Injury to All: The Decline of American Unionism*. New York: Verso.

Moreno, Angel M. 1994. "Presidential Coordination of the Independent Regulatory Process." *Administrative Law Journal of the American University* 8.

Murray, R. 1988. "Life After Henry Ford." *Marxism Today* (October).

Naples, M.I. 1986. "The Unraveling of the Union-Capital Truce and the U.S. Industrial Productivity Crisis," *Review of Radical Political Economics* 18, nos. 1–2 (Spring–Summer): 110–31.

————. 1986–87. "An Analysis of Defensive Strikes." *Industrial Relations* 26, no. 1 (Winter): 96–105.

————. 1988. "Industrial Conflict, the Quality of Worklife, and the Productivity Slowdown in U.S. Manufacturing." *Eastern Economic Journal* 14, no. 2 (April–June): 157–66.

Navarro, P. 1983. "Union Bargaining Power in the Coal Industry, 1945–1981." *Industrial and Labor Relations Review* 36, no. 2 (January).

The 9 to 5 National Survey on Women and Stress. 1984. Cleveland: 9 to 5: The National Association of Working Women.

Nolan, P., and Edwards, P.K. 1984. "Homogenized, Divide and Rule: An Essay on *Segmented Work, Divided Workers.*" *Cambridge Journal of Economics* 8: 197–215.

Norsworthy, J.R., and Zabala, Craig. 1985. "Worker Attitudes, Worker Behavior, and Productivity in the U.S. Automobile Industry." *Industrial and Labor Relations Review* 38, no. 4: 544–57.

Oliver, N., and Wilkinson, B. 1992. *The Japanization of British Industry: New Developments in the 1990s,* 2d ed. Oxford, Eng.: Basil Blackwell.

Olsson, Sven E. 1990. *Social Policy and Welfare State in Sweden.* Lund, Sw.: Lund University.

Pack, Janet R. 1991. "The Opportunities and Constraints of Privatization." In *Privatization and Its Alternatives.* In William T. Gormley, ed., *Privatization and Its Alternatives.* Madison: University of Wisconsin Press, 281–306.

Palloix, C. 1975. "The Internationalization of Capital and the Circuit of Social Capital." In Hugo Radice, ed. *International Firms and Modern Imperialism.* Harmondsworth, Eng.: Penguin.

Parker, M., and Slaughter, J. 1988. *Chosing Sides: Unions and the Team Concept.* Boston: Labor Notes/South End Press.

Pastore, Manuel. 1987. "The Effects of IMF Programs in the Third World: Debate and Evidence from Latin America." *World Development* 15, no. 2: 249–62.

Perelman, Michael. 1993. *The Pathology of the U.S. Economy: The Cost of a Low Wage System.* New York: St. Martin's Press.

Phillips, Andy, and Dunayevskaya, Raya. 1984. *The Coal Miners' General Strike of 1949–50 and the Birth of Marxist-Humanism in the U.S.: A 1980s View.* Chicago: News & Letters.

Phillips, Kevin. 1990. *The Politics of Rich and Poor: Wealth and the American Electorate in the Reagan Aftermath.* New York: Random House.

Piore, M., and Sabel, C. 1984. *The Second Industrial Divide.* Chicago: University of Chicago Press.

Poole, Robert W. 1988. "The Limits of Privatization." In Michael A. Walker, ed., *Privatization: Tactics and Techniques.* Vancouver, BC: Fraser Institute, 79–91.

Poulantzas, Nicos. 1975. "Internationalization of Capitalist Relations and the Nation-State." *Economy and Society.*

Proceedings of the Fifth Annual Robert C. Byrd Conference on the Administrative Process. 1994. "The First Year of Clinton/Gore: Reinventing Government or Refining Reagan/Bush Initiatives?" *Administrative Law Journal of the American University* 8: 23–66.

Przeworski, Adam. 1986. *Paper Stones: The History of Electoral Socialism.* Chicago: University of Chicago Press.

Radice, Hugo. 1984. "The National Economy: A Keynesian Myth?" *Capital and Class* 22.

Rankin, T. 1990. *New Forms of Work Organization: The Challenge for North American Unions.* Toronto: University of Toronto Press.

Ranney, David C. 1987. "Combating Plant Closings." *Journal of Ideology* (Winter).

———. 1988. "Plant Closings and Early Warning Indicators." *Journal of Planning Literature* (Winter): 22–35.

Ranney, David C., and Betancur, John J. 1992. "Labor Force Based Development: A Community Oriented Approach to Targeting Job Training and Industrial Development." *Economic Development Quarterly* 6, no. 3 (August): 286–96.

Reich, Robert. 1992. *Work of Nations: Preparing Ourselves for 21st Century Capitalism.* New York: Vintage Books.

Rexed, Knut. 1991. "Swedish Labor During the 1990s." Paper presented at Swedish Information Service Seminar at the Graduate Faculty of the New School for Social Research in New York City (November 16).

Ringen, Karen B. 1988. "Electronic Monitoring." In *Liberty at Work: Expanding the Rights of Employees in America.* New York: American Civil Liberties Union.

Roediger, David R., and Foner, Philip S. 1989. *Our Own Time: A History of American Labor and the Working Day.* New York: Verso.

Rojas, A. 1991. "The Swedish Model in Historic Perspective." *Scandinavian History Revue* 39, no. 2.

Rosa, Kumudhini. 1991. "Strategies of Organization and Resistance: Women Workers in Sri Lankan Free Trade Zone." *Capital & Class* 45 (Autumn): 27–34.

Rosenberg, Sam. 1988. "Restructuring the Labor Force: The Role of Government Policies." In *The Imperiled Economy, Book II: Through the Safety Net.* New York: Union for Radical Political Economics.

Scharpf, Fritz W. 1987. *Crisis and Choice in European Social Democracy.* Ithaca, NY: Cornell University Press.

Schor, Juliet B. 1992. *The Overworked American: The Unexpected Decline of Leisure.* New York: Basic Books.

Schultz, David. 1992. *Property, Power, and American Democracy.* New Brunswick, NJ: Transaction Publishers.

———. 1993. "The Public Use Doctrine." In Julius L. Sackman and Russell Van Brunt, eds., *Nichols On Eminent Domain.* New York: Matthew Bender.

Schultz, David, and Jann, David. 1992. "Business and Plant Closings: The Expansion of the 'Public Use' Doctrine in Eminent Domain." In Julius L. Sackman and Russell Van Brunt, eds., *Nichols on Eminent Domain.* New York: Matthew Bender.

Semmler, Willi. 1984. *Competition, Monopoly, and Differential Profit Rates.* New York: Columbia University Press.

Shaiken, Harley. 1986. *Work Transformed: Automation and Labor in the Computer Age.* Lexington, MA: Lexington Books.

Shaikh, Anwar. 1978. "A History of Crisis Theories." In Union for Radical Political Economics, ed., *U.S. Capitalism in Crisis.* New York: URPE.

———. 1979. "Foreign Trade and the Law of Value: Part I." *Science & Society* 63, no. 3 (Fall): 281–302.

———. 1980a. "Foreign Trade and the Law of Value: Part II." *Science & Society* 64, no. 1 (Spring): 27–57.

———. 1980b. "Marxian Competition Versus Perfect Competition: Further Comments on the So-called Choice of Technique." *Cambridge Journal of Economics* 4, no. 1: 75–83.

———. 1982. "Neo-Ricardian Economics: A Wealth of Algebra, a Poverty of Theory." *Review of Radical Political Economics* 14 (Summer).

———. 1987. "The Falling Rate of Profit and the Economic Crisis in the U.S." In Robert Cherry et al., eds., *The Imperiled Economy: Macroeconomics from a Left Perspective, Book I.* New York: Union for Radical Political Economics.

Sheinkman, Jack. 1991. "Preface: Worker Rights in Central America." In *Worker Rights in the New World Order*. New York: The National Labor Committee in Support of Democracy and Human Rights in El Salvador.

"Solidarity Across Borders: U.S. Labor in a Global Economy." 1989. *Labor Research Review* 8, no. 1 (Spring).

Starr, Paul. 1987. *The Limits of Privatization*. Washington, DC: Economic Policy Institute.

Stellman, Jeanne M., and Henifin, Mary Sue. 1983. *Office Work Can Be Dangerous to Your Health*. New York: Pantheon.

Stewart, P.; Garrahan, P.; and Crowther, S., eds. 1990. *Restructuring for Economic Flexibility*. London: Avebury/Gower.

Stone, Katherine. 1981. "The Postwar Paradigm in American Labor Law." *Yale Law Journal* 90, no. 7: 1509–80.

Stout, Mike. 1986. "Reindustrialization from Below: The Steel Valley Authority." *Labor Research Review* 5, no. 2 (Fall): 19–34.

Suggs, Robert E. 1989. *Minorities and Privatization: Economic Mobility at Risk*. Washington, DC: Joint Center for Political Studies.

Sullivan, Harold J. 1987. "Privatization of Public Services: A Growing Threat to Constitutional Rights." *Public Administration Review* 47, no. 6 (November–December): 461–67.

Sweezy, Paul. 1937. "On the Definition of Monopoly." *Quarterly Journal of Economics*.
———. 1939. "Demand Under Conditions of Oligopoly." *Journal of Political Economy*.

Tabb, William K. 1989. "Capital Mobility, the Restructuring of Production, and the Politics of Labor." In Arthur MacEwan and William Tabb, eds., *Instability and Change in the World Economy*. New York: Monthly Review Press.

Taylor, Frederick W. 1947. *Scientific Management*. New York: Harper & Brothers.

Thimm, Alfred L. 1980. *The False Promise of Codetermination*. Lexington, MA: Lexington Books.

Titmuss, Richard. 1958. *Essays on Social Policy*. London: Allen & Unwin.

Tomaney, J. 1990. "The Reality of Workplace Flexibility," *Capital & Class* 40.

Tool, Marc R., and Samuels, Warren J. 1989. *State, Society and Corporate Power*, 2d ed. New Brunswick, NJ: Transaction Books.

Verkuil, Paul R. 1994. "Is Efficient Government an Oxymoron?" *Duke Law Journal* 43: 1221–35.

Weber, Arnold. 1967. "Stability and Change in the Structure of Collective Bargaining." In Lloyd Ulman, ed., *Challenges to Collective Bargaining*. Englewood Cliffs, NJ: Prentice-Hall.

Weeks, John. 1981. *Capital and Exploitation*. Princeton, NJ: Princeton University Press.
———. 1985. *Limits to Capitalist Development*. Boulder, CO: Westview Press.

Wickens, P. 1987. *The Road to Nissan*. London: Macmillan.

Williams, Rhonda M. 1987. "Capital, Competition, and Discrimination: A Reconsideration of Racial Earnings Inequality." *Review of Radical Political Economics* (Summer).

Williamson, Hugh. 1991. "Japanese Enterprise Unions in Transnational Companies: Prospects for International Cooperation." *Capital & Class* 45 (Autumn): 17–26.

Willoughby, John. 1986. *Capitalist Imperialism, Crisis and State*. New York: Harwood Press.
———. 1987. "The Promise and Pitfalls of Protectionist Politics." In Robert Cherry et al., eds., *The Imperiled Economy, Book I*. New York: Union for Radical Political Economics, 215–23.
———. 1989. "Is Global Capitalism in Crisis? A Critique of Postwar Crisis Theories." *Rethinking Marxism*. 2, no. 2 (Summer): 83–102.

Womack, J.; Jones, D.T.; and Roos, D. 1990. *The Machine That Changed the World.* New York: Rawson Associates.

Yanarella, E.J., and Green, W.C., eds. 1990. *The Politics of Industrial Recruitment: Japanese Automobile Investment and Economic Development in the American States.* New York: Greenwood Press.

Yarrow, M. 1979. "The Labor Process in Coal Mining: Struggle for Control." In A. Zimbalist, ed., *Case Studies in the Labor Process.* New York: Monthly Review Press.

Zimmerman, Jan. 1983. ed. *The Technological Woman.* New York: Praeger.

Zisman, Michael. 1979. "Office Automation: Revolution or Evolution?" *Sloan Management Review* 19: 1–17.

Zoninsein, Jonas. 1990. *Monopoly Capital Theory: Hilferding and Twentieth-Century Capitalism.* New York: Greenwood Press.

Zuboff, Shoshana. 1988. *In the Age of the Smart Machine: The Future of Work and Power.* New York: Basic Books.

Index

About the Editors

Cyrus Bina is an economist and an affiliate-in-research at Harvard University's Center for Middle Eastern Studies. He specializes in international and energy economics, economic methodology, and global capital-labor relations. He received his Ph.D. in economics from the American University, Washington, DC. Dr. Bina has served as a professor of economics at Providence College, Rhode Island, and was formerly director and professor of economics at Olivet College, Michigan. He has published extensively on subjects such as labor and globalization, transnationalization of capital, economic rent, global oil and OPEC, and the "new world order." He is the author of *The Economics of the Oil Crisis* (1985) and coeditor of *Modern Capitalism and Islamic Ideology in Iran* (1992). As a leading authority on the globalization process, he was nominated for the Grawemeyer World Order Award in 1991.

Laurie Clements is director of the Labor Center at the University of Iowa. Before joining the Labor Center in 1985, Clements was senior lecturer in industrial relations, Trent Business School, Trent Polytechnic, Nottingham, England, and a visiting professor in labor studies at Indiana University at South Bend. He is coeditor of *Trade Unions Under Capitalism* (1977). Clements has written extensively on privatization and is an internationally known expert on the topic. In addition to privatization, his areas of specialization include collective bargaining, alternative pay systems, and labor economics. He is currently vice president of the University and College Labor Education Association, Editorial Board member of the *Labor Studies Journal,* and a member of Workers' Education Local 189, CWA.

Chuck Davis is director of private sector programming and a member of the graduate faculty at the Labor Education Service, Industrial Relations Center,

University of Minnesota. He received his Ph.D. in economics from the American University, Washington, DC. Dr. Davis has published and educated extensively on labor studies and political economy. His areas of specialization currently are labor, labor process and globalization, and collective bargaining in the railroad industry in the United States and Canada. He is a former vice president of the University and College Labor Education Association and is a member of Workers' Education Local 189, CWA.

Contributors

Elaine Bernard is executive director of the Trade Union Program at Harvard University. Before assuming the post at Harvard, Dr. Bernard was director of labour programs at Simon Fraser University, Burnaby, British Columbia. She is an internationally known lecturer on political economy, labor studies, and women's studies. Elaine Bernard received her Ph.D. in history from Simon Fraser University in 1988. She has authored several articles and books with a special emphasis on technology and the labor process, including *The Long-Distance Feeling: A History of the Telecommunication Workers' Union* (1982).

Victor G. Devinatz is associate professor in management and quantitative methods at Illinois State University. Professor Devinatz earned his Ph.D. in industrial relations from the University of Minnesota in 1990. He has also worked as a union organizer. He has published articles in *Journal of Labor Research, Labor Studies Journal, Journal of Collective Negotiations in the Public Sector,* and *Labor Law Journal.* Currently Dr. Devinatz's interests include labor history, the study of shop floor unionism, union representation elections, and industrial ethnography.

Norman Eiger is professor emeritus in labor studies and industrial relations at Rutgers University. Dr. Eiger was chair of the Department of Labor Education, and director of the Labor Education Center at Rutgers. Professor Eiger has taught and written in the field of labor studies for more than twenty-eight years. Among the awards he has received was the 1988 NUEA award for innovations in continuing education for a series of labor seminars at twenty state universities that compared Swedish and American labor movements.

David Fairris is assistant professor of economics at the University of California at Riverside. He received his Ph.D. in economics from Duke University in 1984. Dr. Fairris has published several articles in the areas of labor economics and political economy. His book *Shopfloor Matters* is forthcoming from Routledge. Dr. Fairris is currently shop steward of AFT Local 1966, University of California at Riverside.

Philip Garrahan is head of the School of Social, Political, and Economic Sciences at the University of Northumbria at Newcastle, England. He received his Ph.D. from the Department of Politics, University of Reading, in 1979. Dr. Garrahan has published extensively on the politics of the auto industry and the politics of regional economic development. He is coauthor of *The Nissan Enigma: Flexibility at Work in a Local Economy* (1992) and coeditor of *Urban Change and Renewal: The Paradox of Place* (1994).

Vernon Mogensen is assistant professor of political science at Manhattanville College, Purchase, New York, and a writer in the field of labor and American politics. He received his Ph.D. in political science from the City University of New York in 1993. Dr. Mogensen is author of *Office Politics: Video Display Terminals and Public Policymaking in the Postindustrial Economy* (1995) and is currently working on a political history of occupational safety and health policymaking in the United States.

Michele I. Naples is associate professor of economics at Trenton State College. Her Ph.D. in economics is from the University of Massachusetts at Amherst. Dr. Naples's work has appeared in the *American Economic Review, Capital & Class, Cambridge Journal of Economics, Industrial Relations,* and *Review of Radical Political Economics.* She is coeditor with Nahid Aslanbeigui of *Rethinking Economic Principles: Critical Essays on Introductory Textbooks* (1995). Dr. Naples received the 1991 Otto Eckstein Award for best article published in 1988 and 1989 in the *Eastern Economic Journal.* She is currently serving on the Board of Directors of the Eastern Economics Association.

David C. Ranney is acting director of the Center for Urban Economic Development and is an associate professor in the School of Urban Planning and Policy, University of Illinois at Chicago. He has his Ph.D. in sociology and urban planning from Syracuse University. Dr. Ranney is the author of three books and numerous articles and monographs on issues of employment, labor and community organization, city planning, and politics. Currently he is working in the areas of labor and globalization, job creation and retention, and assistance to dislocated workers.

David Schultz is a visiting professor of political science at the University of Minnesota. He has a Ph.D. in political science from the University of Minnesota. Dr. Schultz has previously worked as a municipal administrator, as a planner for a community action agency, and as a union organizer. He is the author of six books, which include *Property, Power, and American Democracy* (1992) and *The Jurisprudential Vision of Justice Antonin Scalia* (1995), as well as numerous articles on plant closings and economic development; employment discrimination; and law, courts, and the political process.

Paul Stewart is a lecturer in the Japanese Management Research Unit of the Cardiff Business School, University of Wales, United Kingdom. He received his Ph.D. from the Department of Sociology, University of Leeds, in 1986. Dr. Stewart's areas of specialization include the sociology of work and employment, and the sociology of Northern Ireland. He has published extensively in these areas and is coauthor of *The Nissan Enigma: Flexibility at Work in a Local Economy* (1992) and coeditor of *Urban Change and Renewal: The Paradox of Place* (1994).

DATE			